The View From the Bottom Up

Growing Up Fast in World War II

Robert Gilbert
S/Sgt.
U.S. Eighth Air Force

MILITARY MONOGRAPH 117
Bennington, Vermont
2012

First published in 2012 by the Merriam Press

First Edition

ISBN 978-1468049879
Merriam Press #MM117-P

Printed in the United States of America.

This work was designed, produced, and published in
the United States of America by the

Merriam Press
133 Elm Street Suite 3R
Bennington VT 05201-2250

E-mail: ray@merriam-press.com
Web site: merriam-press.com

Both the author and the Publisher welcome and encourage comments and corrections to the material appearing in this work. Please send them to the Publisher at the above address.

The Merriam Press is always interested in publishing new manuscripts on military history, as well as reprinting previous works, such as reports, documents, manuals, articles and other material on military history topics.

Patch of the 533rd Bomb Squadron

381st Bomb Group
U.S. Eighth Air Force
Ridgewell, England

Aerial Gunner Wings

THE VIEW FROM THE BOTTOM UP

Contents

THE VIEW FROM THE BOTTOM UP

Prologue

OUT of the harshness of the Great Depression were produced the people who would fight World War Two in the factories and on the battlefields. Though very human in their failings, they were a generation or so of people who were not particularly self-absorbed or frivolous. As history has shown, they were able to face with fierce dedication the terrible forces of the Axis Powers and beat them. This story observes one of these young persons as he grows rapidly to adulthood, along with his peers, experiencing love, fear and having deep feelings of dedication to protect his country...and is told at times with some humor.

In that fateful time during World War II, there were many theaters of war operations throughout the world. This memoir takes place in one of those theaters, the European Theater of Operations (ETO). The air war in the ETO involved the heavy bombers of the U.S. Eighth Air Force and the fighters and medium bombers of the U.S. Ninth Air Force.

In World War II over Europe were the greatest air battles ever fought by manned aircraft. Surely future air battles in the history of man will be technologically superior to these. But none will ever be as personal or as doggedly contested.

As the war progressed, the U.S. Eighth Air Force attacked Germany's industrial, transportation and fuel resources with onslaughts of massive forces of four engine bombers launched from England. A determined *Luftwaffe* and effective anti-aircraft artillery met these efforts with deadly accuracy. Upon entering the air war in Europe, the United States 8th Air Force decided to conduct its bombing operations in the daylight hours rather than at night as did the British and the German air forces. Though such daylight bombing efforts were more perilous to the American crews, it provided greater accuracy on hitting industrial and transportation targets as was its strategic goal.

This memoir is written against that historic backdrop and takes place during the Fall and Winter of 1944/45, when the USAAF and the RAF bombing reached its peak. It is not as much about the war as it is *of* the war and its effect on the young people involved.

Most history logically enough is written viewing from the top down which is needed to understand the scope and extent of what, why, when, how and where events happened. What did the world leaders, the politicians, the generals, the commanders, the military professionals think and what did they want to achieve with their chess-like matches of men and materiel? Those are the questions that need to be explored and defined for history. But, what of the human story? Viewing the people involved at the "point of the spear" more interestingly illuminates the human events. Not from the top down, but from the bottom up.

This memoir is the story of a young aerial machine gunner, on a B-17 Flying Fortress bomber, who had to grow up fast. He participated as a teenaged enlisted man in the World War II Big League of air war...the ETO. In his turret hanging under that storied bomber, he was positioned to defend his bomber from the *Luftwaffe's* deadly fighter aircraft. This compelling story presents his perspective of the committed life he and his peers brought to manned bomber warfare, which is *The View From The Bottom Up...* literally and figuratively.

Author's Notes

MY experiences as a Ball Turret Gunner on a B-17 Flying Fortress bomber during 35 aerial combat bombing missions over Germany and German occupied territory are the basis of this memoir. Personal background and experiences, as they influenced and were influenced by these events, are also explored. In writing this very personal story, every effort has been employed to make it truthful as to facts and honest as to my opinions. However, it is logical that unintentional selective memory may have played some part in this story's content ...as surely it must in any memoir.

Where historical facts are involved they have been researched and are accurate to my knowledge. The official Certificate of Operational Missions issued by the 533rd Bomb Squadron, Operations Officer, provides the basic time-line used for the combat events. Personal observations are based upon events seared into my memory and also my contemporaneous notes, which have been corroborated with the various reference sources identified in References. These referenced sources were also used to provide some historical background information for story continuity. Where specific documentation did not exist, a thoughtful presentation was created based on known facts to provide a logical sequence of events as they likely occurred.

The content, and detail facts, of this story are written such as to be of interest to the general reader as well as the air warfare aficionado. I have purposely avoided the almost mythic daring-do of World War II aviators, as in some stories, and related a story of the non-heroic Americans I knew just doing their jobs. For clarity to all readers, background information at times is given and technical terms or jargon are minimized.

The period of combat represented is October 1944 through February 1945, which was statistically less deadly for the Eighth Air Force over Europe than the earlier months had been. This memoir is therefore more of a human-interest story, with aerial combat as the background rather than as the focus. The context of this memoir is the period of time spanning my early teen years to my late teen years upon returning to the United States just after VE Day in May 1945.

Where there are quoted conversations, they are faithful representations of the content, but not necessarily the exact wording, of those dialogs. Although such quotations are primarily a story telling device they do accurately record events and situations as they actually occurred.

The names of non-historic people used herein, including "Pat" and her family, are fictitious and any similarity to the names of the real people in the context of this story is purely coincidental. The names of publicly known and historic persons are true as well as are those of my fellow crewmembers and hut-mates in Ridgewell, England.

Any inaccuracies that may have been included in this memoir were unintentional and are my fault All opinions and emotions are mine alone, for this is my memoir after all.

ACKNOWLEDGEMENTS

A big thank you is due to Ruth Herrmann for her insistent prodding and editing advice without which this project would not have happened.

To my wife Althea, for her first draft proof reading, her patience and encouragement throughout these many, many months, a heartfelt thank you, thank you!

To our youngest daughter Lynn Kearney, for her thoughtful insights with her teacher's mind's eye, thank you. A special thank you also to her son, Joey Kearney, who took time from his busy life to read and comment on this story that took place so very long ago. Their caring inputs helped immensely for me to be assured it was a story that could relate to the younger generation.

And to Ralph Engleman and Marcus Tremble, two other surviving Goldin crewmembers, who helped me on some points of accuracy... thanks guys. Also in the area of accuracy, I need to acknowledge the encouragement and historical data input from Christer Bergstrom, the Swedish World War II air war historian and author. Finally from the British standpoint, a big thank you to David Osborne, 381st Bomb Group historian and author and to Brit Roger Kent, a fellow golfer, who helped refresh my memory on wartime London and England.

We did not have an official crew photo taken by the bomb group. Thus had it not been for Frank Hrehocik and his snap shots, which he shared with us, there would be no photo record of us, and the other Blue Room guys, during our combat tour. A post mortem thank you is due to Frank... thanks buddy.

—Bob Gilbert
Murrieta, California

Chapter 1

The Boy Awakens

We know what we are, but know not what we may be.
William Shakespeare
Hamlet, Act IV

ICELAND, SEPTEMBER 1944

IT was dusk in a cold barren land. I had lost on a low card draw competition between the enlisted men on the Goldin crew as to whom would have to guard our airplane during our overnight stay in Iceland.

We had flown this beautiful new B-17G, Flying Fortress, from Hunter Field, Georgia, by way of Bangor, Maine and Goose Bay, Labrador, to Reykjavik, Iceland, on our way to England. This was the first time I, and probably any one else on our crew, had been outside of the United States. We were anxious to start our great adventure as a bomber crew. Our crew of very young men, who were strangers just two months ago, was flying alone across the Atlantic Ocean to our destinies in the World War II air war over Europe.

We were ferrying this new bomber, as well as ourselves, to join the U.S. Eighth Air Force for aerial combat against the forces of Nazi Germany. After a long flight from Labrador, through the broken clouds, land appeared ahead...it was Iceland our next destination. We swooped in low over the choppy Atlantic Ocean and headed for Meeks Field at Reykjavik. As I stood looking out of the waist window, Iceland seemed devoid of vegetation and was a forbidding panorama of icy-snowy rock and earth. It appeared more barren than the desert had in Nevada where I attended gunnery school—it was appropriately named "Iceland." After landing our pilot, Sam Goldin, was directed to a designated spot where he parked our plane to spend the night in Iceland. Someone had to be with her over night to protect the ship and our belongings—and that unfortunately was I. After a hearty hot meal in the mess hall, Marty Tremble, our flight engineer, rode with me back out to our bird. He left me alone with her in a remote area of the large air base with a firm warning to not let anything happen to her!

I was doing a walk-around inspection of our ship, and the tie-downs that secured her to the tarmac, when a chilling wind began to pick up. My cap blew off and I groped for it in the growing darkness with stiffening fingers as the temperature dropped sharply. Here I was, an 18 year-old kid from the beaches of Southern California, in this desolate sub-arctic world feeling like a shivering fish out of water. Of course I had some trepidation about my upcoming participation in the war being fought in the skies over Germany. But of more immediate concern was making sure nothing untoward happened to our ship while she was my responsibility. I slowly climbed through the access door into the waist area of the plane to spend the night as her lone companion.

In the by then black night, the wind became a vicious gale and produced a kind of moan in our bird as she vibrated and lurched to the building storm. I was sitting in the radio room looking through the radio operator's window to see what I could of the storm. As I watched, first one engine cover and then another flapped in the wind with a whip-like cracks and began to come loose. Our ship's four big Wright Cyclone radial engines had canvas covers tied on to keep them protected from the elements while she was parked. Now it appeared they might well be torn free and blown away in the storm.

Being alone it was my problem to solve, I scrambled out of the access door in the waist area of the ship into the frigid weather to secure those protective covers before they were lost into the night. Fighting to keep the wind from ripping them away, I finally got control of, and retied snugly all the restraints on those cumbersome covers. I then went to the tie-downs for the aircraft itself, which was rocking in the wind, and retied them as tight as I could.

Fingers numb from the battering of biting sleet and sub-arctic wind, I climbed back inside my 48,000-pound charge and sought extra coats or anything I could wrap around me for warmth. Inside the non-insulated aluminum skin of the unheated airplane, I was at least dry but freezing. I wondered what I was going to do to be warm and to keep the frost from my bones. Moving forward through the ship to the flight deck, I eased into the command pilot's seat. Scrunching down I pulled coats and blankets around me and looked out through the windshield at the now raging storm. Sleet slashed at the ship and tore by the windshield. As I stared out, almost transfixed, I became less aware of my coldness. I felt as if I were actually flying this magnificent machine through a storm.

In Long Beach, California, when I was growing up, curled up under a tree in our backyard, I loved to read pulp fiction magazines based on the World War I air battles. It was my fantasy that I would some-day become a fighter pilot such as those about whom read. And now here I was actually sitting in a pilot's seat. Not the seat of a fighter, as I had fantasized in my backyard, but of the storied Flying Fortress bomber! As I snuggled deeper into my multi-coat/blanket cocoon, my mind went back to how I got here at this time... September 1944. My mind went back, back to Long Beach and into the years of the Great Depression when we grew up.

CALIFORNIA IN THE THIRTIES

We had a great time to grow up in, my brother, Bill, and I, and our buddies. Because "times were hard" for the adults, they had little time to be involved in our day-to-day activities. We, and our friends, were given the freedom to be boys exploring our world without much adult "help." It was a little like Dickens and his line, "It was the best of times, it was the worst of times..." The Depression was the worst of times for the parents. They had to solve the problems of feeding, cloth-ing and housing of the family with very little government help. Un-employment at times stood at 30% without unemployment insurance. There was no food stamp program. We did have the Los Angeles County dole of basic foodstuffs of flour, sugar, beans etc, to the needy. We never went hungry or unsheltered. Our folks and their generation did what they had to do to get by in those difficult times leaving us to explore life pretty much on our own.

For youngsters like us, it now seems to me, these were the best of times. In the West Long Beach area, where most of those years were spent, there was a mixed collection of industry, commercial and resi-dential sites and empty lots. According to Mom this was not a proper area to raise children, but Dad had taken over the ownership of the Shamrock Bottled Water business on State Street which included a house...so that was where we were to live. This was a great area in the minds of young boys; empty lots for kite flying and the building of forts. We would roam the factory areas and go through their trash piles to look for "keen junk" with which we would make stuff. The near-by Los Angeles River, which is really a flood control seasonal riv-er, provided exploration opportunities of hobo camps and rafting after a rain.

Close by on Anaheim Street were the junkyards and wrecking yards of Long Beach. They smelled of used oil and contained all sorts of automobile, marine and aviation wrecks and junk. There was no better place in the world for prepubescent boys to explore, use their imagination. Just a couple of miles farther from home was the Port of Long Beach. We would go there on our bicycles to look at the freighters in from all over the world unloading their different cargos. Strange materials and containers, often with exotic aromas, would load the docks. This was before the era of the bland shipping containers of today. The harbor was an interesting place that stimulated our young minds about places beyond Southern California. During the 1930s and the start of the 1940s, there were many ships from Japan docking and off loading a variety of cargos. But the cargo they were hauling back to Japan seemed to be primarily scrap metal. The adults, seeing all the large trucks on Alameda Street carrying that scrap iron heading for the Los Angeles and Long Beach harbors, would solemnly predict, "We'll get that scrap iron back one day when the Japs shell us just like they are doing to China." They were right, but we as a country continued to send this precious cargo to Japan right up until they made their sneak attack on Pearl Harbor in December 1941.

With all this wonderfully unfettered exposure, each of us developed his own future plans without adult reminders of sensible limitations to guide him. For me it was to be a pilot, maybe like Lucky Lindy who flew to Paris or the World War I fighter Ace Eddie Rickenbacker. I was going to fly in an airplane soaring among white fluffy clouds in a clear blue sky free of earthly constraints. There never were dark clouds in my young mind.

Our depression era lives went by in this somewhat carefree and unfettered manner until world events caught up with us.

GERMANY RUMBLES

While America was working its way out of The Great Depression, Europe was unraveling with an aggressive Germany once again threatening her neighbors and ultimately invading them one by one. Then, in September 1939, as Europe was rolling under German control, Britain, and France for just a few months, stood up to the Nazi forces. Our carefree days were waning slowly but surely. In my high school years, I listened to the radio news and avidly read of the war in Europe as country after country, and finally France in June 1940, succumbed to the seemingly unstoppable Nazi war machine. Early on the only effective resistance to Germany was the British Royal Air Force (RAF). I read of the great air battles being fought by the gallant RAF against the

　　　　　　　　THE VIEW FROM THE BOTTOM UP

dreaded Luftwaffe and my heart went out to that little island in the North Atlantic and her gallant people.

Not being a particularly war-like person, the thought of actually engaging in kill-or-be-killed warfare was foreign to me. My friends and I did talk about maybe the U.S. might join Britain as we had in World War I, but it was a little iffy. The notion that we might become involved in the war in Europe was bandied about in the newspapers, but there was a strong isolationist movement in our country that would fight any such action. We were told later that much of the funding for the isolationist movement was coming from the German-American Bund, which was directly funded by Nazi Germany. Germany needed to keep the U.S. isolated in our continent at any cost.

President Roosevelt had to engage in bits of chicanery, such as the Lend Lease Act in March of 1941, to send equipment to Britain under the guise of a business deal without becoming legally involved in the war. While Mussolini had joined with Hitler in the Mediterranean, Japan was rampaging unchecked through the South Pacific and China. The stories of Japanese bestiality, particularly in China, were horrifying, but these events were thousands of miles away from us. The world was a checkerboard of aggression by the Axis Powers. We high school kids watched and wondered. We knew we were the prime ages to fight a war should one come, but the decisions were in the hands of our leaders in Washington and the world events even out of their control.

As we young guys talked of such things, we would argue some about which would be the best service to join if it came to that. Having grown up in a Navy town, as Long Beach was in those years, we mostly seemed to favor the Navy. It did offer some technical jobs and a clean dry atmosphere in which to serve. At Long Beach Polytechnic High School I had focused on radio science (today it would be called electronics). I was in the Radio Club, along with the other nerds, and took Radio and Aviation Science classes as my primary interest. I wanted to become a pilot someday like those I had read about. But it seemed very unlikely that I could qualify for pilot training, which required a minimum of two years college as far as I knew. However, I began to research all the ways it was possible to get into the Army Aviation Cadet program. We knew there was no rush. There was time to decide which service to join if war came about and maybe we could get in some college first.

Or so we thought.

THE VIEW FROM THE BOTTOM UP

Chapter 2

From Long Beach to Tampa

Our World Changes

AS the USA watched the world overseas come apart, we one day had our own problems. On a quiet Sunday morning, December 7, 1941, without warning we were viciously attacked by the Imperial Japanese Navy at Pearl Harbor, Hawaii. Close to 3,000 Americans were killed and our Pacific Fleet suffered a major loss of ships lying at anchor on that fateful Sunday morning. At the same time, Japan also attacked American bases all across the Pacific from Guam to the Philippine Islands.

On the Monday following, December 8th, we sat in our homerooms at Long Beach Poly High School and listened to President Roosevelt addressing the joint Houses of Congress. Based on the now infamous Japanese attack, he asked Congress to declare war against Japan. Of course everyone from Washington, D.C., to the streets of Long Beach was intensely angry at Japan and wanted to get even for their treachery. We heard congress cheer the President and felt their eagerness.

I was troubled by some contradictory emotions; on the one hand wishing I were older so I could join the fight against Japan, but also being afraid of what war was going to mean to all of us young guys and our families at home. We seemed so vulnerable here on the West Coast just as Pearl Harbor had been. But filled with anger for the callous treachery of Japan, and with our usual American confidence, we all knew ultimately we were going to win the war.

On the following Thursday, December the 11th, Germany and Italy declared war on the United States to support their ally Japan. Action quickly followed by the President and Congress and war was then declared by the United States against Germany and Italy. Now in a matter of four days after the Japanese sneak attack on our sleeping nation we were fully engaged in World War Two. Those five days forever changed the lives of millions of people.

Southern California, where we lived, was a center for aircraft production. Around the major aircraft manufacturers; Douglas, Lockheed, Northrop, North American, Vultee and Consolidated were hundreds of aircraft sub-contractors and materiel suppliers. Southern California was quickly being filled with aviation war work. The area shipyards also began to build up to meet the country's demands for boats and ships. In addition we had numerous petroleum refineries and oil fields in the Los Angeles basin. A major part of the Pacific Fleet was based in San Diego and in Long Beach. With so many vital resources immediately accessible for any aggressive sea borne attacks on the United States, we lived in a prime target area.

We were under dim-out controls for factories, homes and streets to minimize the glow from land sources outlining our shipping and industrial sites to Japanese submarines plying our coastal waters. Periodically we had black-out drills for the whole Los Angeles basin to prepare us in case of an enemy attack. Most everyone was concerned about another Japanese attack somewhere on the U.S. mainland such as happened in Pearl Harbor

Then on February 25th, 1942, just two and a half months after the Pearl Harbor attack, the war came quickly to the Los Angeles area. At 2:25 AM we were awakened by a massive thundering of loud explosions all around us that we believed were the sounds of bombs being dropped by Japanese bombers. My family and I all naively ran outside to see what was happening. We saw the sky was filled with searchlights sweeping back and forth across the dark night sky. There were shapes, which at the time we thought could be airplanes, occasionally being lit up by the searchlights. We could hear the clinking as pieces of shrapnel fell on the Spanish tile roof of our house and all around us. As we stood shivering in the cold night air, awe struck by the spectacle above us, our neighborhood Air Raid Warden urgently shooed us all back into our homes. Hindsight would indicate those shapes illuminated by the searchlights were probably residual smoke from the flak bursts not aircraft. There were no radio broadcasts to tell us what was going on as radio silence prevailed. Later that morning our local newspapers were calling it the Long Beach air raid by "mysterious forces." To this day the truth of the events of that night remains unexplained, but it was certainly not an air raid...as it turns out. Was it nervous over eager anti-aircraft gunners or a more devious plot by the Government to stir us up? We still don't know. A positive effect, however, was for those who hadn't believed we were in a full-fledged war. They were now onboard with the rest of us who knew we had a war to win.

We young guys' decisions on whether to try and enlist or to await the Draft were now upon us. I had finally decided I was going to find a way to join the Army Aviation Cadet Program and become a pilot rather than leave it to the chance of the Selective Service Draft. However, it was necessary to have two years college as an entrance requirement. I would be getting out of high school when I was 17 years old and thus I would be 19 before completing two years college. The sticking point was, we all had to register for the Draft upon our 18th birthday and then we were eligible to be drafted at any time into the Army or Navy as there was a need for recruits. After diligent researching, I discovered an exception to the Army Air Corps enlistment rules. One could be accepted for the Aviation Cadets if; you had graduated from high school, were still 17 years old, could pass a two years college equivalency test and a flight physical. One would thus avoid registering for the Draft and would be called-up directly into the Air Corps and the Aviation Cadet program upon turning 18 years old.

Upon graduating high school in June of 1943, I began to study the subjects I had found would be tested by the Air Corps to determine a two years college equivalency in knowledge. I crammed on mathematics, physics, language, reading and logic, to prepare for the test. Within a month or so, I felt ready to take the Aviation Cadet entrance test. I drove up to Los Angeles to make the necessary application. As a part of that application, we were given the two years college level equivalency test. Upon completion of the test, we were then scheduled for an all day flight physical at March Field in Riverside the following week.

I was notified, after a tense couple of weeks, I had successfully passed both of those tests and was directed to subsequently appear before a board of officers for an Aviation Cadet Candidate interview. They asked a series of questions to determine why I wanted to join the Air Corps and if I were a suitable officer candidate. Finally getting past this very tense meeting and having met all of the Air Corps' requirements, I was sworn into the Enlisted Reserve Corps on 20th of September 1943, 37 days before turning 18 years. Being in the Air Corps ERC, I was not required to register for the Draft when I turned 18.

As an alternative to immediate call-up upon turning 18, I was given a deferment to attend one year of college, which would have been completed in June 1944. I enrolled in Long Beach City College in September 1943 and sent my enrolment evidence to the Air Corps. That summer I also went to work for Douglas Aircraft in the new Long

Beach assembly plant. I worked swing shift as an installation mechanic on the C-47 cargo aircraft center wing section. My days and nights were full and in a way interesting. In the evenings I was doing war work at Douglas and getting to know my fellow workers who were mostly women. During the days I began to attend college. After a little while of this, I grew restless and didn't want to continue to wait until the next year to get involved in the war.

I decided to withdraw from college and asked the Air Corps for call to active duty when I was eligible on my 18th birthday, October 27th, 1943.

We have all heard of how one simple decision could have a major affect on someone's whole life. Such as upon a whim one door is taken instead of another along side it, or the chance decision to turn down one street rather than another. Sometimes these spontaneous unplanned actions put in motion events that will set the stage for the rest of one's life. And so it was with me, because that one decision had a dramatic effect on my future. If everything had happened as arranged when I was enlisted into the Air Corps, I would not have been called to active duty any sooner than July of 1944 after my year of college. I can't know what would have happened had I waited until then, but it is certain my whole military experience would have been quite different. There is no way I could have been involved in flying combat missions over Germany with the U.S. Eighth Air Force. I would have missed The Big Show.

Just days before I turned 18, I received a notice that my "...request to change [my] assignment order date," was being acknowledged and that I would be called to active duty in November 1943. Unfortunately, I had made the request for immediate call up without consulting or telling my parents. So this letter was very startling to Mom and Dad. To their credit they never criticized my decision just my lack of consideration of them. Days later in early November I received my orders to report for active duty in the Army Air Forces on November 20th, 1943.

I was ordered to report to Fort MacArthur, in San Pedro, for active duty call up into the Army. My orders to report included a voucher on the streetcar from Long Beach to San Pedro, which I insisted on using. Though my folks wanted to drive me to Fort Mac I didn't want to appear to be a little boy with his folks driving him to report for duty. Upon arrival at Fort Mac, we were issued our uniforms and given the basic routine shots. We were exposed to some minimal basic Army instruction as we awaited orders to ship out.

THE VIEW FROM THE BOTTOM UP

About the only thing I can remember was great emphasis on memorizing your serial number so you would know it instantly for the rest of your life, which I still do. When there were enough of us Cadets at Fort Mac to form a troop train, we were shipped to Buckley Field, Colorado, to join others waiting further orders in the Aviation Cadet Program.

PILOT TRAINING?

When we arrived at Buckley there appeared to be some sort of delay in our entrance into actual Aviation Cadet training. There were several hundreds of us who were awaiting assignment. We had a lot of marching and calisthenics and some lectures on military protocols. There were rumors we were to be assigned to Denver University for College Training Detachment (CTD). We heard the results of the traditional football games back home and then Christmas came. It was a lonely time and my first Christmas away from my home and family as it was for most of the guys. Also for me another first was seeing snow fall. Then came the unhappy news at this time the pipeline of guys training to be pilots was too full for the then projected needs of the Air Corps.

As a reduction-in-force technique at Buckley, we were given an all-day test called the psychomotor test. It was used in this case as a screening method to reduce the number of Cadets in the program. A few days later we were assembled in the base theater and told that most of us were to be eliminated from the Cadet Program for the Convenience of the Government (COG).

We who were eliminated COG were to be given six weeks of Army Air Corps basic training there at Buckley Field prior to being shipped out to our various duty assignments. We were moved to another part of the big air base and housed in tar papered barracks. These buildings were "temporary" single story bare affairs having no insulation and with one small coal stove in the center for some protection from the cold snowy days and nights. Nearby there was a latrine for our toilet and bathing needs that supported several barracks.

Air Corps Basic Training was not as rigorous as that given to Army or Marine Corp rookies, but we did have a very intensive six weeks training. We learned all of the necessary basic military skills. We were taught about weaponry such as rifles, bayonets, hand grenades, etc. We learned the basic military courtesies and protocols. There were poison gas drills and we went on a seven day bivouac where we camped out in deep snow and qualified on the .30 cal. carbine.

An event about our bivouac that I remember with some embarrassment involved a night guard duty I had during a snow storm. There was a main gate into the bivouac area that I was posted to guard. I was to walk back and forth across the entry into the area and stop all vehicles and ask for identification of who wished to enter. Except, I was instructed to NOT stop any ambulances or staff cars. However, it was snowing so heavily I couldn't see more than a few feet in any direction. I only stopped two vehicles that night, as their headlights appeared out of the night, a staff car and an ambulance. I must have looked rather forlorn standing there with my carbine at present arms position, heavy snow swirling around my naïve young face, shouting HALT to the only people I was not supposed to stop!

During all of this, we learned how to get along with and use the military system. It became a matter of honor to beat the system and to out-fox non-commissioned and commissioned officers. The military system teaches conformity and obedience as the epitome of conduct. Most of the guys I was with thought we had not been fairly dealt with by our COG elimination from the Aviation Cadet program, so we thought we had to get even with the Army. Further, the dismissive treatment we basic trainee privates received by everyone only stimulated our creative instincts to get even.

MESSING WITH AUTHORITIES

Work details such as KP or other physical tasks the Army needed done were not pleasant and to be avoided if possible, but were an accepted reality. It was the snobbish disrespect that really angered us. One odious practice at Buckley Field that sticks in my mind still was at the evening movies at the base theater. Officers and their guests were allowed in the theater first. We enlisted personnel had to wait in-line outside in the cold Colorado weather until there were no more officers wishing to see the movie. The attitude of the officers seemed to be leisurely. They strolled up to the theater, arm-in-arm with their lady friends, while we waited standing on the snow-covered ground. These and other arrogant displays taught us to learn and practice the art of "malicious compliance" to the orders of superiors.

The more pompous the officer or NCO the more fun it was to obey their orders to the letter without question, even though it was clear they meant something else. We also developed the ability to screw-off to a fine degree; the more elaborate the deception to avoid work the better. I adopted the name Robert Baker to be used when asked my name to be added to a duty list if I didn't have to show my ID tags. For instance for KP duty, a duty clerk would come into our barracks at 4:00 AM, or so, wake us up then ask our names, which he put on the KP duty list. I would respond Robert Baker as he added me to his list. We were ordered to get dressed and form a group outside to be marched to the mess hall. At the mess hall the night kitchen staff would feed us our breakfast as their final duty of the night. After eating breakfast we were to take over the various duty stations while the night guys left to return to their barracks. I would join the night guys as they put on their coats to leave. With my belly full, I'd put on my coat, leave the mess hall and return to my cot for a nice morning nap, or go to the Service Club to read a magazine or two.

Upon discovering they were one man short, the search would go out for Pvt. Baker who was in a lot of trouble. I have often wondered if there was a Pvt. Baker at Buckley Field who had to account for his time and various minor miss-deeds. Anyone who could successfully pull off one of these stunts was held in high regard by his peers. Perhaps this was the start of learning the crew mentality of working together against an enemy...in this case superior officers.

Later we were treated with appropriate respect as we progressed into our combat training and combat duties. But at Buckley Field it was we against them...whomever "them" happened to be. However, as an antidote to life at Buckley Field, the people of Denver were the most generous and caring folks I ever experienced while in the service. As an example on Christmas Eve day 1943 in the late afternoon I was waiting for my date to get off work from Woolworth's. While standing on the sidewalk outside the store I had two families offer me a chance to come to their home for Christmas! My date had in fact also asked me to spend Christmas with her family. It seemed to me no service man or woman had to be alone at Christmas time in Denver.

After completing basic training, we were assigned to our next duty stations. The bulk of our guys were either sent to the Infantry or to the Engineering Corps. Out of our one hundred or so guys, only seven of us remained in the Air Corps. We seven were sent to Flexible Gunnery School at Las Vegas, Nevada, and were to stay in the Air Corps, though no longer as Aviation Cadets.

When I thought I was going to be trained as a pilot, I figured it would be a year or more before I would actually see combat. But now I was going to gunnery training, which was for only six weeks. Of course, I'm thinking I can then go to a technical school such as flight engineer or radio operator and add up to six months before combat. As you can readily see, as combat gets closer I'm more interested in training than actual combat.

GUNNERY SCHOOL

When we arrived at Las Vegas Army Air Field, the ubiquitous "corporal with a clipboard" greeted us as we assembled along side of the train. He yelled his greeting,

"Men, this here is Las Vegas aerial gunnery training school! After graduating here you will be assigned to a combat crew and sent overseas.

If you ain't been to no tech school, you ain't goin' to no tech school!"

So much for my dreams of some kind of additional specialized technical training after gunnery school.

I loved the shooting part of gunnery training! I had never owned a gun larger than a BB gun in my life. In aerial gunnery we fired all sorts of guns from a BB firing machine gun to 50 Cal. machine guns that fired at moving and fixed targets. I took to all of this like a duck to water. It turned out I was well suited to be a gunner. With bright and shiny 20/10 eyesight, I could find the smallest speck in the distance and seemed to have natural coordination for tracking moving targets.

Finally we began to be treated as if maybe we were something more than grunts. We were not required to do the usual Army work assignments such as KP or other work details. We were in Student Squadrons and lived very strict lives but with some respect. We had the usual physical training and classroom work learning about guns, ammunition, turrets and shooting at moving targets, and how to install, repair and set up guns and turrets. The afternoons were usually dedicated to actually shooting various sizes and types of guns. This was for the most part fun although there was a certain amount of standing around in the sun, when we would be told "Take ten; smoke if you got 'em." As yet I didn't smoke cigarettes, so I just found a place to sit and relax.

Becoming intimately familiar with the Browning 50 Cal. machine gun was the focus of much of our training. We learned to disassemble (detail strip) it and assemble it blindfolded. We also could field strip it (major components disassembly) blindfolded and also with gloves on. Along with hours of classroom training on the care and repair of the Browning we began to get a variety of lessons on shooting at a moving target from a moving base. We also had a number of shooting training sessions wherein shotguns were mounted in top turrets and ball turrets shooting at clay pigeons. This was the most fun but also the trickiest, because it was difficult to get the turret to track fast enough.

But, it wasn't all schooling. One of the best diversions for me was at the base Post Exchange (PX). They had a doughnut-making machine operated by a curvy young woman. She had striking blonde hair under her little waitress cap and was always smiling. We would wait to get the plain doughnuts she had freshly made. They were hot with a crisp outer side and needed no coating to taste delicious. I would have two or three of those crunchy delights, along with a cup of hot cocoa, and make small talk to the girl when she wasn't busy. Nothing before or since has ever tasted so good. Maybe it was the girl or maybe the doughnut recipe.

The day we had our first exposure to the skeet shotgun range was really scary for me. I had never fired a shotgun before and was not really sure of myself. We used shotguns that had ring and post sights welded on them so we could get trained to use the sighting method for leading a moving target as used on aerial machine guns. Our aiming positions used the standard skeet range clock positions when shooting at the clay pigeons. Each of us had his turn at shooting at the clay pigeons from each clock position. We were taught to yell pull; then the bird would be flung out of the shed, you were to track it, then fire and attempt to hit the clay pigeon. On my first firing position, I nervously fired the shotgun first then yelled pull! The gunnery instructor, a large red-faced man who looked as if he would be at home in chaos anywhere, firmly explained to me the proper sequence of actions. He said,

"First you yell, pull! then you shoot the damn bird, OK?"

Luckily I scored 21 out of 25 birds on my first attempt which score was very good. And I got a begrudging,

"Not bad, son." from him.

In fact, our instructor offered a crisp new $5 bill to any of us who could get 25 out of 25 birds during our training. I don't recall anyone getting the five bucks. I believe the best I ever did was 23 out of 25. There was one demanding shotgun range wherein we stood on the bed of a traveling pickup truck. It moved through an area of randomly placed trap houses, from which were flung clay pigeons in random patterns. This was so much fun that I thought it would have made a great civilian life game except for the expense.

Along about this time, I had a small epiphany. Each morning before breakfast we had a formation along side of our barracks for roll call and orders of the day. Our no nonsense training NCO, Sgt. Bell, as a part of this formation, gave us a visual inspection for general appearance. One morning the early Nevada sun was shining on us standing at attention, as the sergeant walked past me he stopped and said,

"Soldier, you need a shave!"

It seemed the bright morning sun had illuminated my peach fuzz coated upper lip. It was the highlight of my week. I told everyone about how old sergeant Bell had,

"...really chewed me out because I needed a shave."

Wow, I had arrived.

COMIC RELIEF

The student squadron commanding officers mostly were pilots grounded for one reason or another. Our squadron adjutant had been grounded for six months for buzzing, with his B-17, a control tower containing a bird Colonel. Lieutenant Crab (as we called him) was a youngish looking fellow with a thin dark mustache, who seemed to blame us for his current desk duty...he was not a happy pilot. He would conduct unannounced barracks inspections to keep his mind occupied. Once in our barracks, as we stoically watched, he demanded that the sergeant help him look into the attic for what God only knew. As he shined his flashlight into the attic he yelled,

"Sergeant Bell, there is crap in here from World War One! Give me a boost up here."

He climbed into the attic and promptly fell through the ceiling up to his crotch on a rafter. As the desert dust and pieces of paper filtered down from the attic as it was disturbed by our thrashing leader, we wiped away our tears and stifled our laughter as best we could. We lost our weekend passes but it was worth it; the attic needed cleaning anyway.

UNAUTHORIZED TRIP

Being in Las Vegas, I was just a few hundred miles from home and yet I couldn't legally go there on a weekend pass. It was frustrating. Our passes were limited to 100 miles from the base and Long Beach was around 300 miles away. I decided I would go home anyhow. When I signed out on the Pass Log on Saturday morning, I put down my destination as Long Beach, California. I reasoned that being truthful about where I was going might avoid any seeming evidence of desertion if someone caught on to what I was doing.

I took a local bus into Las Vegas and got out on the highway to Los Angeles and put out my thumb to hitch a ride. I had considered taking a commercial bus to Long Beach but didn't have the money to do it. Rather than having to borrow money, I decided to hitch hike, which of course is free. I was also concerned that the MPs might have checked my pass when I got on a bus for California. After a while, a young woman driving a new looking convertible with the top down stopped for me. Pushing wind-blown, long blonde hair away from her attractive face, she pleasantly asked where was I going, when I answered Long Beach, she said,

"Hop in."

We drove west out of town toward California. I don't recall our conversation very much but I think I must have missed some essential information. I was very surprised when in about two hours along our way, she suddenly announced, "This where I turn," pulled over and stopped the car. You have heard people speak of "the middle of no where," right? Well, I now knew where that is. It is about two hours westward from Las Vegas in the Mojave Desert. She silently watched as I got out of her car then drove northward into the empty desert with a small dust cloud rolling down the dirt road after her. She had turned onto a narrow road that had no marker of any kind. If life were a video tape, I would like to rerun her words to me, prior to dropping me off, to see what I had missed.

Even though it was wartime, and a man in uniform should not have trouble getting a ride, no one stopped for me for hours as I baked in the sun. Then along came a Mexican farmer driving a battered and dirty pick-up truck. With a slightly accented tired voice, he told me he was going to Barstow and I could ride along...but I had to ride in the truck bed. He had no one else in the cab with him so I guess he was not too sure of what I was doing out in the "middle of nowhere." I gratefully rode in the back of that noisy and windy truck until we got to Barstow at around sundown. Achy and dusty I climbed out of that truck, thanked the farmer, and looked for a diner to grab a burger and a large coke.

Watching me as I stiffly moved away from the truck, an MP immediately came up and wanted to see my pass. I guess it was my wearing an Air Corps patch on my uniform that triggered his interest in me. It seemed Barstow had a lot of soldiers in their area but no airmen or air bases.

He noted the pass was restricted to 100 miles from Las Vegas and asked what I was doing in Barstow, which is 160 or so miles from Vegas. I told him a sad story of my mother being sick and of my hitch-hiking to see her before I went overseas. He took me to see the Provost Marshall, a spiffy 2nd Lieutenant who on that Saturday night was the officer in charge of the Military Police, and had me repeat my story to him. I pointed out to the officer that I had actually signed out for Long Beach as my destination on the Pass Log in the squadron Orderly Room. I then innocently asked, "I wouldn't have done that if it weren't OK to go to Long Beach, would I?"

After considering his options, he told the MP to take me to a pay phone and have me pay for a call to my Student Squadron orderly room to verify my story. It was by now well after dark and no one would be there except the Charge of Quarters (CQ) who was just a GI stuck with the duty that night. After I finally got through on the phone and the CQ answered, I asked him to verify where I was signed out for on the Pass Log. I then gave the phone to the MP and he was able to verify I was indeed signed out for Long Beach...so they let me go on my way.

After having a quick meal, I tried for a while to hitch a ride out of Barstow, but by now there was virtually no traffic. Finally, I called my folks and we decided I would meet them the next morning in near-by Victorville where my Grandma Labelle lived.

On my way to finding an economical motel, I came upon a group of local toughs beating up on a lone boy with long stringy hair. He had a pair of shoe type roller skates tied around his neck and was cowering on the sidewalk. Emboldened, I suppose, because of being in uniform, I ran up and ordered them to leave him alone and "...be on your way!" I surprised them, and myself, and they ran away leaving the scared youngster alone. He told me he was hitch hiking his way to Los Angeles to get a part in some show or movie featuring roller skating. Not trusting the locals to leave him alone, I suggested he stay in the motel room I was going to get so he would have a safe rest that night. I got a room with two beds and never once thought how this may look to anyone else. It was a different time and I was quite naïve, though I did hide my wallet in my pillow case to protect it while I slept. I left the room very early the next morning while he was still asleep and found a café open for breakfast.

Standing on the highway on that Sunday morning I was able to get a ride with a family going to Victorville for church services. I waited by the park and Mom and Dad soon arrived, with my five years old brother Donny and Grandma Labelle. We all spent the day together for a nice normal Sunday. The war seemed far away, which of course it

THE VIEW FROM THE BOTTOM UP

was, and it was not the big topic of conversation. They brought me up-to-date on family matters and I told a little of my gunnery training. Donny had always been a precocious and curious boy but he seemed to have grown a year or two since I had last seen him six months ago. He had many questions about airplanes and guns. He also gave me advice on how to assure my safety during the war.

Finally it was time for me to return to Las Vegas. As it turned out Mom hadn't been too well, so my concocted story for the MPs wasn't entirely a lie. We believed that this Sunday together might be our last time before going overseas—so it seemed worth the troubles involved in the past two days. Dad gave me the money for a Greyhound Bus ride back to Las Vegas and I arrived back in time to not further violate any Pass restrictions or military orders. Whew!

BOMB BAY STEW

For the air-to-air and air-to-ground shooting we were moved to Indian Springs aerial gunnery flight facility some miles away from Las Vegas. For me, and most of the guys, this was to be our first time in any kind of airplane, let alone a bomber. We were each issued a belt of 50-caliber ammunition color tipped with marker paint, which was a different color for each student. As the fired round hit the tow target the color would rub off on the target to identify each gunner as the bullet hit the target. With goose bumps I remember the pride I felt walking out in that bright desert sunlight on the flight line with a belt of .50 cal. ammunition slung over my shoulder. Walking in amongst parked Flying Fortresses, which seemed so large, I felt I had finally become an airman. We would be flying in tired B-17s along with a veteran gunnery-training sergeant. Most of these guys had combat experience and really seemed to know their stuff not only book information but from the gut. Unfortunately many of them seemed to take dark humor type pleasure in telling us we were 'goners not gunners', referring to the then high casualty rates on bomber crews. Fortunately for us by the time we reached combat, things were getting better for the combat air-crews.

I vividly remember that first gunnery training flight. After donning our parachutes, we loaded into the waist area of the ship, I was feeling an exciting fear of the unknown. As we taxied out to the end of the runway for take off, I tried to appear as blaze' as an 18 year old can. The pilot revved up those four big radial engines with the old ship vibrating in anticipation. I was standing at the waist window hanging on to a mounted machine gun for support and watched the burnt out desert begin to rapidly move by. I couldn't believe how noisy that ship was as she pounded down the runway for the takeoff. Conversation other than on the interphone was only by yelling directly into someone's ear. Once airborne, though, she had a kind of graceful strength that gave one confidence in her. As we lifted off the runway, she made a slight dip then rose effortlessly into the bright blue cloudless desert sky. We were flying! For the first part of that flight, we took turns shooting at targets being towed by another plane. Our hits left a color dab identifying whose ammo was involved in successfully hitting the tow target. Later when we saw the results of our shooting, I was surprised at how many of my shots as well as the others had missed the target. It was apparently a lot harder than it looked. Over time, as we experienced many training flights, we would get pretty good at hitting those tow targets.

For the rest of that first flight, we had air-to-ground shooting at airplane cutouts mounted on the desert floor. In order to do this shooting, it was required that we fly very low to the ground; on-the-deck as it is called. This was exciting but very rough because the Nevada heat created many thermals rising off the desert floor. As a result our ship bounced and dipped constantly. One of the students got air sick lurched forward and vomited into the empty bomb bay. We had all been told to use the bomb bay if we had to vomit as was fairly common with new flyers. I got very queasy also just smelling that vomit and moved back by the tail wheel for the fresh air that gushed around it and took a nap.

When we got back to the base it was time for our noon meal. As we student gunners filed into the mess hall, tired and still a little queasy, there was a big kettle situated at the front of the mess serving line. On it was attached a large sign with bold lettering, "Special Today—BOMB BAY STEW." The sign was just a not too gentle reminder of the airsickness recently experienced by numbers of students. Oh, those wacky cooks! It seemed we were a constant source of amusement for these poor fellows "stuck" out at Indian Springs...an hour's drive to Las Vegas!

SILVER WINGS

We returned to the base in Las Vegas to complete our training and testing. There was a 10 to 20 per cent washout rate during gunnery training. We did have a few guys along the way who had been removed

THE VIEW FROM THE BOTTOM UP

from training, usually for fear of flying. Flying duty was voluntary after all.

The six weeks of training had passed all too quickly. It seemed only a short while ago we were standing along side of the train that brought us here from Buckley Field, and wondering what lay ahead. On the final Saturday morning we had a formal parade and graduation ceremony where we were presented with our silver wings. We were told this was a lifetime award and the right to wear them could not be withdrawn at any time in the future. After the ceremony, we were taken to the base theater where we were given a lecture by a Flight Surgeon. His theme was the gunner's silver wings would present more chances for catching venereal disease. This slant to the usual VD lecture given to GIs was in fact a source of some pride for most of us. We hadn't had much experience in chasing females away. He called our Gunner's Wings the "silver leg-spreaders" and warned of their power to get one in trouble. One could only hope, we jokingly thought.

Mom and Dad came over from California for the graduation. We were given passes to spend time with our guests. Dad knew of a cooler recreation area above Las Vegas called Mount Charleston. We went up there for a leisurely meal, relaxation and conversation. It was kind of sad and yet nice... our little bit of family time. We didn't know when we would see each other again. My training was winding down and soon the next step was to be in a combat assignment somewhere. We didn't talk about it, but we knew that maybe this would be our last time together

I left the next day on a troop train for Plant Park in Tampa, Florida, to become part of a combat crew. Our troop train was in fact a civilian style Pullman car not the normal Army Troop Sleeping car. The Pullman porters were a source of information about all things involving railroad travel. They were very helpful and let us ride in the vestibule between cars on the boarding steps while we steamed along the countryside toward Florida. We rode on that troop train from Las Vegas up to Chicago and wound randomly on various rail lines down to Florida for a span of a week or more. It seemed a troop train did not have priority over most war materiel laden freight trains. So our train would be pulled over onto sidings while high priority trains roared past us with blaring whistles. I had a lot of time to rubberneck at America as we crawled our way along through the Western, Midwestern and Southern farms and towns. What wonderful sights to this naïve youngster from Long Beach.

We once sat in a siding along side of the Missouri River for several hours waiting for a high priority freight train to pass us. I lounged on the cool shady riverbank and inhaled the moist woody smell of the languid river sliding by. I was transported back in time to a young Huck Finn poling a raft down the river with his best friend Tom Sawyer, on a high adventure trip to somewhere. I loved my home state but in the southern part where I was from we didn't have wonderful tree lined rivers like these.

The engineer would give us a long whistle warning when he was ready to resume our trek so we could get back on board.

In St. Joseph, Missouri, when we stopped there, a group of ladies from the town came out and went through the train handing out milk, Hershey bars, cookies, magazines and books. They were very friendly and wished us well. It was a thoughtful generous gesture and one that makes me think well of those wonderful folks of St. Joseph to this day.

As we made our way through the humid verdant Deep South and into Florida, I realized that this was it. I mused, *"Soon I will be joining a group of strangers to become a part of a combat crew to be sent somewhere. God, I hope it will be England."* It seems odd to me now, but my deep desire was *to* go to England and become a part of the war against Nazi Germany; not Japan who had attacked us directly at Pearl Harbor. Further, my family living on the West Coast had every reason to fear that any further attacks from Japan would be on them. It would seem my natural desire would be to engage the Japanese who were more of a threat to California than was Germany. In spite of this logic, my heart was to be a part of the U.S. Eighth Air Force flying out of England and attacking directly Hitler's Nazi industrial backbone, which had been the bane of Europe for so long.

Next stop Tampa and combat crew assignment...at last.

THE VIEW FROM THE BOTTOM UP

Pvt. Robert Gilbert, Buckley Field, Colorado, circa February 1944.

The View From the Bottom Up

Chapter 3

E Pluribus Unum

PLANT PARK

THE troop train slowly pulled into the Tampa area. I was eagerly looking out my window at anything I could see trying to anticipate what this place was going to be like. I really enjoyed being able to see orange groves again. It was quite a contrast to the starkness of Nevada and Colorado where I had spent the last several months and, in a way, it looked like my California. It was a warm comfortable feeling. We were to spend the summer here in the Tampa area but I soon found appearances aside, Florida and California have quite different summers. The active summer thunderstorms in Florida would at times bedevil our flying training schedules, and make going into town on pass an unpleasant sweaty experience. One could put on a freshly pressed suntan uniform and by the time you got to town it was sweat stained and wrinkled.

Closely across the river from downtown Tampa was an area called Plant Park. In the park there were the usual grass and trees features of a city park with benches and paths. But next to the public area was the USAAF replacement center by the same name. It had a grandstand, remnants of a radio broadcasting booth and some kind of racing track. I believe it had housed state fairs and such in peacetime. Our mess hall had partially screen walls that abutted a sidewalk in a Tampa neighborhood. It seemed strange to see civilians walking by chatting a few feet away while we ate. It was quite different when compared to the almost desolate sites of both Buckley Field and Las Vegas Army Air Field.

Bomber air crewmen of all disciplines were gathered at Plant Park and eventually assembled into combat crews. While awaiting crew assignment we mostly tried to keep out of trouble. There were the usual Venereal Disease (VD) lectures where we were told, as we had been about every other place we had been in the Army; Tampa (supposedly) had the highest VD rate in the state. So beware. We went swimming over at Davis Island, rode the ferry out to St. Petersburg sightseeing, and generally goofed off.

Then we were given a chance for a two-week furlough. I immediately jumped at the chance to go home for a last visit. Of the 14 days I had for my furlough, I spent 10 days onboard train chair cars (non-Pullman sleepers that is) going to and from California. These trains were really crammed and filthy, but I was going home! Because of the war effort and lack of gasoline for automobiles, many train cars had been pressed into service that were in poor shape. They were noisy, rickety and smelly from the coal smoke.

During one night of my trip, there was a sweet pretty young woman in the seat beside me. She had soulful brown eyes and a wonderfully soft southern accent. We talked the usual talk of strangers on a train. She was going to spend time with an Aunt somewhere before going off to college "up north." The evening got late and we both started to doze so she spread her coat, made of some kind of white fur-like material, over both of us while we slept. In the morning we saw the soot had drifted down from the ceiling of the train car and spread over her coat like black snow! She left the train in the morning, with her now dirty coat that had protected us, wearing a big smile and a, "Good luck, soldier."

Later, as the landscape whizzed past, with the background sound of the pulsing rhythm of iron wheels on rails, and the occasional *ding ding ding ding* of a crossing signal as we flew by, I mused about my being here at this time. A year ago I had just gotten out of high school and generally was not yet doing much of anything productive. At that time I had only been outside of California once and then briefly to visit relatives in Reno. Now, here I was on the brink of a wartime adventure of a lifetime and on a train by myself traveling 3,000 miles to see my family. I had had a pretty girl talk with me as if I were somebody. Things were changing rapidly in my world.

The four days at home went too quickly and are mostly a blur in my memory. We had one day that was a get-together day with our family members who lived locally. Mom, who was a great cook, had fixed a buffet of snacking type goodies. There was also iced tea, cold beer and watermelon for anyone who stopped by to say hello and good luck and God's speed. I remember a neighbor who said unthinkingly, "Well, I guess we won't see you again until you come back from overseas." As if it were a sure thing. I was not optimistic about surviving a combat tour in a B-17 and he seemed to be dismissive about any risks in such an effort Maybe he was trying to give a positive spin to his words, but I felt he was sadly unaware of what aerial combat risks were. And I guess I didn't mind risking my life for my country, but I

THE VIEW FROM THE BOTTOM UP

wanted people to appreciate that fact. Not a very noble state of mind...but I was very young.

The next day it was time to go. We drove up to the beautiful Union Pacific train station in Los Angeles where I caught the train to New Orleans for my trip back to Tampa. Mom had fixed me a bag of her great fried chicken and baking powder biscuits to take with me. I ended up sharing some of it with fellow passengers because there was so much and it wasn't going to keep without refrigeration.

D-DAY

The trip back to Tampa was highlighted by the news announcement of the long awaited invasion of France by the Allies...at last!

The invasion of the European continent was eagerly anticipated by everyone. Attempting to cross the 50 miles of the English Channel had historically stopped the Spanish Armada, the French Navy and even Germany's military might. For the Allies to achieve this historic undertaking, Britain had to be the base from which American, Canadian and British forces would attack Hitler's so called Fortress Europe. That small island was crammed with hundreds of thousands of troops and thousands of tons of equipment and supplies. The first day of this monumental effort was known as D Day to the military planners and became the symbol to the world that the Germany was not unbeatable. That first day involved 160,000 Allied troops and resulted in 10,000 casualties. By five days later (D Day + 5), 326,000 Allied troops were landed on those beaches in Normandy leading the way to the ultimate defeat of Germany 11 months later. These were to be a hard fought and deadly 11 months with much work to be done.

President Roosevelt rightfully said December the 7th, 1941 would be a date that will live in infamy; I believe June the 6th, 1944, should be a date that will live in records of honor and noble accomplishments of the United States and her valiant allies primarily Britain and Canada. Whether it will be so remembered by future generations, time will tell, but I doubt it. As this is being written in 2006, the D Day Anniversary is not particularly acknowledged by the media and is generally ignored by the American public—except for the older generation who lived it.

It was June 6, 1944. Our train stopped briefly at a town in New Mexico and we were able to get copies of the area newspapers. They were ablaze with the first news flashes of that monumental and massive happening on the beaches of Normandy. The papers were enthusiastic about such an historic event, but they, and we, had no idea of its magnitude. It wouldn't be until later that we were fully aware of the incredible bravery being displayed on the beaches and cliffs of Normandy by our landing forces. This largest sea borne invasion in history would ultimately involve over three million men.

My return trip to Tampa was a five-plus days in a chair car, with a memorable stop in New Orleans for a few hours. I went with a couple of other GIs to a bar near the train station where we had a marvelous hamburger and a JAX beer. I had never been in a bar before and this was quite an experience. The food was quite good and better yet a fight broke out between two guys who were apparently regulars of the bar. Boy! That was heady stuff. Unfortunately I later ran out of money and had to get $10 from the Red Cross when I was in Montgomery, Alabama, so I could eat until I got back to the Plant Park in Tampa. I was a day late, but we were given a one-day grace period to cover unexpected events while on furlough. Then just outside of Tampa my train hit an automobile where we were delayed for some time while the accident was investigated. I was close to violating my one-day grace period but I finally just got back in time.

THE BIRTH OF A CREW

Not long after we all returned from furlough, around the middle of June, we were assembled into crews. We gathered in the grandstand area of Plant Park and our names were called out as being a part of a crew the identity of which was the first pilot's name. I was to be a part of the Goldin crew, named for Second Lieutenant Samuel Goldin our pilot. After we were assigned, we gathered around Sam and introduced ourselves. It was strange for me to be so closely associated with commissioned officers; up until now it had been them and us, officers and enlisted men. Lt. Goldin was the pilot and it was his crew of which we were a part. He quickly got over to us the idea that, although he was not our buddy, formal officer-enlisted man relationships were not practical for a small group who were to work so closely together. We were in fact to be a crew of specialists each having his own job to perform. We were expected to know our equipment and tasks letter perfect. It seemed to me that to him being liked was not as important as being respected for our individual abilities. We were ten guys who were to be fused into one unit, a bomber crew. Truly *E Pluribus Unum* as our founding fathers declared, Out of Many, One. Later as we got into combat that definition of a crew would prove to be very apt.

The Goldin crew represented the whole United States from the

East Coast, The South, the upper Middle West, the South West and the Far West. .Sam Goldin, our Pilot, was from Philadelphia. Alfred Reynolds, Jr., our Co-Pilot, was from Battle Creek, Mich. Robert Anderson, our Navigator, was from Evanston, Ill. and Stuart Newman, our Bombardier was from Ft. Lauderdale, Fla. Leo Nothling, our original Flight Engineer was replaced later by Marcus Tremble from Wisconsin. Jack Bressie, our Radio Operator was from Angus, Texas. Mifsud, our original Armorer Ball Turret Gunner, was later replaced by Frank Clements, from Dothan, Ala. Robert Gonnering, one of our original Waist Gunners, who was later removed when we went to a nine man crew, was from Greenleaf, Wis., and Ralph Engleman, our Tail Gunner, was from Spring Valley, Ill. Finally, I the other original waist gunner, was from Long Beach, Calif.

DREW FIELD

We were transported to the near-by 327th AAF Replacement Training Unit (RTU) at Drew Field for our combat crew training. Drew Field was out in the boondocks some miles from downtown Tampa, and is today the site of the Tampa International Airport. Nearby to downtown Tampa was Mac Dill Field and it had the new B-29, Super Fortresses, which with their longer range capabilities were slated for the Pacific Theater. Whereas Drew had B-17s and were slated for the European or Mediterranean Theaters. Though that beautiful B-29 looked so new and "modern," I still had my heart set on going to England, joining those valiant people on their small island and thus serving on the Flying Fortress, which I had admired for years.

Our first processing chore as we checked into Drew involved getting our records of next-of-kin finalized and the signing of a Last Will and Testament. For an eighteen-year-old guy, it was unusual to be talking about signing a will and certainly made a little more real what lay ahead of us.

Drew Field was neither a comfortable nor a pretty place. We enlisted men lived in one-story tarpaper barracks similar to what we had at Buckley Field that had no ventilation or cooling other than the ambient swampy wind as it may occur. I have no idea what the officer's quarters were like, but probably no worse than ours. We were issued mosquito netting for our cots, which at times was the only covering we used at night it being too hot and humid for even a sheet.

I had never seen bugs so big and plentiful. To reduce the bug population, we would empty out our footlockers, squirt lighter fluid into the seams and set it on fire to get rid of the insect eggs. Then one day appeared a corporal with a box of spray cans and, of course, a clipboard. We were called outside the barracks where he addressed us, with a high-pitched voice like the late actor Don Knotts:

"Men... this material we are issuing to you today is called DDT. It is a brand new insecticide developed for your use by the Army to help you clean up your barracks. Now, we aren't sure it will kill these monsters we have here at Drew, but it *WILL* blind them and they may then stagger off into some one else's barracks!"

I guess it was his standard gag line he used every day, but it did give us a chuckle and got our attention. The DDT actually performed fairly well, however the supply of bugs was beyond anything the DDT could handle other than minimal control. On a night mission, while we waited 'till sundown to take off, we would figuratively be eaten alive by the bugs. So Sam, taking care of his men, would start up one engine and we would all sit in its prop wash, which created a cooling breeze and too much wind for the bugs to land. I can remember on high altitude missions seeing the flying bugs drop for lack of oxygen and appear to be dead. But they were tough to kill, once we got back down to lower altitudes they would come alive and be hungry again for human blood.

We gunners who had not been to any tech school were called "career gunners." There were three of us so designated; we were to be taught to back-up one of the specialist gunners; the flight engineer, radio operator or armorer. I had been assigned to back-up Jack Bressie our Radio Operator. Tex, as he was called, was a baby faced likable guy who was only 5' 2" tall. He was short for any airman but for a Texan? Unheard of! He and I became instant friends maybe because of our mutual interests in radio. At the time I was a waist gunner and immediately available to the Radio Room if needed. Further, I had quite a bit of training in high school on the operation and building of radios. So Tex and I would go out to the flight line during our spare time where he taught me all I needed to know to operate the radio should he become unable to do so. This arrangement made sense when I was a waist gunner, but when I ended up in the ball turret that assignment no longer made sense but it didn't change. Fortunately, it never became a problem.

Ralph Engleman, our tail gunner, was a big guy with a straightforward forceful manner. I used to say he looked more like a Marine than a flyboy. When Ralph would meet someone he would thrust out his big hand palm side up and say, Ralph Engleman, E N G L E M

AN, glad to meet you. It was the most non-threatening gesture for a strong hand-shake that I have ever seen. His nickname was Foon, which was given to him by his high school friends. Foon was short for Ralphoon as he was sometimes called by them. When we got into combat he would put an extra flak vest covering his tail gunner's seat to assure he would be a father someday after the war...and he was. I think Foon was the only one of us not to smoke cigarettes or a pipe. To his credit he was not strongly influenced by peer pressure as most of us were.

I became the ball turret gunner by a twist of fate. The guy originally assigned to the ball was a little unsure of it so I volunteered to fill in for him from time to time to help him get used to it. I had found the ball fascinating in gunnery school and was at ease in using it, which he wasn't. Unfortunately he had an appendicitis attack and ended up in the hospital and so was removed from the crew. The ball turret was unique in many ways. It was the only position on the B-17 where the crew-member was completely enclosed in a structure isolated from the aircraft structure. As the name signifies, the ball turret was a spherical mechanism within which the gunner rode and operated his sight and two 50 Cal. machine guns. The ball hung outside of the fuselage in the air stream just aft of the radio room and the bomb bay. [See photo at the end of the chapter.] Of necessity it was designed for a small man; most ball turret gunners were probably 5 feet 6 inches or under. At 5 feet 10½ inches I was too tall for the ball. I couldn't wear a parachute, a flak helmet or a flak vest. The two foot-pedals in the ball operated the compensating sight and the interphone connection respectively. I had to scrunch a little sideways to contain my long legs and use only one foot-pedal at a time. I couldn't use the gun sight and the interphone at the same time. In training this was never a problem but in combat, as you shall read later, this was a difficulty

To replace him Sam was able to get Frank Clements (Clem) from a pool of available experienced gunners. He was about 5 feet 10 inches with the lean look of a hunter. Frank was from Alabama, a very good card player and crapshooter. He had flown 30 missions previously with the Eighth Air Force in England and as such was a valuable addition to our crew. I was made the permanent ball turret operator at this time because Clem didn't want it and I kind of liked it, though it was cramped for me.

Although this memoir is focused on the enlisted men, our officers, along with Marty, had the most important assignments from an aircraft operational standpoint. Sam Goldin our command pilot was a very talented pilot but not too close with the enlisted men. He was not there to be our buddy but I would trust him with my life...and did many times. Al Reynolds, Jr., our co-pilot, was a quiet and efficient officer who was not too happy to be stuck being a co-pilot on a bomber crew. Other than the pilots, the other officers we had were Andy Anderson the navigator and Stu Newman the bombardier. Andy was a fun loving friendly guy without pretensions of any kind. He was probably closer with the enlisted men than any of the other officers. Stu was the steady studious type who seemed closer to Sam than the other officers. He was a strong steadying influence on our crew.

Our instructors at Drew were for the most part combat veterans. They were no-nonsense kind of guys, but were very effective teachers. They were just what we needed to be prepared to operate effectively a four engine bomber on a combat mission and to return to the base.

As we all began to learn and refine our jobs on a combat crew, one of us had it tougher than the others. Al Reynolds (called Buster by the officers), was a trained fighter pilot. He and other fighter pilots had been pulled out of fighter transition training and sent to bomber crew assignments where more pilots were needed. He did not like flying in a "big lumbering bird." I recall once when Sam was trying to explain something to Reynolds about simultaneously controlling the throttles for four engines. In frustration, he said to Sam, "Let me fly one engine and you can fly the other three!"

We all could understand his disappointment at being saddled with a bomber co-pilot's job. But we all had to do what we had to do. He developed into a very good bomber pilot whom we had faith in when he was doing the flying. Latter in combat he was given his own crew for a while then was returned to the Goldin crew after an accident that cost his navigator a leg.

THE 15-MINUTE PILOT

In order to assure that any one of us could actually fly our plane temporarily, if needed in an emergency, Sam had each crewman come up front and fly the plane for 10 or 15 minutes. He spent time with each of us explaining the controls, how to set the Auto Pilot, etc, and letting us have the feel of actually piloting the Fort. As I sat there with the control wheel in my hands and my feet on the rudder pedals, making a 90 degrees turn at 7,000 feet over the Gulf Of Mexico, I knew I could do this in an emergency if needed. It was a feeling of power like nothing I had ever felt. To actually be piloting a Flying Fortress was a

THE VIEW FROM THE BOTTOM UP

dream come true for this 18 year old. I didn't want to turn the controls back to Sam, but this had to end. Boy, I thought, if my buddies back home could see me now!

TRAINING GETS REAL

Combat crew training was designed to refine each of the various skills required in a bomber crew individually and collectively. As we honed our specialty skills, we learned how we each performed in support of, and integration with, each other. We had much ground training on equipment operation and repair, oxygen safety, aircraft recognition, etc. There was about 200 hours of flying time invested into each our flight training operations. We had quite a bit of time in formation flying practice, which could be tricky and dangerous because of so many large airplanes flying very close to each other. Unfortunately accidents did happen during such training. There was a bit of black humor among crewmen about these training dangers, "A plane a day in Tampa Bay" was the mantra often repeated by the B-17 crews. However, this bit of dark humor originally referred to the B-26, Martin Marauders flying out of near-by Mac Dill Field, which reportedly had some tricky flying characteristics.

I lost more friends in training than in combat as a matter of fact. On July 21, our training class had one mid-air collision, during a formation-flying mission, between B-17s that reportedly killed 10 guys and injured 11 others. A number of guys were from the next barracks and our touch football buddies. Fortunately we didn't witness this awful event. One of the guys we knew, who ultimately survived, had frozen at the waist exit door afraid to jump out, when someone from the inside of the damaged bomber pushed him out. The man who saved the fear frozen gunner never made it safely out of the plane and perished. The survivors were given furloughs to go home for a bit of rest. These events were a damper on our youthful enthusiasm for a while and caused even more stringent training requirements. The American public never had a clue how many casualties occurred everyday during training by the various military branches in the United States during World War II.

Flying during the summer in Florida meant flying in what was at times very tempestuous weather. The azure skies would begin to reveal wonderfully beautiful puffy clouds marching across the horizon. These visitors would slowly change into angry darkening monster clouds filled with dynamic forces accompanied by lightening flashes. We had to fly in and around the massive thunderheads generated in the tropical climate boiling up thousands of feet into the sky. Of course they were to be avoided if at all possible. We did have a few occasions when we ended up in one of those violent clouds and it was very scary. We were told that Sam had been nicknamed, by some of the other pilots, Thunderhead Sam, because he would fly into them when others wouldn't. Whatever plane we were in would creak and groan with the violent thrashing about inside one of those thunderheads. Foon sitting back in his tail position in these times of rough weather would bounce about more than any of the rest of us, but he loved his little house-like tail gunner position.

Sometimes in the middle of one of those thrashing clouds, we could see glowing blue-white electrical discharges dancing along the wing or in the propellers like a halo of light. This phenomenon is called St. Elmo's Fire and was a sure indicator that lightning could be generated at any time in those super-charged clouds. I had never heard of a B-17 being torn apart by a thunderhead, but I did think it was going to happen on more than one such wild forays. All we in the back could do is hang on tightly to something, do a little praying and plan our next steps if the plane began to come apart. The real work was up front with the pilots whose flying skills were being tested.

On one morning when we were scheduled to fly, it was like a mini hurricane with wild winds and drenching rain. When asked if we were going to fly that day, the Operations Officer's response was, "Once we see birds flying again you will fly!"

We found out that birds will fly in perfectly awful weather and so also did we that morning.

OPEN HOUSE STAR

At one point during our time at Drew, the Base Commander decided, or was required by higher authority, to have an open house to let the public know where their tax dollars were going. There was to be a demonstration of all the various combat crew activities in which we crews were trained. Our crew was selected to be one of two crews demonstrating the ditching procedures because we had one of the two best times during training.

Ditching is a crash landing on water of a land-based airplane. It requires many things to happen right and in order for the plane and its crew to survive. After the pilot has hopefully been able to put his plane down on top of the water without it breaking up, there are only minutes before it will likely sink. There must be an organized routine established to get the crew out of the crashed plane, with their emergency gear such as inflatable rafts, emergency radio, water, etc, in a minimum amount of time. In the ditching training set-up, there was a B-17 wreck mounted on pilings in a pond to simulate a plane that has just ditched. During the demonstration, as in a real event, half of the crew is waiting in the radio room and the rest are up front in the flight deck area. As the whistle was blown, we in the radio room were to leap out of the hatch and on to the wing.

Once out of the radio hatch and on the wing, a side hatch was to be opened; the emergency raft and other gear pulled out, the raft to be inflated by a CO_2 bottle and put in the water. The emergency radio and gear were then to be put in the raft. The crew was to jump in the water, swim while pushing the raft to the tail where they would join up with the other life raft and the rest of the crew. Finally, the two rafts were to be tied together and all the crewmembers were to get into the rafts. At that point in time, a whistle was to be blown signaling the end of the demonstration followed by a big ovation from an adoring public. Well, that's how it happened during the demonstration by the first crew.

Then for the second show came the Goldin crew. When the whistle blew to signal the start of our demonstration I, being an eager young lad, shot out of the radio hatch first. Unbeknown to us the first crew doing their demo had splashed water on the wing and left it very wet. As I hit that wet wing I slipped, fell on my butt and slid off the wet wing into the pond. We were wearing our flight suits complete with GI boots. My boots filled with water and I began to sink deeper into the silent eerie dark green of the pond. Not being able to swim up fast enough with my GI boots filled with pond water, I pulled the cords on the CO_2 cartridges for my Mae West vest. As the vest inflated, I shot to the surface and ended up under the raft that had, in the mean time, been deployed upside down. Coming up inside the upturned raft, I immediately began to thrash at the bottom of the raft, which helped to flip it over and right it. Seeing the raft floating along side me, self-preservation kicked in, and I climbed in it instead of staying outside and help pushing it to join with the other raft.

Now, in a properly performed demonstration we were not supposed to get in the raft until we had pushed it back to join up with the other raft. But I had had enough of that scary pond. I just sat in the raft as the others swam and pushed the raft back to the tail area. Well, let me tell you I was the hit of the show! The visiting public thought it was a comedy routine done on purpose. As I rode along in the raft, and heard the laughter and applause, I nodded my soggy head and waived in acknowledgement of their applause. Pushing the wet hair out of my eyes all I could think was, "Sam's going to kill me, he's going to kill me and then kick me off the crew." I don't think he was happy with me, but he did neither. Walking back to our barracks after the show we stopped into the PX for a Coke and a bag of potato chips. We were still wet from being in the ditching training pond. Our GI boots squished out water when we walked. Upon noticing we were attracting attention due to our wet flight suits and shoes, Bob Gonnering and I began to ad lib a dialog between us about how scary it had been bailing out over Tampa Bay when "our ship went down." As they attentively listened to our ad-lib story, the rest of our guys quickly joined us in our charade. Thinking back now I believe show business missed the discovery of some fine actors and future stars by not being there in the boondocks of Florida on that Saturday in the Summer of 1944.

Gonnering was one of the quieter members of our crew. He was the waist gunner who, unfortunately, got removed from our combat crew in England when they cut the crews to nine guys. Bob was of German extraction and grew up in a Wisconsin area with a large Germanic population. He claimed to be able to speak German well enough to get by. He had a plan that if we got shot down over Germany he and I would seek out a couple of fräuleins and hide out with them until the war was over. He taught me some German drinking songs and a few phrases that might be handy to attract girls and avoid German troops. Very fortunately neither of us had the chance to employ his "sure fire" Germany vacation plan.

WEEKENDS

We had one night training mission each week and the Air Corps in its evil cleverness scheduled those for Friday night. These were six-hour flight time missions and we didn't take off until well after sundown. We didn't return to base until the wee hours of the morning. There were no classes scheduled for Saturday so we got to sleep in on our own time. The night flights were fraught with the problems a lot of other aircraft flying in the same area can create. We would have to flash our landing lights whenever we thought we saw another plane in our area. These flights were usually navigational training and others for the flight crew. We in the back end didn't have much to do unless called up to the flight deck to help watch for aircraft. So it could be

　　　　　　　　　THE VIEW FROM THE BOTTOM UP

boring unless there were city lights to look at.

After a night mission, I looked forward to going to the Flight Line Mess Hall that was open 24 hours a day. Most of us would go there and have anything from breakfast to dinner. My favorite was the freshly cooked southern fried chicken along with a large sweating glass of cold milk. This was a good time for light conversation and the general kidding that goes on between guys who work together. Our bellies full, we would stroll back to our barracks as the sky began to lighten on a dewy fresh Florida morning. Weekend plans were discussed and some times Tex would get us to sing some country song he had taught us. We would crawl into the sack with the netting tucked in all around to discourage the mosquitoes and try to get four or five hours sleep in the day-lighted barracks.

On Saturday nights there would often be a poker game or a game of craps mostly if it were payday. Clem, our veteran waist gunner, was an avid and successful gambler. He loved to shoot craps when he needed to get money to go to Tampa. He had a habit of folding the bills he had won in half length-wise. He would then interweave them between the fingers of his left hand to where they looked like a green fan. We would try to hurry him up to head for town and his answer was always, "Wait until these look like a tight head of lettuce!", waving his left hand, "then we can go."

Tampa was not too friendly a town, at least to enlisted men. I encountered no open hostility but I didn't feel particularly welcome at most places. Mostly we were tolerated or ignored. Perhaps it was the huge amount of service men and women that flooded their town, I don't know. Denver, which also had a great influx of service folks, had been, on the other hand, extremely generous and accepting of GIs. Being less than 21 years of age there was not much to do in Las Vegas so I never got into town to experience their hospitality when I was there. In Tampa we would just go to a movie or a USO dance during the evenings. In the daytime my favorite was to ride the ferry out to St. Petersburg. It was a free ride, thanks to the cities of Tampa and St. Pete, and was a great way to get to St. Pete, which seemed a more receptive place for us.

COMBAT CREW TRAINING IS FINALIZED

Our training was progressing smoothly when our original flight engineer developed hearing problems and had to be removed from flight status. Sam then was able to acquire Marcus Tremble (Marty) who was a highly experienced flight engineer in the B-17. Marty was an unflappable guy in the air or on the ground. He had a bushy mustache, smoked a pipe and looked older than his 25 years.

The flight engineer assisted the pilots in monitoring aircraft systems in flight. He was the primary on-board expert for trouble shooting aircraft systems problems. If that weren't enough, he was the senior enlisted man on a bomber crew and the man that Sam looked toward to handle the rest of us. Marty was perfect for that task and a strong asset for our crew. He moved into place on our crew as if he had been with us the whole time. He was the oldest man on the crew and was a stabilizing influence; but he was not too interesting as a travel companion unless you wanted to look at buildings or historic sites. Our crew, as it would be when we reported for duty at our overseas base, was now in place.

Over the weeks we had gotten to know and respect each other. We enlisted men worked and played together 24 hours a day and seven days a week. We were still teenagers, except for Marty and probably Clem, and we did enjoy playing sports and games of any kind. We played highly competitive touch football in an area between our barracks and the latrine. The main problem with that site was that one of the goal lines was a ditch. Of course one day someone from another crew going for an extra yard broke his leg in the ditch as he scored a touchdown. A combat crewman being deleted from a crew for such a frivolous reason caused great concern and a general chewing out of these fractious young guys.

The officers lived in a separate area of course and as required we didn't spend our off-duty times or socialize with each other. However, we did have easy, respectful and friendly relations with each other during our duty times. We were a coordinated crew with a single focus on our purpose in being. And that was to haul and dump accurately, explosive materials on enemy strategic or tactical targets while contending with the defensive attacks of that enemy.

Throughout our training we had been tested and supervised at each phase. As we neared the end of our two months combat crew training at Drew, we would undergo final checkouts to assure our capabilities, and our medical and dental condition. Unfortunately for me all dental fillings had to be replaced to assure there were no air pockets in them. Any such pockets of air at high altitude would expand in pressure several times normal and would cause severe pain. Sudden tooth pain at altitude could affect a crewmember's performance at the wrong time. I had a mouth full of fillings that had to be dug out and replaced in one session.

It was an administrative goof that had let the dental check go until there wasn't enough time to do a proper job. But I had to live with the consequences of that screw up. I had the corners of my mouth torn open during an all day session in the dentist chair by a clumsy and tired dentist.

Prior to the final medical and dental checks and as a thank you to his crew, Sam took us all out for a last night in Tampa. We had a festive meal in a nice restaurant. Then we went to a local nightclub and saw a great floor show with scantily clad dancers (my first such experience). One of the officers, Andy I believe, pushed my chair against the stage, which was only about two feet high, and blocked my chair so I couldn't move away. As the dancers played to our group of young airmen I was uncomfortably close to them and beet red with embarrassment much to the delight of everyone else. I complained about it then, but I remember the event now with fondness. This was a nice social occasion after all our hard work and mighty thoughtful of Sam who probably paid for it out of his own pocket.

THE GOLDIN CREW

The Goldin crew was now set, as follows:

The Officers
2nd Lt. Samuel Goldin — Sam — Pilot
2nd Lt. Alfred Reynolds — Buster — Co-Pilot
2nd Lt. Robert Anderson — Andy — Navigator
2nd Lt. Stuart Newman — Stu — Bombardier

The Gunners
S/Sgt. Marcus Tremble — Marty — Flight Engineer
Cpl. Jack Bressie — Tex — Radio Operator
Sgt. Frank Clements — Clem — Armorer
Cpl. Robert Gilbert — Gilbert — Ball Turret
Cpl. Robert Gonnering — Bob — Waist
Cpl. Ralph Engleman — Foon — Tail

On September 9, 1944, having done all they could do to get us ready for combat bombing operations, the personnel of the 327th AAF Base Unit of Drew Field, Florida, shipped us out to Hunter Field, Georgia. The Goldin Crew, along with 54 other crews, began the first step to being assigned to combat in a war theater-of-operations somewhere...as yet unknown to us.

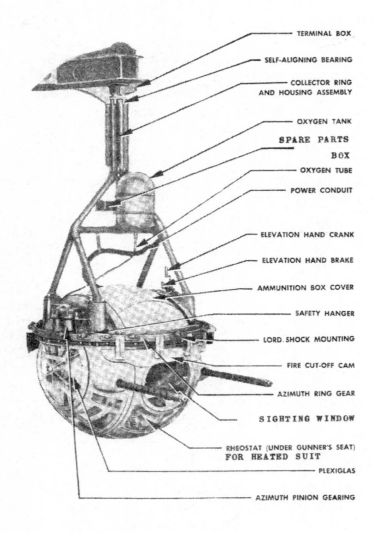

TERMINAL BOX

SELF-ALIGNING BEARING

COLLECTOR RING
AND HOUSING ASSEMBLY

OXYGEN TANK

SPARE PARTS
BOX

OXYGEN TUBE

POWER CONDUIT

ELEVATION HAND CRANK

ELEVATION HAND BRAKE

AMMUNITION BOX COVER

SAFETY HANGER

LORD SHOCK MOUNTING

FIRE CUT-OFF CAM

AZIMUTH RING GEAR

SIGHTING WINDOW

RHEOSTAT (UNDER GUNNER'S SEAT)
FOR HEATED SUIT

PLEXIGLAS

AZIMUTH PINION GEARING

Figure No. 9
SPERRY LOWER BALL TURRET

-26-

The Ball Turret—My assigned position. [USAAF]

Me in cold weather flying gear issued at Drew Field in July in Florida. A laughing matter. [Engleman]

Me with Bob Gonnering, Drew Field, Florida.

THE VIEW FROM THE BOTTOM UP

Chapter 4

Bon Voyage

STATESIDE WRAP-UP

HUNTER Field, Savanna, Georgia, was a mass of new crews and new airplanes. Their job at Hunter Field was to get us all ready to go to our overseas assignments in the best shape possible. For the next few days, we were processed and equipped for overseas deployment. Among these activities, and one that was unique for aircrews, was the "escape pictures" that were taken of each of us. For these we put on a false civilian looking outfit that was a front only. We were given several prints of this photo to be carried at all times on a combat mission. The intention was they could be used in fake documents by underground organizations in enemy occupied areas. These would help us to avoid capture and to escape should we be shot down in enemy territory. This was a seeming contradiction to our instructions to not be caught wearing anything other than our uniforms or else be in violation of the Geneva Convention and thus eligible for execution as a spy.

I believe it was at Hunter Field we were issued the flight crew B-4 clothing travel bags. The B-4 is widely copied today as the hanging travel bag that folds in half for carrying suits. Like the A-2 leather flying jacket, which would be issued later when we were at our English base, the B-4 travel bag was a kind of status symbol issued to flying officers and enlisted men alike.

I remember when at Hunter Field we, and dozens of other crews, were assembled out in an open area where a training film was being made. This film was staring George Montgomery, who was then the singer Dinah Shore's husband, as a crewmember arriving at Hunter Field for deployment overseas. We were told to bring our B-4 bags and just stand attentively along side of them as background to the dialog action. I believe we did a very good job of standing but never did hear from Hollywood for any more work.

On our last night when we could get a pass to go into town, the whole crew went together into Savanna. We had dinner in an Italian restaurant and then went cruising various recommended bars/night-clubs. One of these bars had a gambling room in the back with slot machines and a crap table. We tried a few coins in the slots and made our contributions to those one-armed bandits. Mostly it was just a good time with the guys with whom we were fated to face our war...wherever that was to be. I was getting anxious to know where we going and wanted to get going—all the while hoping it would be England.

We were assigned a new B-17G, S/N 43-38607, to fly to our overseas destination. She was outfitted with temporary luggage racks in the bomb bay to carry all of our personal and issued belongings. Each crewman conducted an inspection of the plane's equipment for his area of responsibility to assure all equipment was in place, in good visual condition and working order as applicable. We then took her out for a three-hour check flight, which was really fun for we gunners with no further duties to perform. It was like having a giant aluminum limousine take us around Georgia and environs. At one point, Sam put her on the deck at about 30 feet or so above the ground and flew along side of a passenger train at the cruising speed of around 150 miles per hour. Every window on that train was filled with smiling faces and there was much waving back and forth. My heart was pumping with excitement and I'm sure I had a grin from ear to ear. Sam was so proficient and careful a pilot that I never had any concern for our safety being so low to the ground roaring along the countryside. We didn't know where the people on the train were going but I guess they knew we were on our way to the war in a few days.

As we completed our various last minute tasks needed to be ready to go to our combat assignment, I began to realize that I might not be returning to my home and family. I was enjoying the flying and the preparations for combat, but at night reality crept in as I lay awake in my cot and thought of home and my family. I was fatalistic about my own fate but worried what it would do to them should I not return. When I knew we were shipping out the next day, I decided to place a phone call home just to say hello and hear their voices once more. Today placing such a call would be quick and easy. But that was not so in 1944, because long distance line access was rationed just like everything else in our country and personal calls had the lowest priority.

I called a long distance operator, placed a call to my folks and was told there would be a two hours wait. In an area with dozens of other crewmen, I sat in a hard chair trying to read and listened for my name to be called that my call was ready. After three hours or so, I called long distance again and was told there still would be a two hours wait for my call to California! I finally cancelled the call after about six hours of waiting. It was around mid-night to 1:00 AM when I gave up waiting for a connection to California. I had work to do in just a few hours. Later I questioned my decision to not wait any longer for my phone connection, but nothing could be done to assure when my call would be actually connected. As it turned out, it would be eight months before I would hear any of their voices again. There was no way to telephone home from overseas during World War II, our only connection was by mail.

INTO THE WILD BLUE

When it was time to leave Hunter Field, the tarmac was jammed with new B-17s awaiting their turns to fly overseas. Out at our new bird as we were making final preparations to leave, it was so hot we had removed all of our clothes except our GI shorts and shoes...then unannounced appeared a Red Cross staff car. The doors opened and two laughing Red Cross girls got out with packages of goodies for each of us. They shook our hands and wished each of us a *Bon Voyage*. They didn't seem to notice our minimal attire, but I was sure uncomfortable.

After they left Sam had to taxi our plane safely through this huge collection of bombers in order to take off. To assure we didn't hit any other ships as we taxied out, he had two of us sitting on the wing tips. We were to signal to warn him of any reduced clearance between our plane and any others. I, on the right wind tip, took this "E Ticket" ride very seriously but with joy. That wing tip riding assignment made me feel important and it was reassuring to be trusted by Sam. Once clear of the parked aircraft, Sam stopped taxiing. We two wing tip riders carefully slid down the wing to the fuselage to the ground and climbed back inside through the waist door.

We finally cleared Hunter Field air space and started our 1,000 miles flight up the East Coast to Dow Field in Bangor, Maine. We did a bit of sightseeing of the East Coast areas along the way up north. Looking out of the waist windows, the United States looked so beautiful and peaceful. It was hard to remember we were a nation at war, and in those pretty towns were people working hard to arm and equip us younger guys to fight that war.

Bangor, Maine and its surroundings was a visual treat of trees, trees and more trees. We spent the night at Dow Field. They provided us a steak dinner that evening as our last evening meal before leaving. It was a first class meal with which we were very impressed. We received our final orders for our overseas destination as we departed the next morning. The orders were sealed and couldn't be opened until we were airborne. Once clear of the Dow Field air space, Sam, as our commander, opened the orders and read them to us over the interphone. We all shouted with enthusiasm when he read our destination was the Eighth Air Force in the United Kingdom! We were to fly by way of Goose Bay, Labrador, then to Reykjavik, Iceland and finally to Valley, Wales. It was the best possible news to me and I think the others as well; we were to be a part of the Mighty Eighth Air Force flying out of England.

Flying northeast over Canada toward Labrador all we could see were forests with here and there a lake or two. It was a vast area without signs of mankind. During our six hour flight I couldn't help thinking how little of the Earth's surface was being used by humans. On September 17th we proceeded to Goose Bay, which was located in the northern area of Labrador just off the Labrador Sea. The base itself appeared to be carved out of pristine forests replete with wild streams. At the base they had all the comforts of home (well almost) with movie theaters, bowling alleys, etc.

Reynolds developed a bad head cold so we were grounded an extra four days at Goose Bay until he got better. The B-17, unlike the B-29 and all modern aircraft, was un-pressurized at altitude. He could develop a disabling headache if his ears due to the cold plugged up with changes in air pressure from the higher altitudes. We could not fly with a co-pilot in that condition.

While there Andy discovered someone had stolen a case of whiskey he had stowed in the bomb bay luggage rack. So it was decided that the crew would have to post a guard with our plane every night because Goose Bay's MPs couldn't watch all the many planes that were parked there. This unhappy lot of course fell to the enlisted men. We decided to draw cards from a deck and the low card was the designated guard for that night. I never lost for the several nights that we were in Goose Bay. I would stop by and shoot the breeze after the movie or whatever with whomever had the duty. I felt sorry for the poor boob who was stuck with the guard duty out there all alone while we were bowling or going to a movie. The time to finally leave came for us. We had only one more stop before we hit the UK so my odds for not getting that last guard duty were pretty good. Right? As the reader knows from the start of this memoir, my luck ran out in Iceland and I caught the duty guarding our airplane in a blizzard.

Our flight to Iceland was uneventful and boring for us gunners.

With nothing to see, we soon grew tired of trying to talk with each other over the constant roar of the engines. I took a nap. I believed in the old military axiom that goes: don't run if you can walk, don't walk if you can stand, don't stand if you can sit, don't sit if you can lie down and don't just lie down if you can sleep. And that's just what I did during our night in Iceland when I was our plane's guardian in the storm as was described in Chapter 1.

THE ADVENTURE BEGINS

After my night of riding out the Icelandic storm in the pilot's seat, and reminiscing about my boyhood and how I got here, I was awakened from my reverie and fitful sleep by Marty sitting in a winterized Jeep and honking the horn.

"Shake a leg, Gilbert," he yelled, "if you want a hot breakfast before we leave for England!"

I slowly uncoiled myself from the coats I had scrunched around to keep me warm during the storm, and made my way out of the waist door. I stretched and walked to the idling Jeep. We drove off toward the base facilities in the cold first light of the quiet after-the-storm Icelandic morning. The breakfast was good and the coffee hot, God was in His heaven and all was right with the world, as the old adage goes.

It was September 23rd when we climbed aboard our ship and were refueled for the last leg of our solo trans-Atlantic ferry mission. The destination was Valley, Wales. The flight crew had the serious work of navigating and piloting to direct us safely for our 1,000-mile leg to Wales. But there was nothing to do for us gunners. At some point along the way, we were joined briefly by a flight of three Douglas A-26 attack bombers. The A-26 (later changed to B-26 designation) airplane was a new model speedy medium bomber made at Douglas Aircraft, Long Beach, where I worked after high school and before entering the Air Corps. When I was at Douglas, the first A-26 was in final assembly in a walled off area of an assembly building as a secret project. Now 15 months later we are all on our way to the war in Europe. They slowed down along side of us for a few minutes as we all waved at each other. Then with an easy burst of speed and a wing waggle, they quickly left us behind and alone once again in the sky over the Atlantic Ocean.

After spending some time looking out of the waist window at endless miles of open sea and clouds, we passed the time reading and napping as the hours went by. Finally after about a six hour flight, as we droned along alone, Stu spotted a green land up ahead jutting out of the sea. He and Andy confirmed for Sam it was indeed Wales and we were right on course. We were at last in view of the mainland of the United Kingdom (UK). It was exciting as we crowded the windows looking out and realizing that this lovely pastoral landscape coming up was Wales. Sam brought our plane in for one of his butter-smooth landings and we had ended the start of our Eighth Air Force tour of duty. Sam taxied behind a Follow Me Jeep in our beautiful new B-17 to a designated area where we were to turn her over. We removed our belongings and stood aside as our plane was quickly checked, signed over and accepted by USAAF personnel. We had grown attached to her, this beautifully gleaming new bird, and wished we could take her with us to our Group assignment. But she was to go elsewhere for other crews to fly at another base from ours. I learned in later years that she was shot down over Berlin on March 18th, 1945, with several of the crew killed and the rest made POWs. Rest In Peace fellow airmen.

At Valley we were billeted in a Nissen hut for transient personnel and fed in a near-by mess hall. The Nissen hut was a very basic form of housing widely used during World War II. It consisted essentially of a half pipe shape of corrugated steel mounted to a concrete floor. The ends were wooden panels with windows.

Our first taste of British politeness was at Valley the night of our arrival. While it was still daylight, we were shown where there was an enlisted men's club we could visit later that evening. By the time we were ready to go to the club, the sky was deep black. The base was under total blackout of course and it was a cloudy moonless night. So we edged along in the complete darkness to an area where we believed the club was. We finally found a door to a Quonset hut which is a larger and more versatile version of the Nissen hut. We tentatively went into the bright light inside. We found it to be a very nice club with a snack bar where we bought peanut butter sandwiches and Coca Colas from a pretty English girl. They took our American money and tried to explain their money to us. As we pondered over these strange coins, one of our guys commented, "Man did you ever see so many women in one place before?"

Then one of the young women, who had helped us with the money explanations, said, without snide innuendo,

"This is a Women's RAF club and men are not allowed."

We were then directed across the street to the men's club, which we had missed in the dark. This was a great introduction to British civility.

In the morning, after chow in an RAF mess hall, we were trans-

THE VIEW FROM THE BOTTOM UP

ported by truck to the train station in Valley. The Welch children ran after the trucks yelling for "Gum, chum?" They and the town seemed somewhat dirty or sooty to me. I tried to observe and not judge as best I could. These kids seemed a happy bunch running down the street yelling at the Yanks. This was the start of what we call culture shock today. However, shock is too strong a verb for what I felt. Wales was different than back home but I loved the differences, which seemed quaint and enduring.

We traveled by train to a replacement center called Stone for processing into the 8th Air Force. We were told that normally crews were sent to theater schools to be instructed on how things were done here in the European Theater of Operations (ETO). But we were needed now at our operational Group so we were to be transported directly there from Stone. We found our assigned Group was the 381st Bomb Group (Heavy) at Station 167, Ridgewell. As our crew excitedly talked together, the scuttlebutt was that the 381st was a first rate outfit. It was a part of the First Combat Wing of the First Air Division of the Eighth Air Force and had a very good combat record.

CAMBRIDGE

On September 27th we were sent by train to Cambridge to await a truck from the 381st Bomb Group, which would pick us up later in the day. We were given a few hours to sightsee around Cambridge. Wow! What a gorgeous ancient city, I thought. I recall vividly the incredibly green grounds in the area of the many churches and chapels. Walking inside a chapel of one of the colleges seemed like being in a cathedral to this boy from Long Beach. I quietly gasped looking at the soaring gothic architecture and many stained glass windows; it was awe-inspiring.

The sight of Cambridge University students walking around and riding bicycles wearing those historic flowing academic gowns was surreal to me. I had been prepared for the valiant country at war with all the barbed wire and stern British soldiers on guard everywhere, but here we saw the centuries old traditional student gowns still being worn. The ancient buildings and narrow streets with discrete signs identifying the occupant shops or businesses rather than bold neon signs looked wonderfully archaic. Cambridge seemed unfazed by time and a temporary thing called World War II. Of course that was not true. It was just tangible evidence of human, and particularly of British, quiet adaptability to the most difficult of conditions. It was finally real to me that we were here in England and seeing first hand places I had only read about but never expected to actually see.

Soaking up the local atmosphere and experiencing England first hand was exciting and interesting, but we were anxious to see Ridgewell, our home for the next eight months or so, God willing.

Eventually, we were picked up and transported the 30 miles or so along narrow roads through a picture book countryside to Ridgewell. It was a scaled down country it seemed to me. Most everything was smaller than back home; the cars, the roads, the trains, etc. I hung out the back of our truck gawking as we roared through quaint villages complete with country inns, churches and farm homes built with thick straw thatched roofs. All looking like pretty faded illustrations in a book.

Our GI driver seemed intent on straightening out these winding roads. His truck was at times brushing against berry bushes as he sped along with little regard for the scenic value of our trip. There were fields of farms separated by rolled barbed wire put in place to deter potential enemy parachutists. In the fields along the way there were many young women doing the farming. Later we were to learn these were the WLA girls (Women's Land Army) who were an important force to help replace the many men away in the military. We got to know the WLA girls later at dances held I believe in Yeldham. We finally slowed down as we entered the village of Yeldham. It was quiet and quaint with a small train station by a lovely inn nearby named "The Waggon [sic] & Horses." Our base was just down the road a couple of miles.

RIDGEWELL—STATION 167

Finally, we arrived at the unimposing main gate of the Ridgewell AAFB guarded by a bored MP. We were taken to our respective Squadron areas. The officers and enlisted men of course lived in separate areas. We enlisted men were delivered to Site Five near the 533rd Squadron Orderly Room. This was a rather bleak site with scattered Nissen huts and rock lined pathways, but few trees or plants I can recall. As we disembarked from the truck with our belongings, the Squadron Adjutant welcomed us to the 533rd. He gave us a brief hello and told us that they were glad to have us here. He introduced a sergeant who would get us started settling in, and who would answer any questions we might have. The sergeant escorted us to Hut 5, our home for our time in Ridgewell, and gave us the directions to the supply

THE VIEW FROM THE BOTTOM UP

room where we could pick up our bedding.

As we walked to our hut, quite appropriately the familiar sound of B-17's big Wright-Cyclone engines from near-by could be heard penetrating the chilly autumn air as mechanics worked into the twilight. We stopped and turned toward that familiar and comforting sound. We were here, it had been a long time in training and a lot of preparation, but we were here at last. I was filled with nervous excitement and some sober concern for what was ahead for us as we were about to enter the Big League of air war over Europe.

"Well let's go in and meet our hut mates," someone said, as we opened the outer door of Hut Five, Site Five, Ridgewell. England.

HEADQUARTERS THIRD AIR FORCE STAGING WING   G-ALT-1
Office of the Commanding Officer

SPECIAL ORDERS)   Hunter Field, Ga.
           :   15 September 1944
NO   259)   E X T R A C T

*   *   *

    2. Following B-17 Repl Crewsie asgd Shipment FK-350-BJ (Project 92840R) and WP fr Hunter Field, Ga, immediately by air to Dow Field, Bangor, Me, rptg to CG ATC for temp duty pending further dispatch to overseas destination:

FK-350-BJ- 78

P	1091	2nd Lt SAMUEL GOLDIN	0825837	Ap No. 43-38607
CP	1054	2nd Lt ALFRED J REYNOLDS	0823154	(B-17-G)
N	1034	2nd Lt ROBERT H ANDERSON	02064500	
B	1035	2nd Lt STUART G NEWMAN	02061321	
EG	748	S/Sgt Marcus J Tremble	12034687	
ROG	757	Cpl Jack L Bressie	38436975	
1 CG	611 (757)	Cpl Robert B Gilbert	19207435	
2 CG	611 (748)	Cpl Robert J Gonnering	36834645	
3 CG	611 (612)	Cpl Ralph C Engelman	16188783	
AG	612	Sgt Frank E Clements	34161883	

    a. See Annex "A" to this order.
    b. This shipment will use APO 16500-BJ78 c/o Postmaster, New York, N.Y.
    c. Pers will be clothed and equipped in accordance with List H, Individual Clo and Equipment, 15 Nov 43, as amended. Acft will be equipped and loaded in accordance with List C.
    d. O baggage not transported by air may be shipped to New York P/E for movement by water to destination.
    e. TDN 501-31 P 431-01, 02, 03, 07, 08 212/50425.
    f. Auth: Ltr Hq AAF 370.5 (21 Aug 44) PUB-R-AF-M subject: "Movement O, Shipment FD-350" dated 22 Aug 44.

*   *   *

    By order of Colonel FITZMAURICE:

                                        DAVID S CARTER,
                                        Capt, Air Corps,
                                        Adjutant.

OFFICIAL:

ARTHUR L TSHOEPL,
Capt, Air Corps,
Asst Adjutant.

DISTRIBUTION: 5-CG ATC Dow Field, Bangor, Me (via airmail)
                     plus regular combat crew distribution.

Our shipment overseas orders.

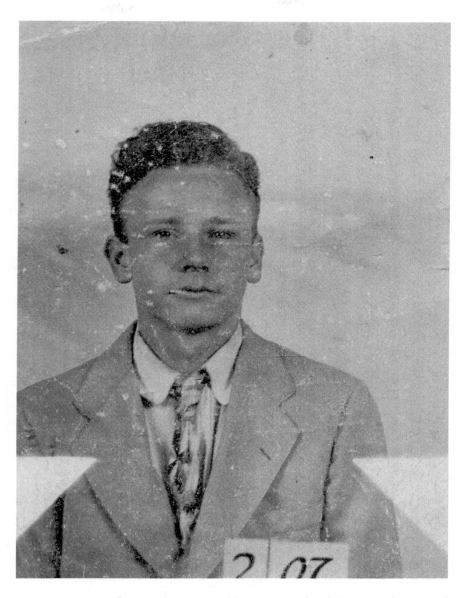

Escape picture taken at Hunter Field, Georgia, for fake identification if needed to facilitate evasion or escape from enemy forces. The shirt, tie and coat were a one-piece fake for the picture.

THE VIEW FROM THE BOTTOM UP

Chapter 5

And So It Begins

AS we tentatively walked into the hut, we were greeted with a round of good-natured raucous greetings mostly having to do with being a rookie crew. My first impression of the hut was it was messy like guy's rooms end up being if they are left alone. It had a warm friendly feeling and smelled of cigarette smoke, which was usual in those days. Each guy had his own little arrangement of boxes, shelves, poles and wires for his area. This gave the hut a somewhat jumbled non-military look that seemed to satisfy most airmen at that time because they took pride in being non-military.

The hut was utilitarian in its simplicity. Like all Nissen huts, it was a half pipe of corrugated steel on a concrete slab with a small coke stove in the center. For those who may not know, coke is a fuel derived from coal. It comes in hard nuggets of the residual material from coal when it is processed to make a cleaner handling and slower burning fuel.

There were no windows on the sides as there are in Quonset huts, but there were windows of wire reinforced translucent glass, as you see in some restrooms, on both ends. On one end, where we had entered, was a storm door arrangement with a little foyer-like space to contain the winter air blasts as one entered.

We came into the hut and dropped our bags as our new hut-mates met us with smiles; hands outstretched, and introduced themselves. They were from the Steinwinter crew, Bill Hiney, Tom Guilfoyle, Dan Adair, Frank Hrehocik, and Jackie Nickols. These guys would become our best friends and the information source for just about everything we needed to know to get along in Ridgewell. As in any military organization, one is given all sorts of official information in directives and orientations, but the real information comes from those who have been there. Our hut-mates would give us the low-down on people, places and things. Their information made adjusting to this new place relatively easy. What I really wanted to know from them was what combat was like, but I didn't ask for fear of appearing too anxious.

There were six empty cots along one side of the hut for us to pick out and set up our own little worlds. In time we would arrange each of our areas to our individual tastes also adding to the general male ambience. We went to Supply and picked up our bedding as directed. We found these were RAF issue items of bedding because Ridgewell had been originally an RAF base. They didn't have mattresses as such. They used three square pads called biscuits. The biscuits were then stuffed inside a mattress sack by us and thus functioned as a mattress. The biscuits had an unfortunate habit of spreading apart inside the sack and providing a gap for the cold air to crawl through in the middle of the night.

WELCOME TO THE ETO

We were setting up our areas and making our beds when an unusual deep-throated noise could be heard outside along with the roar of a fighter and machine gun fire.

"Oh my God, it's a buzz bomb real close!" someone said.

We all ran outside; to see it or go to the bomb shelter, I didn't know which. Everyone skipped the bomb shelter and stayed to watch the battle in the sky. What we next witnessed was more exciting than any movie I had ever seen. With wide-eyed excitement, I eagerly watched as an RAF Spitfire made passes while firing his machine guns at the buzz bomb. Frank Hrehocik, I believe it was, explained to us that the Spit was trying to detonate it in mid-air before it fell to earth and exploded on people or buildings.

The buzz bomb, called the V1 by the Germans, was a pilot-less flying bomb. It was designed to drop on the ground after a crude preset timer signaled time to fall and explode or when it ran out of fuel. This very imprecise targeting method explained why Ridgewell was in what was called "buzz bomb alley." We were just north of London; the real target of the buzz bombs, thus a V1 that overran London was likely headed our way. The buzz bomb onslaught of London started in late June 1944 a few months before our arrival. This was a renewal of the London Blitz by Germany but this time by pilot-less drone aircraft. It was said the buzz bombs were Germany's attempt to destroy London in response to the invasion of Europe by the Allies on D-Day.

We watched the buzz bomb with bated breath as it came toward us. The V1 seemed slow when compared to the speed of the nimble Spitfire. The deep throaty sound of the V1's pulse jet engine reminded me of a diesel truck laboring up a steep hill with a heavy load. The RAF pilot in his magnificent sweeping Spitfire finally scored a direct hit and the doodlebug blew up in mid-air with a bright flash of light and a massive explosion. The explosion was so near that the concussion knocked me off my perch on a fence where I had climbed to get a better view. Wow, I thought, what an introduction to life in the ETO! However, that event was unique and we never again were to witness such a spectacular destruction of a buzz bomb. In the future, we would many times hear that ominous sound of the V1 drone and just wait. When the engine stopped it fell to the ground and exploded. So we would listen for the beast to keep making its unique noise and fly by us and to drop harmlessly in an open field somewhere. But we saw no more magnificent Spitfire attacks.

It being chow time by now, we went to the Combat Mess for our evening meal. It was a pleasant surprise to find our meals were served on china and not on the Army's usual formed steel trays. We discovered at Ridgewell, combat personnel were catered to as much as possible. An example of that was the Combat Mess, which served the combat crewmen both officers and enlisted men. It had a common kitchen with two mess halls; one for the officers and one for the enlisted men. We didn't fraternize during our meals as is required by the Army, but we did eat the same food prepared by the same people. It was the best food available at the time.

A bicycle was the favorite mode of transportation on our base when one couldn't get a ride. While we were walking back to the hut, the Steinwinter guys pointed out to us we should probably buy bicycles to get around the base. Mostly guys would acquire the bike of someone going home or perhaps lost in action. In a hut near ours we were introduced to a gunner named Frank who restored damaged and worn-out bikes as a sideline. Frank was a whiz of a mechanic on bicycles. He would get bits and pieces of wrecked aircraft to replace brake pads, control cables, bolts, etc, on old bikes. His restored machines lacked nothing except fresh paint and the price was right. We were to buy our bikes from him in a few days when we had the time to be interested in such things.

Somewhere in this time frame I learned to smoke cigarettes on purpose to look like an experienced airman...or so I thought. Of course it was a pathetic way to bolster my self confidence but it was what I chose to do. It seems so silly, and even stupid, now but then it was important and helped me feel I belonged

The day after our arrival, the Goldin crew was called together by 533rd Bomb Squadron Operations officers and the crew was immediately changed. In the 381st we were to fly with only one waist gunner. They had removed the radio room machine gun on all their aircraft because it was thought not to be particularly effective. If things were to get hot and heavy with fighter attacks, the radio operator would then fill in the open waist gun position. To comply with this directive, Sam selected Bob Gonnering as the gunner to be removed from the crew. Bob went into a pool of gunners that was used to supply spare gunners when a regular gunner was sick or injured. He later was trained as and became a togglier, which was an enlisted man bombardier.

The Goldin crew was then given the in-theater training we needed to operate as a part of the 381st Bomb Group and the Eighth Air Force. We learned what was expected of each crewmember in combat operations as well as day-to-day normal routines. We were familiarized with how things were done in this theater of war and in our Bomb Group. Our orientation sessions were at times job specific, such as gunners only or pilots only while others were general crew level information. During eight days of constant ground training and orientation, we had one training flight of two hours on the 6th of October. It was part check-out of the crew and part routine training of air-to-air gunnery and navigation. We were found to be ready for combat and assigned to flight status. On our first four or five missions Sam would be flying as co-pilot with a combat experienced pilot flying as First Pilot and Reynolds would stand down.

During this time we were outfitted with our personal flight gear as needed including an equipment bag in which to store them. A leather shoulder holster with a Colt .45 automatic pistol in it was issued to each man. We were also issued our A2 leather flight jackets. [See photo at the end of the chapter.] These had become the symbol of an airman in the United States Army Air Corps as much as anything. I was as proud of that jacket as of my gunner's silver wings. Somewhere in this time frame we who were corporals and then to sergeant. No one flew over Germany at that time and place as any grade lower than sergeant. On the seventh and eighth of October, we were on flight status but no missions were scheduled due to bad weather. We anxiously awaited our first combat bombing mission assignment with trepidation and muted excitement.

We took these couple of days as a chance to acquire our bicycles. We went over to Frank, the bicycle guy, and selected our bikes. Mine appeared to have been red in an earlier life so I named her Ole Red. Frank had put all new brake cables and pads on her. The tires seemed to be holding air though they didn't look too new, but Frank assured me they were fine. Although we had been warned about the difference in braking systems between American and British, most of us, including me, had to learn the hard way...crashing. At this time in the states the common bicycle braking system was the New Departure brand brake. With it, to slow or stop your bicycle, you moved your pedal backwards with varying pressure to increase the stopping time. While it was fresh in my mind, I did fairly well using the hand brakes instead of the more familiar back pedal system. Within minutes of getting my new bike, we were happily flying down a road when a hump suddenly appeared in our path. I carefully back-pedaled to slow down. When that didn't seem to be working I back-pedaled faster only to continue flying into the hump. At the last second, and too late, I remembered and squeezed the hand control for the brakes. Not stopping in time, I hit the bump and was thrown by Ole Red as a lesson of tough love I guess. Most times I remembered the hand brakes, but I had a few more lapses of memory about her British braking characteristics. We also found that beer didn't help memory very much for any of us. There were many stories of back pedaling into chaos on the way home from the base pub.

As we waited for our time to start our combat tour, we rode our bikes around the base checking out such facilities as the base pub and the Aero Club. The Aero Club was a pleasant place attended to by Red Cross ladies. One could read, play pool, have a light snack and just generally relax. Out of curiosity I biked down to the flight line and took a look at these veteran aircraft as they waited quietly on their hard stands for their next call to combat. Some were bare metal finished and gleamed in the daylight. Most were camouflage painted and bore oil stains streaming back on the wings from the many hours of hard work by their Wright-Cyclone engines. I was looking at one old bird with many patches on her olive drab skin and wondered how well she was able to fly in her seemingly distressed condition. An airplane mechanic who was walking away from the bird said, "Hi, you a new gunner?'

Startled, I said. "Yeah, does it show? Ha ha."

"Sure." He said. " I see you guys come down here to the flight line when you are just starting your tours all bright eyed and asking questions. Then later after a few missions, you only come down here when you have to. You take it all for granted."

I felt ill at ease with this veteran mechanic who didn't seem too happy with my being there. So just to say something, indicating the battered old bird he had been working on, I said, "She sure looks kind a beat-up."

Seeming to have taken offense, he proudly said, "Let me tell you something Sarge, she has taken crews to Germany and delivered their bombs over fifty times and always came back no matter how battered she was. There ain't no quit in her...ever!"

Then the obvious came to my mind. We bomber crews had such things as flak vests and helmets as flak protection gear, but maybe our biggest protection was the unparalleled toughness of the Boeing Flying Fortress itself and our hard working ground crews. We all had seen pictures of ships half blown away and still getting back to their base. For sure they weren't bullet or flak proof, but they would take the best the enemy had to offer and still keep coming back. The Fort reminded me of a tough veteran prizefighter who would take punches round after round, looking really beat-up, but still answer the bell for the next round. Boeing had done a great job in designing probably the hardest bomber to shoot down that had ever been produced. I thought from now on I'd look with more respect at these beat-up looking veteran birds, which were still actively fighting the war, and the tireless ground crews who took care of them.

THE FIRST MISSION

On the night of October 8th, I had trouble getting to sleep. We were scheduled to fly on the next mission the Group flew and I had some anxiety about what lie ahead and how I would perform my job. Finally I drifted off into a sleep for a couple of hours when at around 3:00 AM, on October the 9th, the duty orderly awakened us. He read off our names and announced, "You're flying today. Breakfast is at 3:45. The trucks will pick you up by the orderly room in 30 minutes."

One of the guys from the Steinwinter crew said, "I just realized today is the Group's 200th mission. There was supposed to be a big party tonight, but it was nixed by Division or Wing. Too bad, you guys could have really started off your tour with a celebration!"

Not really caring about any Group celebrations, we went out into the icy and quiet black night for our first mission. My first time to face what ever the Nazis wanted to throw at us...that was more important to me. We straggled over and got on the trucks waiting to take us to the combat mess. The mess hall was warm and friendly with crews comfortably chatting over steaming cups of strong GI coffee and having their last meal until suppertime. I don't recall actually eating that breakfast, but I do remember the feeling of being with all these combat veterans casually eating and chatting. After breakfast we "nonchalantly" walked out to the trucks waiting in the dark to take us to the flight line. The conversations I heard were the usual GI banter along with predictions of where we were going today. Someone said, "A guy I know over in Operations said we were going on a short mission to France today so we'd be back early for the 200th mission party."

"Riley, you're full of it!" said someone else, "The party's been cancelled. They're afraid we'll get drunk and hurt each other like happened at other outfits on their 200th mission party."

And so it went. This casual conversation took some of the edge off my first mission anxiety.

In the 381st, the gunners, other than the flight engineer and the radio operator, didn't go to the mission briefing. They would get the information they needed from their crewmembers who were at the briefing. We picked up our equipment bags and caught a ride out to our plane for today a venerable ship named Princess Pat, which some months later crashed and burned on the continent. We went about cleaning and re-assembling our guns to assure they were in perfect operating condition. We installed them in Princess Pat and awaited our pilot and the others who had been to the mission briefing. While waiting for the rest of our crew, we busied ourselves with double-checking our personal equipment and guns. While standing away from our plane, I busied myself nervously smoking a few cigarettes and relieving the morning's coffee. I was most of all lost in my thoughts of what the day was going to be like. Would it be a tough raid today? I had always taken our technical training seriously and felt competent with my assignment in the ball turret, but would I do my job as I knew how to do it once the action started? What if we have major damage by flak or fighters will I have time to get out of the ball and into the waist where my parachute is stored? What does it feel like to see flak up ahead and know you must fly through it? That question is what I wanted to know most of all, but had never asked anyone. The morning coffee was bitter on my edgy stomach.

I looked at that old warhorse, Princess Pat, with all her damaged and patched areas, and remembered the mechanic who told me about his battered airplane which had "no quit in her"

I thought, well old girl, if you can do it over and over again so can I. The sounds of; shouted orders, talk and random laughter, the clanging of wrenches, of trucks grinding by and of auxiliary power units putt-putting away all drifted to us through the cold dark early morning air. It was the sounds of life all around us. Then, suddenly I remembered I hadn't written to my folks for a while. I had intended to write before my first mission and tell them how much they meant to me. It was awkward trying to write about my feelings because we could not mention we were flying combat, and because of censorship I couldn't write one of those "tell them what was going on with me letters." But, I had intended to write a note to just communicate with home. And now I realized I had forgotten even that simple gesture.

With our breaths making visible vapor in the cold predawn morning air, we anxiously waited for the rest of our crew.

Standing in front of Hut 5, our home in Ridgewell, England, in my A-2 leather jacket with the 533rd Bomb Squadron patch. [Frank Hrehocik]

Chapter 6

Return to Schweinfurt

BACKGROUND

SCHWEINFURT, Germany, had been a highly defended target with devastating results on the two prior famous missions there. On the first Schweinfurt raid, on August 17th, 1943, the Eighth AF lost 36 bombers out of 188 sent. The 381st lost 11 out of 18 bombers sent...a devastating 61% loss. On the second Schweinfurt raid, on October 14th, 1943, which became known as Black Thursday, the Eighth AF lost 60 out of 229 bombers sent. The 381st was fortunate this time and "only" lost one aircraft out of 15 sent. When we were in training in the States, Schweinfurt was well known to all the aircrews as the toughest of the toughest targets in Germany.

When the rest of the crew arrived at Princess Pat for our first mission, our command pilot Lt. Dale Windsor called us inside the waist area to talk with us. He introduced himself as our temporary first pilot and gave us a quick pitch on what he expected of each of us. So far so good, but he was holding something back. Finally, he said, "I'm sure you have all heard of Schweinfurt and the ball bearing plant there? As you may know, the past missions there have been a little rough. Today we are returning to Schweinfurt."

Our pilot continued, "We believe that things will be much better there today than in the past, but you will all have to be on your toes. Sam tells me you are well trained and up to the challenge. Good luck."

As for me I would have been uneasy no matter what the target was. The target being Schweinfurt added some concern of course but mostly I just wanted to get this day behind me. The first time you do anything there is some concern about how it will go, how you will do, etc. For the crew, except Lt. Windsor and Clem, this was going to be the first time anyone had shot at us with the intent to kill. I was buzzing inside with anxious anticipation.

I have often thought of that veteran command pilot, Dale Windsor, having to shepherd a green crew on their first mission and then the target turns out to be Schweinfurt! He sure deserved an Atta Boy for his calm leadership that day.

When the green flare signal came to start engines, from all around us we could hear the familiar sounds of B-17s coming alive with a belch of smoke and that powerful engine rumble. With the double green flare signal, each ship began to taxi out of its hard stand and move in-order along the perimeter track. We gunners in the rear areas of the ship were all hunched in our required take off positions in the radio room.

The sounds of bomb laden four-engine bombers waiting, and then moving in line toward the head of the runway, filled the air of the otherwise quiet Essex morning. At thirty seconds intervals, each of these veteran bombers turned into the runway. As our ship reached the end of the runway, its engines were throttled up to take off power, the brakes released and we roared down the runway to lift off in the pre-dawn cold morning sky with a full load of gasoline and bombs. Take off was a critical part of each mission because the bombs and aviation fuel would make a massive explosion should we crash. .

With a sigh of relief as we were airborne, I wondered about the farmers, and others who lived all around us, and how these very loud noises affected them. They didn't need any alarm clocks or cock's crowing to wake up to each morning...they had us.

After each bomber became airborne, they flew in an orderly manner into their assigned spot in their Squadron formation. Then the Squadrons assembled into the Group formation. During Group Assembly operations, while we were still over England, I remember watching out the waist window with some wonder at the actions of all these bomb and gasoline laden aircraft as they gracefully moved into their formation positions. We had done this in training in Florida, but this time someone was going to try and shoot us out of the sky. I felt some tension in anticipation but busied my mind on my job.

I had made my ball turret ready to be entered on command. As a normal routine, shortly after take off the ball turret gunners would be ordered to get their turrets ready. We would unlock and hand-crank the turret until the guns pointed straight down. In this position the access door was in position to be entered. Then we would lock the turret in place, open and leave open the turret door to make it immediately accessible As one looked out at the formation, all the ball turrets had their guns pointing down and were ready to be entered. It was a formidable sight!

At 10,000 feet, Sam, serving as co-pilot, ordered everyone to put on his oxygen mask. We buckled our masks on and connected the oxygen supply hose to the mask and checked the oxygen regulator indicator to verify the oxygen system was working. Sam there after called for an oxygen check for each guy starting in the tail gunner's spot with Ralph Engleman and moving forward to each of us in order. As long as we were above 10,000 feet we had oxygen checks every 15 minutes or so throughout the day.

No one needed tell us to connect and turn on our electrically heated suits because the temperature drops dramatically as we gain altitude and you know you need heat. With oxygen, however, you can die for lack of it without realizing you are in trouble. In fact paradoxically the first symptom of anoxia, the lack of adequate oxygen, is an unusual sense of well being or elation.

When the order came for me to get into the ball turret, I, aided by Tex, entered the turret and made the connections to the interphone, the heated suit and the oxygen. I latched the belt across my back that would keep me from falling out of the plane if my door should come open. After making sure I had my connections made, Tex closed the door over my back. I latched it; released the brake, turned the power on and rotated the turret backwards so the guns were horizontal. That first movement took some getting used to because it gave one the scary feeling of falling backward into space. All of our actions so far have been those we have done many times during our training, which has been extensive and has prepared us well. I was now in my place where I would remain for the next six and half hours or so and where I would participate in my first combat mission.

I sat rolled up in my private world in the ball turret. I breathed the cool dry oxygen/air mixture while the Group roared along its way over the English Channel and France toward Germany and our target... Schweinfurt. We were at 24,000 feet altitude, with a temperature of minus 38°F, and moving through a clear brilliantly deep blue sky.

Throughout this memoir I have recorded the temperatures for each mission as a general statistic. It becomes routine to note the temperatures, but to give scope to these temperatures it must be kept in mind that our modern household freezers are set for 0°F, whereas our missions were carried out at up to 70° below zero. These bitter cold conditions were an added hazard on each mission.

Below us Europe and the ground war were completely obscured by bumpy gray wool-looking cloud coverage. I could see our little friends (P-51 Mustangs) the fighter escorts moving about and keeping track of us. It was a comforting sight. So far no bandits (enemy fighters) reported. Good!

Interphone conversation was kept to a minimum and primarily for essential information only. As an unforeseen problem, we had new oxygen masks with the microphone built in. This was supposed to be an improvement over the old throat mike but it had problems. At altitude the moisture from our breaths collected and froze and caused the mask mikes to garble our voices and in some cases blocked the oxygen. This problem gave an added difficulty to be worked around. We each experimented with ways to break up the ice and clear our mask mikes with limited success. Fortunately our veteran pilot had a throat mike so he could be heard loud and clear. With no real emergencies, we would be all right. But because of this experience we all elected to go back to throat mikes for our future missions even though they were less convenient. At least we will be able to understand each other.

A bomber formation is a dynamic thing and never a static fixed grouping as it may appear from the outside the formation. All the aircraft are moving relative to each other, up and down and sideways, as the pilots work to keep their positions with as little jockeying as possible. From my unique observation position hanging under the ship in the ball turret, I watched all the planes along side of, and below us, and marveled at this ballet of massive machines. I don't think bomber pilots got enough credit for their difficult and arduous assignment in formation flying.

Rotating my turret and keeping on the lookout for bandits I could see scattered inaccurate flak around our group but not too close to our plane. The term flak is an acronym of the German words *flieger abwehr kanone*, meaning anti-aircraft artillery. This was our first sighting of flak and it didn't seem too ominous so far. For me at that time, I didn't appreciate fully that each of those little black bursts were the center of an explosion that was throwing hunks of steel through the air. As we started our bomb run, I rotated my turret forward to watch the bomb bay doors coming open. My job on the bomb run was to visually track the bombs as they fell from the bomb bay and to observe and mentally record the bomb strikes. I looked forward at the bomb bay area awaiting the 'bombs away' call from Stu Newman. Upon release of the smoke bomb from the lead ship, Stu released our bomb load, and announced, 'bombs away'! Our ship softly lifted as the weight of the bomb load was removed. I followed the bombs all the way down as they disappeared into the clouds. On this date of course there were no bomb strikes to be observed because we were bombing by radar through clouds. When we could see the results of the bombing, I was to tell what I saw to the Intelligence officers during interrogation after the mission. This input form the ball turret gunners provided a human back-up to the bomb strike photos. I liked this assignment because it helped keep my mind busy.

Having dropped our deadly cargo toward Schweinfurt, the bomb bay doors slowly closed and we headed for home back across Germany and France. Hopefully, we would avoid any more flak and not be attacked by Luftwaffe fighters. As it turned out, we had no further encounters with flak or fighters on our way back to Ridgewell. Once over England, we were talking back and forth about our first experience in combat over Germany. Then Clem brought a bit of reality to us when he said deliberately, with his Alabama drawl, "I hate to tell you boys, but that was a full fledged milk run. You ain't seen any combat yet. They ain't all gonna be like this, trust me."

He was right of course, but it sure felt good to us to have gotten our feet wet this way.

After the mission we removed, cleaned, oiled reassembled and stored our guns. We returned our flight equipment to the equipment building and went to Interrogation to make a verbal report to the Intelligence Officers. We stood around in a smoky anteroom waiting to be called to give our reports. The Red Cross was there with hot coffee, hot chocolate and doughnuts. Also, available from the Medics, was a shot of Scotch whisky if you wanted or needed it. I don't recall any of our guys taking the Scotch this date. Each crew was called into Interrogation as a group and significant information would be related plus observations any crewmember wished to make. Once finished with interrogation, we were free to go to chow. We really looked forward to that meal because it had been around 12 hours since breakfast. Prior to taking off we had each been given a small box labeled High Carbohydrate Ration, which contained hard candy, fudge and Chiclets chewing gum. These were snacked on during the mission to account for the sugar burned by adrenalin and assuaged the hunger to some degree.

After chow and back in the hut, our hut-mates quizzed us about our first combat mission.

"Well, there was bad news and there was good news," we told them.

"The bad news was that it was Schweinfurt...and the good news was it was a milk run!"

But, we had finally started our combat tour of duty on this 9th day of October, 1944.

The ensuing missions were not so benign. My second, third and forth missions were to the train marshalling yards of Cologne, Germany. Cologne of course is an ancient and historic city with a famous beautiful cathedral, which had been saved from destruction by careful bombing. [See photo at the end of the chapter.] During World War II Cologne's strategic location on the Rhine River made it very important. It was a transportation hub for Germany and an entrance to the German homeland from occupied France.

On October 14th, the Goldin crew, except for Foon and Stu who both had been hospitalized with pneumonia, was assigned to fly combat again for our second mission. When we found the target was the rail yards of Cologne we knew we were in for a more difficult mission than our first had been. Poor weather had caused missions to Cologne to be scrubbed in the past few days. But the 8th Air Force was scheduling the 381st to Cologne again, meaning it was of immediate importance to the U.S. military campaign. A further indication that this was an important target, was the fact that today our Squadron Commander, Lieutenant Colonel George G. Shackley, was leading our Group as it led a five Group task force. Usually our commanding officers took the lead role when a mission appeared to be particularly difficult or important.

Our plane this date was Rotherhite's Revenge a veteran ship that had endured scores of prior missions against German fighters and anti aircraft guns. She was in a battered condition with holes and patches all over. She was often assigned to newer crews because, I suppose, of the higher incidence of calamitous events happening to them. She was named for a London borough flattened by the Luftwaffe in attempt to break the English spirit. They didn't understand the English people very well. That action only pissed them off. The English subscribed to war bonds in the amount of money to buy a Flying Fortress then asked the 381st to name a new bomber after their destroyed town. Serial number 761 was dedicated with this name in formal ceremonies at the base when she was new. Originally she was the aircraft of our squadron commander, but by this time in her combat career she must endure rookie crews like us. However, she ultimately survived the war. After the war she was sent to Arizona to be turned into scrap metal, which probably became pots and pans for America's young families after the war. Not a dignified retirement but she, and the other ships who came home, continued to serve in more quiet times and ways.

Mission preparation and early stages of assembling of our five Group task force went routinely and we headed for Germany. As I sat in my turret constantly moving and scanning the clear blue sky over heavy cloud cover, I began to sense this was not to be a milk run today. My face in the oxygen mask breathing the cold dry air-oxygen mix felt a little stiff. Maybe it was the minus 38°F cold or maybe it was my anxiousness about what lay ahead.

As we hit the IP (initial point) and turned on the bomb run I could see a massive flak field ahead which we were about to enter to drop our bombs on the target. Flak when it explodes leaves a residual black double puff that remains for several minutes. Seen from a distance the puffs of spent explosions and of current explosions combine together into a field of black puffs that look impenetrable as one flies toward the target. Of course the danger is not the black smoke puffs, but rather the invisible hunks of metal being propelled out from each burst through out the sky. This was our first look at serious flak and it was scary to see and feel. Our venerable ship was bounced about by 88mm anti aircraft shells exploding near us. I felt tension in my cramped body with nothing to do but hope my number was not on any of those pieces of metal hurtling through the sky. One trouble with flak is that mostly there is no defense from it...just hope and prayer. A flak vest and a flak helmet could have helped me some, but due to my size I was not able to wear any such protection while in the turret.

We, along with the other bombers in our task force, continued on the bomb run through the flak field and dropped our bombs by radar because of cloud cover of the target. We continued to be attacked by flak until we left the target area behind us as other groups were plowing through it. We returned to Ridgewell without further incidents.
Our combat veteran Clem said, "That was the real thing today, guys. You don't have to take a back seat to anyone anymore!"

When we got back to the hard stand at Ridgewell we all were excitedly talking about the days events. There was animated conversation reliving what had happened and what each of us had seen when we experienced our first taste of flak. I was on a little bit of a high and felt gratitude because we finally experienced what being shot at was like and had survived while performing well. As we walked around the trusty old bird that brought us home, we spotted 14 obviously new flak holes but no major damage. Some of us picked up small souvenir pieces of flak that had pierced the skin of our aircraft and lay on the floor in the waist area. In the future, we didn't bother to routinely look for and count holes; the novelty having worn off rather quickly

The next mission was on October 15th, we returned to the marshalling yards of Cologne. Apparently we had left some work to be done. It was another day of looking at cloud cover as our group formed up and we went on our programmed route to Germany. Somewhere along the way I began to realize something was wrong with my heated suit. My upper body and gloves were comfortable but my feet were becoming stiff and very cold. I reported to Sam that I was having difficulties and thought my feet were freezing due to heated suit failure. He told me that I must stay in the turret until he felt it was safe to leave it.

The anti-aircraft gunners of Cologne were hard at work again with accurate and moderate to heavy flak just as the day before. But my personal concern for the possible freezing of my feet took some of the concern for the flak away. I later recorded in my log that we had had slight battle damage but no mention of the number of holes this time. Clem had a piece of flak that caromed off his ammo belt and just missed him. He picked it up from the floor of the waist area and saved it. Though we bombed by radar again, I could see the target in spots through small breaks in the clouds. It appeared to me we did hit the rail yards. My feet were by this time were completely numb.

Andy called me on the interphone after we left flak field of the target area and asked me how my feet were doing. When I said I had lost all feeing in them, he said, with no bandits having been reported in our area, I should get out of the turret. I immediately unplugged my interphone so I couldn't hear any countermanding order from Sam and rotated the turret to the guns down position. When I opened my access door, there were Tex and Clem standing there worriedly looking down at me. They pulled me out and got me to the radio room. There they plugged me into oxygen, removed my flight boots and put electric heated muffs on my feet. At first I couldn't feel their heat at all. In time I began to feel pain as my feet thawed. The heated muffs had brought feeling back to my now hurting feet and probably saved them from frostbite and serious damage.

Our flying temperature this date had been a bitter –43°F, which is 75°F below freezing and didn't help my feet problems. I got chewed out for not routinely checking my heated suit before we flew, although, it had worked before and when I first got into the turret that morning. Sam thought I should more carefully verify the suit was OK each time before we flew, because he didn't like the ball turret being unmanned for any amount of time. I believe I had my first shot of Medics issued after-mission Scotch this day because of my painful feet.

On October 17th I flew with the Steinwinter crew as a replacement for their regular ball turret gunner who was sick. To be selected as a replacement gunner after only three combat missions was a compliment of sorts. In any case, the Group returned once again to Cologne and its rail yards, which by now must look like a huge field of bomb craters with twisted steel rails sprouting up like rust colored dead trees. The temperature was a –41°F with at times very heavy but widely scattered flak. We witnessed one ship, in another group behind us, blowing as a result of a direct hit by an 88mm anti-aircraft shell. I watched for, but didn't see, any parachutes...all of those crewmen apparently perished.

I didn't record any comments about battle damage to our ship probably because you couldn't tell a new hole from an old hole. We had our initial sighting of Germany's, and the world's, first combat jet propelled aircraft. We thought we were seeing the Me 262 jet fighter but it may have actually been the Arado 234 jet bomber. I couldn't see if they were attacking anyone or not, but their speed was startling as they streaked across the sky much faster than any propeller driven fighter. It was odd for us to see an airplane without propellers although we did know of the development of jet-propelled fighters. At this point in history, these were the only operational jets anywhere in the world. If Germany had gotten its production going sooner, the Me 262 would have been a deadly peril to the bomber formations of the Eighth Air Force. Thankfully, that is today only an if and not a reality.

On October 19th, my fifth mission, the target was a tank factory in Mannheim, Germany; even though the target was partially visible we bombed using radar again. We had a –58° F air temperature reading as we were now getting into what would prove to be a record breaking cold winter in Europe. We encountered scattered flak continuously for 30 or 40 minutes as we approached the target. It was, however, not very accurate as far as our Group was concerned. I did see a group ahead of us, and one behind us really catching accurate flak. They must have suffered a lot of battle damage.

DREAMBABY

My records indicate we were flying *Dreambaby* on this date, although I can't be sure because other records I've checked don't agree. It is relatively unimportant except to say she was our favorite plane whenever we got her assigned to us. All the crewmen from the pilots on down were in love with *Dreambaby* for her toughness, reliability and fly ability. [See photo at the end of the chapter.] For her combat career, *Dreambaby* flew 73 combat missions and brought her crews home every time. At war's end she was flown back to the USA with 20 of the Group's personnel to complete her wartime service. Even though she was our favorite we flew a series of planes as assigned because no crew could fly the same plane every time.

I'm afraid the movies were more romantic than accurate when it came to crew assignments to specific aircraft and thus many think bomber crews flew one ship all the time. As a military matter, the mission assignment was handed down from Eighth AF Command to the Group. A certain number of planes were required from the Group on a given mission. The Group would establish each Squadron's portion of the Group's responsibility. At the Squadron level the assignment of planes and crews would take place in rotation based on availability of personnel and machines. Older crews probably had some influence on what plane they flew if it were ready to fly considering repairs and maintenance. In fact our crew flew two missions in another squadron's planes when our squadron didn't have enough flyable planes. Perhaps fighter pilots did have personally assigned aircraft that they always flew I don't know. But the bomber crews when we were flying would fly any ship that was fit to fly as assigned by Operations.

We returned from Mannheim to Ridgewell. I had what turned out to be minor damage from flak hitting my turret. It gouged out a hunk of metal about a ¼ of an inch from the edge of a *Plexiglas* panel along side of my head. A small rotation of my turret a second before would have allowed that hunk of flak to rip through the *Plexiglas* and into my head. When back on the ground we marveled at how close it had been to coming through, but we didn't note any other damage on the ship. I was a little reflective on the randomness of chance and the nearness of that hit, but at 18 years you don't invest much time in what could have been.

We cleaned and oiled our guns and put them into storage by the hard stand. Jumping on a passing weapons carrier truck we rode over to Interrogation for our crew report of today's actions. The hot cocoa along with a doughnut from the friendly Red Cross girls made for a pleasant time while waiting to be called in for our report. Then it was off to the Combat Mess for our supper.

BASE FAMILIARIZATION

During this time of the year the weather was consistently miserable to the point there were several days without any ships flying. This became our chance to check out some of the facilities on the base. We have been on the go since our arrival here on the 27th of September and up till now haven't had much chance to look around. So we checked out a few places. The PX, first on our list, was just a single large room in a Quonset hut with some of the basic and niceties of life but everything, if available, was rationed. As a combat crewmember, our ration cards were over-stamped COMBAT thus giving us first preference at those things that were so scarce they weren't available for everyone. We had Class B passes issued to us, which would allow us to go anywhere in Essex or Suffolk Counties and Cambridgeshire, when not on duty, between the hours of 6:00 A.M. and 1:00 A.M. We may have used these during this period of time but I don't recall if we did.

The barbershop was a one-man affair in a Nissen hut decorated with pin up pictures [see photo at the end of the chapter], and a radio playing music from the Armed Forces Network (AFN). The AFN played many records from home and rebroadcast some radio shows. They as well had live broadcasts by groups such as the Glen Miller Army Air Force Band that were pleasant to hear. There was a Day Room over by the Squadron Orderly Room where we could read or play ping-pong. The Red Cross Aero Club was a really nice place for the enlisted men as I've already mentioned. The pool table there was a snooker table, which is a lot tougher than a regular pocket pool table. It is larger and has smaller pockets. I was fortunate because Clem was usually my partner and he was an expert snooker player. He claimed he lived over a pool hall in Dothan. I don't know if that was true or not, but when we got our turn at the table we usually didn't have to leave it until we wanted to because of his skill. This was a friendly and warm place due to the Red Cross ladies always being there keeping things light.

Since our first mission on October 9th, we have flown every mission the Squadron has flown excepting one. It was time for our first 36 hours pass. The normal routine at the 381st was you worked 10 days and then got a day and half pass. We had been on the base much longer than that but we had only been on flight status for 10 days. Most of us decided to take advantage of this opportunity to see the big town, London. Someone said, "Let's get into our Class A uniforms and head out!" and away we went to Old London Town.

Example of accurate flak. [USAAF]

Dreambaby, our favorite ship, on a bomb run. [USAAF]

THE VIEW FROM THE BOTTOM UP

Our barbershop. [USAAF]

THE VIEW FROM THE BOTTOM UP

Chapter 7

London

I T may not be generally appreciated today, but during World War II, London was to the world the symbol of England's gallant fight against the devastating Nazi forces of Hitler and his cohorts. To me this indomitable old city epitomized England just as Prime Minister Winston Churchill personified the English people. Back in the States we had heard the radio broadcasts of CBS's Edward R. Morrow back to the States from the rooftops of London during the London Blitz when London burned. We suffered with and admired those Londoners and the RAF in "their finest hour" as Churchill called it. I was now going there and was excited as a sophomore on his first date.

We got to London by taking the *Colne Valley Railway* a narrow gauge train from Yeldham, a village near our base. We Yanks called this train The Toonerville Trolley after a rickety train of that name in a comic strip back home. This doughty little train with its high pitched whistle would get us to Marks Tey a junction where we caught the Norwich to London train into London and arriving at the Liverpool Street Station. I really liked the English trains and their compartment style cars, rather than ours with the rows of seats arranged on each side of a center aisle. On the English trains each compartment had a door to a side corridor as well as its own outside access door so it was quick and easy to get out of at the train station.

The train slowed down as we entered the outskirts of London. We were met with the disquieting sights of block after block of bombed and burned out buildings. At one point, where there was much of this destruction, we could see that the famous St. Paul's Cathedral was basically still intact. It was a stirring sight even to this hick from California. Our minds were on having a good time here in London, but this was a sobering reminder that these people were engaged in the war as much as any combat group.

Of course we had been clued-in by our hut mates as to where to stay and what to do and see when in London. We had been directed to Russell Square where there were several Red Cross hotels. These had no frills, but were comfortable and friendly. The American Red Cross had gone into areas such as Russell Square and set up these hostel-like hotels with several Army cots per room. For a night it only cost two shillings and six pence (2 and 6), which was the equivalent of 50 cents American. The hotel had communal showers and toilets, which was no problem for GIs who had lost their right to privacy the day they enlisted or were drafted. British ladies, perhaps British Red Cross, who offered friendly conversation, and maybe a cup of very good tea if you wished, ran these hotels where everything was quiet and above board.

PICCADILLY CIRCUS

Russell Square was within walking distance of Piccadilly Circus the center of London activity for GIs on leave. It was also right around the corner from the British Museum, but the museum didn't get the interest of the younger GIs like us that Piccadilly did. On this, our first visit to London, when we were ready to go to where the action was, we hailed a taxi and asked him to take us to Piccadilly. Thirty minutes later we were there. We paid what the meter said and gave him a nice tip for his friendly and "efficient service." Later I discovered accidentally that Piccadilly was just a five or ten minute walk from Russell Square. We had had our first introduction to the London con men. They were all just about the same as in any large city anywhere.

Piccadilly Circus was the activity center for the Americans because of Rainbow Corner as the American Red Cross Club there was called. I believe the name came from World War I American soldiers of the 42nd Infantry, Rainbow Division, who first enjoyed that facility in the heart of London. It had a nice snack bar called The Doughnut Dugout that was quite popular. They served sandwiches, doughnuts and hot brewed coffee. There was a pool table and a rather large library in comfortable surroundings.

Adele Astaire, who was the sister and one time dance partner of Fred Astaire the American movie star, was at the Rainbow Corner a lot. She was at this time Lady Cavendish, having married Lord Charles Cavendish before the war and now living in England. She would spend time socializing with the GIs having the usual chitchat of, "Where are you from...etc." It seemed most guys liked to talk about where they were from and what home was like. She understood this well and was a good listener. When I met her she was writing a letter home for a GI who had an injured right hand and thus unable to write at that time. It was a thoughtful thing for her to do. There were a lot of very nice people populating our earth in those difficult times.

The Piccadilly area was also filled with service men and women from many other countries. As well there were British forces from Commonwealth countries around the world. There were *Coldstream Guards* with their Kelly green berets and Indian forces with turbans, etc. It was quite a sight. Such a collection of servicemen presented an irresistible attraction to the many folks who made money off of these young men. The prostitutes were called Piccadilly Commandos and were courteously aggressive, as one would expect from the British. In the evenings the sidewalks were alive with young people looking for action, but mostly titillation. As I understood it, there were no pimps or houses of prostitution allowed. The women who practiced their "craft," however, also had to have a regular productive job... prostitution didn't count. No one was allowed to just loaf about during the war. Even the titled and rich had jobs or volunteer work of some sort.

We rubbernecked roaming about and looking at this famous and historic medieval city's offerings. These ranged from penny arcade type places, much like we had back in Long Beach at The Pike, to places like The Windmill Theater that offered live stage performances. The penny arcades were places with many coin-operated machines from a fortune-teller gypsy to a love meter. The love meter would translate your grip strength into your rating as a lover (useful information). I remember trying to figure out my weight on an English weight scale, which recorded weight as Stones not pounds.

The Windmill was noted for never closing down its stage productions during any time of the war including the Blitz. Leicester Square and Trafalgar Square were also near-by with many cinemas, bars, brasseries, pubs and cafes from which to choose. The Whitehall Theater in Trafalgar Square featured a burlesque type entertainment. The star stripper was a pretty young woman who called herself Phyllis Dixie and the MC comedian went by the name of Snuffy Smith. Obviously by using those names they were catering to the American service men.

In one of the theaters were featured nude female models posing on stage in scenes called tableaus. The tableau would be of some high sounding representation. To a darkened theater an MC would announce the tableau's lofty title, such as, "Occupied Europe Yearns To Be Free." The curtain would open and carefully posed and lit nude models would be revealed showing what yearning for freedom symbolically looked like. The pose would be held for a few minutes, with appropriate background music, and we would eagerly stare at the beautiful nude women 'till the curtain closed for the next scene. These scenes were quite tastefully posed with no genital or pornographic type scenes or movement. As healthy young men, we of course were very pleased to observe such beauty...it was a simpler time.

However, there were no ice cream parlors or drug stores with marble counters; no colorful tin Coca-Cola signs, no gaudily lit juke-box playing in the corner, and no fresh young American girls serving bacon and tomato sandwiches on toasted white bread with a chocolate malted. London was exotic but it wasn't home.

SOLOING

At some point I had split off on my own to observe the life of the city at close range. Walking along these curving streets filled with shops and offices, I was transported to some of the places in my boyhood readings such as Sherlock Holmes. As one got away from Piccadilly, there were fewer and fewer GIs and things looked more English-like. At that time it was hard to remember these folks were in the middle of a war for their very way of life. They seemed to carry that burden with ease.

I wandered through what they called a mall and it was really interesting. I suppose what we call a shopping mall today is modern re-creation of the English mall. It was a narrow lane or alley fronted with small shops on each side and was covered over some stories up with a glass-paneled roof. These shops were filled with a myriad of different kinds of items for sale. It was rather like a Middle Eastern bazaar.

I casually walked into a music store somewhere in my travels. I was looking at the records they had available and was surprised at the variety and quantity of their American records. I came upon a 12-inch record of *Sing Sing Sing* .by the Benny Goodman band. I had tried to find this longer version of *Sing Sing Sing* back home and had been un-successful. I commented out loud about the luck of finding this some-what rare record so far from home. There was an English girl also looking at the records. She asked me if I was going to buy it and take it home. I explained the difficulty of transporting a fragile record all the way back to California. When she found out that I was from Southern California she immediately wanted to know if I lived near Hollywood, had I seen any movie stars up close, etc? Her name was Joyce and she lived in London with her mother and little brother. I asked her about what it was like growing up in wartime London, and she asked me about living in California. We decided to go some place to sit down and chat.

We left the music shop and went to a café close by that was located a few steps below street level. The place was called The Something-Or-

THE VIEW FROM THE BOTTOM UP

Other Brasserie. I read the name a little too quickly and thought it said brassiere. Joyce carefully corrected my mispronunciation and diplomatically explained that a brasserie (pronounced brass a ree) was a café that served drinks as well as food. It had an ideal atmosphere for conversation being quiet, with some sort of soft music playing. There was a bar with a few people seated, chatting and sipping drinks. We had tea and sweet biscuits (cookies). She told me some about what it was like living under these wartime conditions in London. They had moved back from somewhere in the countryside where they had relocated during the awful days of the Luftwaffe's bomber Blitz. Even now London could be a dangerous place. During the Summer of 1944 Germany had started attacking London again, not with manned bombers as during the Blitz, but with the unmanned V1 Buzz Bombs and the V2 rocket missiles. Even with that peril, her mother loved London and it was home. Her father was overseas somewhere in the Pacific I believe.

After a bit we exchanged addresses but, for some reason I don't remember, we never got together again. However, it was nice just to talk to a girl; they are so much more interesting than guys. Besides, I was finding out that the English girls considered American airmen quite glamorous, which was a good ego boost for me who had always been a little shy around girls. The English girls' interest in us probably also explained the antipathy one could encounter every now and then from English men. Ironically enough back home American girls considered an English accent quite attractive and English men were the glamorous ones.

DOGS PLAYING POKER

That evening all of us guys got together for dinner at a Lyon's Corner House restaurant, in Leicester Square. It was a modest restaurant but quite well appointed. As I recall we were served on white tablecloths with cloth napkins I don't recall what I ordered, but I do remember I enjoyed it. It was a good meal served properly. When we asked for coffee, the waiter asked if we wanted a demitasse or a full tasse. We being Yanks, of course asked for a full tasse. We didn't have a clue what the word *tasse* meant. It turned out to be a cup of coffee.

The dining experience had a surreal feeling to it for me. Here I was in the middle of a world war, sitting in a good restaurant in London, enjoying a tasse of coffee and looking at the dessert cart for inspiration as to what to have with that coffee. As we chatted away about the day's activities, I tried to look and act as if this were all quite normal for me. I'm sure the others guys were doing the same thing, but no one mentioned it. I felt we looked as incongruous as one of those "dogs playing poker" pictures we have around today. I guess we were growing day-by-day in our inadvertent rush to adulthood.

We got together the next morning and went to breakfast at George's American Restaurant where ole George made waffles out of corn meal! He had neither butter nor syrup, but he did have orange marmalade and a waffle iron. It was a perfectly awful meal.

SOLO ONCE AGAIN

We all split off on various ideas of what to see this day. I just wanted to get a general idea of the place. So what better way than on one of those famous red double-decked buses? I took off on the buses just to sight-see by myself. I climbed aboard a bus to somewhere and was met by a conductor collecting the fare. I couldn't understand what he was telling me he wanted for the fare. So I filled up my hand with a variety of coins: three pence, six pence, shillings and half crowns and said to the him, "Take what you need"...he selected the proper coins but was not amused. A couple sitting nearby smiled and called me over.

"Sit down Yank," they said, "and we'll help you understand our old but wonderful monetary system."

About all I can remember of what they told me is that it was not based on a decimal system. But, they were able to let me know the American equivalent to their archaic coinage, which information became the Rosetta Stone for me. From then on I was able to use the English money without too much trouble. This was another nice gesture from a people who surely had American GIs up to their eyeballs yet remained friendly and helpful.

I also explored the London Underground system, called the Tube, by riding from station to station and then going up to the street level and seeing what was up there. Their subway system was very well maintained and efficient and quite inexpensive to use. The platforms had bunk beds installed so they could be used as bomb shelters for families who would stay the night. The Luftwaffe did their bombing at night so these Tube station platforms being well under ground offered a safe haven for families with children or elderly to care for at night. At one point on this trip, or perhaps a later one, I was walking along a street when the air raid sirens began to wail that dire sound of a pending air attack. Immediately people seem to move quickly but without any great haste to somewhere, bomb shelters I assumed. I asked a man moving quickly by where was the nearest bomb shelter. He directed me to one near by and then added, "Most of us will just find a pub and wait it out, but it is up to you." I followed him to a pub nearby where we waited for the all clear with a pint of beer and some conversation. The folks in the pub displayed good humor and waited patiently. There apparently was no air raid and after an hour or so with the expected all clear siren we dispersed into the night each on his own separate way.

When it was time to catch our train back to Yeldham, I got on the Tube and went to Liverpool Street Station. During the war train stations were constant beehives of activity. Civilians and service personnel were excitedly rushing to meet a train or someone, or they were just tired weary bundles waiting for a train or someone. I bought my ticket and searched for my buddies as I walked along the loading platform for our train. In all the turmoil, I failed to see anyone I knew so I just got into a compartment that was fairly empty but which filled up soon. It was a friendly ride except for a taciturn older man and a stolid English soldier who did their best to ignore the gregarious American (me) asking silly questions. Remembering what it was like in Long Beach when we became overrun with Iowans and Oklahomans, etc, seeking jobs in the aircraft plants and shipyards, I could understand their reticence to join in.

When we got to Marks Tey, the rest of the guys finally appeared, having been in another car from mine. We met the Toonerville Trolley and proceeded back to Yeldham and home at Ridgewell. I make it a rule to never believe the stories that start, "Boy, you should have been there..." What ensues is at best an inflated version of the truth and often a pure invention aimed to make one jealous of what was missed. As I was being regaled by these glamorized adventures, I retaliated with my stories, which were maybe also a little "polished." It was a nice ride and it was comforting to be with them again, these, my brothers.

London had turned out to be a fascinating place to me. Not the over inflated romanticized place from many of the movies then current. It was a more solid down to earth place with remarkably indomitable people doing their everyday jobs in spite of the best efforts of the Nazis. Maybe the Hallmark of this war was how these ordinary people, and our ordinary people back home, had risen to face down the sophisticated German war machine.

We returned to our hut to await tomorrow and the war.

THE VIEW FROM THE BOTTOM UP

Chapter 8

Of Shots and Chaff

I awoke to a quiet and cold hut. Unfortunately I had a habit of sleeping-in whenever I could and apparently had again this day. I was stretching myself awake and trying to figure what I was going to do on my day of leisure when the door creaked open and an orderly came in. He wanted to know if I were Sergeant Gilbert. I thought to myself, "I knew it, a day off was too good to be true!" In our bomb Group, combat personnel were only required to fly combat and training missions plus ground training. Other than that our time was our own. I cautiously answered that I was indeed Sergeant Gilbert, hoping I hadn't missed some mandatory formation or training assignment. He handed me a note from the Medical Department with my name printed on the outside.

The note required me to report to the Dispensary for a records check. It seemed simple and harmless enough so I set it aside while I slowly got dressed and washed up. As I was eating a candy bar breakfast, and listening to music from the Armed Forces Network on Tex's radio, some of the guys began to return to the hut after having had a real breakfast in the mess hall. When I mentioned I was supposed to go to the dispensary, because of a medical record glitch, and asked if anyone wanted to go along, I was met with catcalls. Bill Hiney, I believe it was, yelled, "I'll bet that girl in London you met called the Bobby's on you because she has found out she has VD thanks to your 'talk' with her."

"Inasmuch as I just met her yesterday don't you think that is setting some kind of medical record?," I grumbled.

"Sure, tell them that so they can fix the record books. My vote is you've got some new kinda VD," Bill came back as a final crack.

I knew he was kidding, but I began to worry about what did the Medics want? When I got there it turned out they had lost my shot records and only wanted my copy so they could transfer the data and update their records. I opened my wallet and rooted though the various pieces of important notes and bits of paper I had carefully stored there in case I ever needed them. I looked for my shot record back-up copy we had to carry on our person. It was not to be found. When I offered to go back to the hut and check my belongings for it, I was told, "On your person, Sergeant, means on your person. So we will now give you all the shots you were to have received before coming overseas and create a current shot record for you."

The total was seven shots.

"Which arm do you want us to put them?" asked a grinning medic.

I remembered that one or more of those shots had really left my arm sore, so I said, "Split them up between my arms," to minimize the effect on any one arm. They did as I asked and put three in one arm and four in the other.

The next morning, October 26, we were awakened at 3:30 a.m. for our sixth mission. As I got out of bed and started to dress, I found both my arms were extremely painful and difficult to move. This was a serious problem for me. In order to operate the ball turret, my arms were in a raised position. I didn't know if I could do my job, but I didn't want to fall behind the rest of the crew in my mission count. That had happened to Foon who missed our second and third missions because he was in the hospital with pneumonia. He flew his next mission as soon as they let him out of the hospital, no matter what he felt like, because no one wanted to be behind the rest of the crew. So I didn't tell Sam of my condition, which was probably not the correct thing to do. He should have had the chance to make the decision on my ability to perform. But I preempted him and unilaterally decided to fly.

It was very painful getting my guns disassembled, cleaned, reassembled and made ready to be installed. I then carefully installed each of them in the ball turret. Each gun weighs about 60 pounds so getting them in place was a chore but I was able to do it with the help of some aspirins. Later as we were getting ready to cross the Channel the next big test for my arms was getting into the turret. With Tex helping me, I was able to connect my interphone, oxygen and heated suit, get into the turret and begin operating it. As I unsuccessfully attempted to move without pain or discomfort, I began to question my decision to fly. I wondered if I should have gone to the Medics and gotten some kind of painkiller. But on the other hand, maybe they wouldn't have let me fly with pain medicine in me and would have made me stand-down for a day or so. It was a gamble I didn't want to take. The turret and the guns can be operated from either the right or left control so I alternated between arms all day. My decision to split up the shots to both arms now seemed ill conceived at best.

As we approached the target, Munster (Bielefeld), Germany, at 27,000 feet and −36°F, we encountered some amount of flak but it was scattered and not too accurate. The inaccuracy was probably due in part to the chaff we were dispensing as we neared the target area. Chaff was narrow strips of paper backed aluminum foil, which were hand delivered by the radio operators upon command of the lead ship. Each radio room on a Fortress had a chute used by the radio operators to push the chaff out into the air stream. These little strips of aluminum foil played havoc with the German's radar giving false echo signals that made radar control of their guns unreliable. I looked down on these millions of glittering strips scattering over the German countryside and wondered what it looked like from their standpoint. Did the little kids know what this stuff was that fell from the sky sometimes? Was it a game to collect all you could? Did the German kids in the middle of this awful war play games? Probably they did. Fortunately for them, and for our own conscience, we did not target non-strategic places such as their towns and cities. If one lived near to a strategic target, however, there could be real danger with the best of our intentions.

Once again we were bombing by radar due to 100% cloud cover of the target. Our bombardier Stu Newman had been removed from the crew and replaced by an enlisted man toggelier as was the case in all but the lead crews. Stu was to become a navigator and apparently a very good one. Our toggelier dropped our bombs, in concert with the lead plane, on the target, which was an aircraft assembly plant. But because of the cloud cover, we couldn't observe the results.

We for whom this was our sixth mission were to be awarded the Air Medal. The Air Medal was awarded for what acts the Air Force decided met the definition of "meritorious achievement while participating in sustained combat operations over Germany and German occupied countries...." At our time of flying, it was six accredited combat missions or else some specific act of meritorious achievement while on a combat mission. Subsequent awards were Oak Leaf Clusters to the Air Medal for each six missions except for the last Oak Leaf Cluster that was for five missions. It didn't necessarily take a brave or heroic act to be eligible for the Air Medal; most times just survival was all that was required. Even so I was proud of that beautiful medal, and also the next day October 27th was my 19th birthday...certainly a time to remember.

We returned home to Ridgewell without unusual incident. The

removal, cleaning, oiling and storage of my two guns was a painful chore, but we were home at last. As we waited in the Interrogation lobby, I took the Medics issued shot of Scotch to help my aching arms and back. After interrogation and a nice evening meal with hot coffee, I began to feel better. I now no longer regretted my decision to fly on this date. It took a few days for my arms to feel OK again. They didn't use the term "tough love" in those days, but I never lost a shot record again.

LIBERTY RUN

Due primarily to lousy weather and our crew's need to get up-to-date on ground training, we didn't fly combat for a number of days. During any time when not on flight alert status, we could go off base for an evening of socializing at a local or nearby pub and stay up late. Each night the Squadron offered rides called the Liberty Runs to various towns nearby. We decided to go to Cambridge for our first Liberty Run. Lurching down country roads I was happily bouncing along in the back of a truck in anticipation. Looking out the back, I was again fascinated by the farmhouses with thick roofs of thatched straw and here and there quaint roadside inns and chapels. It looked like an illustration for an English mystery novel. The quiet idyllic landscape of Essex and Cambridgeshire were in sharp contrast to our air base. At Ridgewell with its round-the-clock activity, there was an almost constant background noise of aircraft engines being worked on and tested. As we rode along I gazed out at this calming sight and thought how lucky I was to be here in this place at this time.

England during the war was on war double daylight savings time. Thus, combined with the long English twilight, it would be fairly light well after 10:00PM. While it was still light, one could do some looking at the historic sites for a while before going to a pub or two for some social time, Cambridge had pubs everywhere. One of the pubs recommended to us was The Eagle, which was very popular with the American aircrews. Some pubs, especially in the smaller towns and family neighborhoods of the cities, were very socially oriented. The neighborhood pubs were not pick-up spots or places to get drunk and start a fight. A family might have a pub night when dad and mum would go and be with their friends who shared the same pub night. As the kids got older they would often join their folks on the pub night. Darts were of course a favorite game with many pubs having a darts team to compete with other pubs. Some of the older guys would quietly play dominoes. To me the most memorable thing about pubs was the singing. The songs, maybe sung *a cappella,* or to some musical instrument, started the evening happily with mostly traditional pub songs such as "I've Got Six-Pence" or popular songs of the day. As the night wore on the songs tended to be more sentimental and often filled with optimism about tomorrow such as "Blue Birds Over The White Cliffs Of Dover".

Unfortunately a few of us Americans were not content to just sit back and enjoy. A few could be quite obnoxious trying to take over and make things their way. Plus, trying to pick up women in a place that was primarily family oriented was rude to say the least, which could understandably cause some resentment of any American. The guys who had been in England for some time advised us when in a family type pub it was best to only be involved in the activities when and as you were asked. And further, they wisely advised if the pub had a lot of British soldier customers, go somewhere else. From time to time fights did break out between American and British service men, but I believe that was mostly in the larger cities. The advice we got was don't be out alone in the cities at night, because the British had a few idiot soldiers just as we did.

These pubs were warm happy havens from the war and war-like things. I loved the friendly atmosphere and the singing. I could never sing in public without the social lubricant of beer, which flowed freely in these places. However, in spite of the easy availability of beer, it was rare to see anyone really drunk.

When it came time to get back to our trucks for the ride home, we had to get moving without delay. If we missed the Liberty Run back, we were in deep trouble. There was no public, or private, transportation available for us. If you were not back by 1:00 A.M., you were Absent Without Leave (A.W.O.L), which was an infraction requiring disciplinary action. We found our Liberty Run trucks without a problem and returned on time. When we got back to the hut it was still warm from the evenings coke fire in our little coke stove. Everyone was soundly sleeping with a snort or snore every now and then. Our arrival didn't bother anyone as I recall.

EVASION AND ESCAPE TRAINING

Our ground training continued with presentations on evasion and escape suggestions and requirements. We got tips from guys who had successfully evaded capture on what they found had worked. I remember one gunner particularly who obtained and wore the uniform of a German Hitler Youth, because he was so young looking he could make it work. That was not a recommended method because it was against the Geneva Convention Rules of Warfare to not wear your uniform and could subject one to execution if caught. However he decided to give it a try by exhibiting an enthusiastic Nazi attitude. Cautiously he moved toward allied held territory by giving the Heil Hitler salute to everyone he saw. When he got close to American held territory he dumped the Hitler Youth garb and in his underwear surrendered to some GIs.

One other that sticks in my mind was a gunner who bailed out wearing an early heated suit which was called a Blue Bunny suit by the crews because it had an outer layer of sky blue felt-like material. They looked like a child's pajamas and would appear strange anywhere to see a grown man wearing one. This gunner had landed without any problems and then had gotten rid of his parachute and harness. In his Blue Bunny suit he was cautiously walking down a road in the direction of allied positions. Then there appeared a column of German soldiers marching toward him on the same road. He decided that to run would draw immediate gunfire so he just kept walking toward the Germans. After they passed he looked back and saw the NCO who was leading them standing in the road looking at him quizzically but without any challenge. He too was able to connect up with our soldiers and get back to England after some explanation to the GIs of his strange garb. While entertaining, these two stories particularly seemed a little farfetched to me. However, these guys were being sent around to all the bases to tell their stories by the Army Air Corps so maybe they were factual.

Evading capture, and if captured escaping, were the duties of airmen who ended up in enemy territory. The potential always existed for us to end up in enemy territory due to enemy action or mechanical failure. Though we went to the bombing targets in formations of many bombers escorted by fighter aircraft, each plane was alone over the enemy's backyard if trouble developed. That was a thought that never left me. The peril of ending up, say, in a German village was first the populace who were not happy with us and second any unsupervised German soldiers. We were told that if capture were inevitable our best protection from being beaten or butchered was to find a German officer or a large group of soldiers seemingly under some control and surrender.

We were issued escape kits before each mission, which had to be returned after the mission. These kits were inside plastic cases that were about the size of a VHF videotape box we use today. The kit included silk maps of Europe, Benzedrine tablets to keep you awake for long periods, a language aid card for German, French and Russian, water purification tablets, some kind of concentrated food, a first aid kit, etc. The kits were sealed to ensure someone hadn't swiped any of its valuable contents. I carried my escape kit in the shin pocket of my flying suit I wore under the electrically heated suit. It was a good idea we were told to also carry some extra packages of cigarettes for use as money if need be.

To familiarize us with the tactics used by all Intelligence officers, we had lectures from both American and British Intelligence Officers. It was our understanding that all captured bomber crewmen and fighter pilots were initially sent to a place called Dulag Luft for interrogation prior to being sent to a stalag for imprisonment. The foremost message the Intelligence guys wanted us to retain was that any item of information could be important to the Germans when combined with other information they had collected. We were ordered to only give our name, rank and serial number to anyone.

We were told that at Dulag Luft, the interrogation center for downed airmen, they had a file on every man who was known to be flying in Europe. The source for much such detailed information was our own American newspapers! German agents collected stories that were printed about this or that local boy who was flying combat out of England and this information was sent to Dulag Luft by way of Switzerland. An example of how such information got out is the record of my citation for the Air Medal. [See document at the end of the chapter.] My hometown's name, Long Beach, California, is noted in the citation block of the form. I'm assuming logically enough that this was for the Public Relations personnel. There is no other reason I can conceive. After the award of the medal, the PR guys sent a publicity release to the newspapers in the airman's hometown. The story in the paper would tell about this local airman being awarded the Air Medal, etc. We were told this type of information was used by the Germans to convince an airman that they already knew much about him, where he was from, his parents names, etc, to disarm him in casual conversation. In this relaxed friendly conversation, he might give some information that, when used with other bits could be useful to the enemy.

These particular lectures were interesting and informative. The best summation of what intelligence gathering and interrogation is all about came from an RAF Intelligence Officer who said to us, "Just remember all Intelligence officers are bastards." He went on to entertain us with stories of the tricks they had used against captured German pilots to illustrate the deviousness they used. Other stories were told of the common ruses being employed by the Germans to extract any small bit of information from downed airmen. These were sobering sessions and ones I listened to carefully.

LETTERS

The rest of October was spent in training and tending to our personal projects. I liked bicycle riding on the nearby country roads looking at the pastoral world of Essex farms. Wild berry bush lined roads led past farmhouses with straw thatched roofs and placid plow horses nibbling at grass. It was easy to get lost in a reverie of peaceful times and places until the sound of bomber engines crowded through the air. I was falling in love with the English countryside.

When the weather was dry there was usually a touch-football game somewhere in our area, which was fun to do or watch. I was usually behind in my letter writing to home, so this was a good chance to catch up. There was one problem with letters home and that was we could not write about our missions, or even the fact that we were flying combat. Reynolds censored our mail; it was another one of the co-pilot's duties that he didn't like. He had to scan the letter for any breaches of security and then sign the outer envelope and letter as the authorized censor. After we had been in England for a while, my mother asked if I ever did anything but go to London because that was mostly about which I wrote.

Mail from loved ones was the highlight of any day. If I got more than one letter, I would space them out so I could savor the moments of reading over several days. I mostly got mail from my mom who gave me all the news of what was going on at home in Long Beach. She would include a letter from Bill or Donny my brothers back home. Every now and then a letter would come in from my grandma or one of my aunts. There were a few from the people I had worked with at Douglas Aircraft, Long Beach, before being called to active duty. I even got a letter from my homeroom teacher at Poly High, Mrs. Hitchings, who must have had scores of ex-students to write to but she didn't forget me, nor anyone else I'll wager. For the guys getting letters from girl friends back home, there was the dread of the "Dear John" letter telling the guy she was moving on. This was not uncommon, unfortunately, because it had been many months and up to a year since some guys had been home.

The Group had been somewhat idle combat mission-wise for the last few days due mostly to poor weather. Our time had been filled with training and a little personal time. We knew this couldn't last, but we were given a 36 hours pass while things were still quiet.

GENERAL ORDERS)
NUMBER   477)

Hq 1st Bombardment Division,
APO 557, 30 October 1944.

Under the provisions of Army Regulations 600-45, 22 September 1943, as amended, and pursuant to authority contained in letter, Hq Eighth Air Force, File 200.6, 23 September 1944, subject, "Awards and Decorations", the AIR MEDAL is awarded to the following-named Officers and Enlisted Men, organizations as indicated, Army Air Forces, United States Army.

Citation: For meritorious achievement while participating in sustained bomber combat operations over Germany and German occupied countries. The courage, coolness and skill displayed by these Officers and Enlisted Men upon these occasions reflect great credit upon themselves and the Armed Forces of the United States.

381st Bombardment Group (H)

ROBERT B. GILBERT, 19207435, Sgt. Long Beach, California.

By command of Brigadier General TURNER:

BARTLETT BEAMAN,
Brigadier General, U. S. Army,
Chief of Staff.

OFFICIAL:
ROBERTS P. JOHNSON, JR.,
Lieut. Colonel, A.G.D.,
Adjutant General

Author's Air Medal Award Letter

THE VIEW FROM THE BOTTOM UP

Chapter 9

The City Girl

IT had been ten days or so since our last 36-hours pass. Normally we were granted the 36-hours pass about every week and a half if possible. Clem and I were heading for London again, but most of the crew was going to check out other towns while on pass. We caught the Toonerville Trolly from Yeldham and off to London we went. I can't quite explain why, but for me London held an emotional pull. It was as if I had lived there in a prior life, if in fact we do have prior lives. Clem, having had been there many times during his first tour of duty, was very familiar with the big city and its many attractions so he was a good traveling partner.

ENTER PAT—THE CITY GIRL

We checked into a Red Cross Hotel in Russell Square, walked to the Tube stop and were going to some destination picked out by Clem. The Underground train car was standing room only with the usual mix of Americans and British. As we rolled along, someone jostled me from the rear. I turned around to apologize and was met with the sweet face of an English girl who had one of those peaches and cream complexions and big blue eyes. We both apologized at the same time, and then laughed. We had spoken a few words to each other when seating finally opened up nearby. The girl, her friend, Clem and I all sat down and got to know each other and eventually paired off.

Her name was Pat and she lived in a section of greater London called Lower Edmonton. We had an almost instant attraction in that teenage sort of way. She asked about all the stripes I had on my overcoat. Oddly enough it wasn't my coat, I had borrowed the coat of Tom Guilfoyle, radio operator on the Steinwinter crew, who was a Tech Sergeant and thus had two rockers under his stripes. I suppose all those stripes appeared a little odd on someone who looked as young as I did. In any case the stripes were the conversation starter. We immediately had a conversational rapport. She asked questions about California, when she learned I was from there, and I wanted to know more about England. It turned out she was 17 years old and out of the English equivalent to our high school about a year or so. Now I was finally the "older" man at 19 years. Clem also seemed to be getting along well with Pat's friend Alice. We decided we would change trains and go to the Leicester Square area where there was more action and forget about the sightseeing Clem originally had in mind for him and me.

In Leicester Square we walked along aimlessly, talking and looking in shop windows. Unexpectedly, I felt a soft warm hand seek mine and I gently held hers. I was hooked, as we walked holding hands in this somewhat austere and cold city. In a back street near Piccadilly, we saw a restaurant that looked quiet and like the cliché continental small café. We entered and took a table near the front window. The owner gave us small stained menus to review. Some of the dishes I'd never heard of but never let on I didn't know. Both the girls were obviously not used to being in this type of place and were a little giggly. Clem and I acted blasé or at least what we though was blasé. On the menu there was something virtually unheard of in wartime England, a steak dinner. I hadn't had a steak since we were in the States and was eager to go for it. I convinced Pat it was OK to order such an expensive meal and so we ordered steak dinners for everyone. The meal was pretty good even though the steak had a flavor that was different for us. The owner was apparently Greek based on his wall decorations. His menu also had featured lots of Greek sounding dishes, so we reasoned it was the Greek seasonings we tasted. On a subsequent trip to London, I led a couple of guys to this café for a quick steak dinner and had a surprise instead. Posted on the door was an official notice that said this establishment had been ordered closed for selling horse meat for human consumption! I don't think I ever told Pat what we probably had eaten on that first evening we had together.

After our satisfying dinner, the two couples split up to go their own ways. I believe Clem and Alice were going to find some place to have a drink. At 17 Pat was under aged and also we were more interested in just wandering and sightseeing. I don't recall any place specifically where we visited. We just enjoyed each other's company. In spite of her easy familiarity with me, Pat was not a cheap girl but almost naively open and honest. I, though I wouldn't have admitted it then, was usually quite shy around girls, but around her I felt sure of myself.

THE MARS BAR AND THE TROLLEY SONG

Somewhere we were in a place where they sold candy and I saw a Mars Bar, which had been my favorite back home. I asked the candy counter person how much for a Mars Bar, he said, "That'l be six pence and a sweet coupon, Yank."

I didn't have any British ration coupons, of course, and said so.

"Never mind," Pat said and went into her purse for the necessary ration coupon and I then paid for the bar. We both took a bite and it was as good as I remembered. I ended up eating most of it because it reminded me of home in Long Beach.

Eventually we rode a red double decked bus to end of the line in Lower Edmonton. I walked her to her home in a two-story row house neighborhood. We said goodnight after exchanging addresses and in her case also a phone number. She then offered to walk me to a train station nearby where we could say another goodbye and I could wait for a ride back to central London. That seems very ungentlemanly to me now, but I was anxious to spend more time with her. We settled down on a bench to wait for the train. At one point, Pat asked me if I had seen the American movie, Meet Me In St. Louis with Judy Garland. And did I remember the *Trolley Song* that Judy sang? She said, "To me our meeting on the Tube was just like in that song."

To explain she began to quietly sing a part of the lyric, "I went to lose a jolly hour on the trolley and lost my heart instead."

"That's me!" she said.

It really sounds sappy now but it sounded sweet to me at the time. We sat in that cold damp train station being romantic and probably felt we were in love as only teenagers can. We agreed to meet the next day in Russell Square at my Red Cross hotel. We just wanted to spend more time together doing something or nothing... it didn't matter.

Pat was to meet me outside my hotel because visitors were not allowed inside. When I walked out of the hotel at the appointed time there was no Pat as we had agreed. I waited a while and began to doubt that she was going to show up. As I was starting to give up and leave, Clem came out of the hotel and told me earlier he had seen a Bobby apparently arresting Pat and taking her into custody! I asked what in the world for? He wasn't sure but the conversation he heard sounded like she had no legitimate reason for not being at her job. I found out later that she wasn't arrested but had been taken to a police site where her dad had to come get her because she was under aged. He was angry with her for his embarrassment and for her getting involved with an American GI. "No good can come from that!" I'm sure he thought. This was a hell of a start to establishing good relations with her family. Later I had tried to call her on her folk's telephone, hoping she would answer, but no one was there. Thankfully, her dad didn't answer the phone while he was still irate or we probably would never have seen each other again.

After missing my connection with Pat, the city girl of whom I had become so fond, I wandered alone, and feeling empty, around the Russell Square and The British Museum area. The song "I'll Be Seeing You" kept going through my head though we didn't really have that kind of history having just met. But we had developed an almost instant attraction for each other for some reason. Hormonal attraction of course played its normal role but there was something more that was a new feeling to me.

Clem had reconnected with Alice and they had taken off somewhere. After a while I lost my interest in aimlessly roaming around London by myself. I went to the train station and returned to the base early. I think Clem stayed on until the evening spending time with Alice. When returning to Ridgewell, I stopped at the Waggon [sic] & Horses Inn in Yeldham for a pint of beer. It was the first time I had been in a pub without a couple of buddies. Quietly I walked inside the cozy smoky warmth of the pub and ordered a glass of beer. There was a low fire in the fireplace taking some of the chill out of the air and a low rumble of quiet conversation. The atmosphere was more reserved that we had experienced in Cambridge. These were older folks...locals.

Just sitting in a corner and listening, I began to really appreciate these resilient people. There was not a lot of conversation, but what conversation I heard seemed laconic with abbreviated sentences for a full conversation. Brief words were said here and there but they seemed to be communicating much. There was a "Hello, Harry" instead of the American approach of, "Hello Harry, how the hell are you? How's Mrs. Harry, she feeling better now? What about this damn cold weather? ...etc." These people seemed to be enjoying each other's quiet company. Finally, someone asked me if I were posted at Ridgewell. I said yes, I was. I introduced myself and slowly we began to talk. Once again when it was found that I lived in California there was some interest in Hollywood, had I been there and so forth. Mostly it was small talk and more importantly I was made to feel welcome. It was the antidote to my melancholy feeling about what had happened to Pat back in London that morning.

I mentioned the Mars Bar incident to them because I thought that the Mars Candy Company was an American company and how surprised I was to see a Mars Bar over here. Then they told me that Mars was in fact a well-known British company. One older lady asked, "Do you realize, Bob, that she gave up her whole month's sweet ration for that bar?" Wide eyed in surprise I replied weakly, "No, I didn't know, sorry.," I lamely apologized.

This jarred my memory of the High Carbohydrate rations we were given before each mission. Many of the guys didn't eat all of that candy we were given and just tossed it away; I'm embarrassed to admit. As I finished my beer, I began to plan how I was to repay Pat for her unselfish gift of her sweet coupon... that is if I ever saw her again.

Back at the base and after evening chow, I got to a telephone and chanced a call to Pat, hoping she would answer and not her parents. After going through a male telephone operator somewhere who had trouble understanding my awful accent, I got through. A young female voice answered but it wasn't Pat I didn't think. A cautiously asked if I could speak to Pat, the voice squealed, "Oh, Patty, its him!," or something like that. I was concerned how loud she was talking, but then when Pat came on the line she said her dad and mum were at the neighborhood pub tonight so 'not to worry'. Her younger sister had answered the phone just as the two girls had been talking about the day's events and this Yank whom she had gone into town to meet from the night before. I noticed her sister called her Patty and asked if I was right in calling her Pat. She said her mother and sister mostly called her Patty and her dad also called her Patty unless she was in trouble...then she was Patricia. But anyhow she said her friends called her Pat and that would be most comfortable for me to use.

Apparently she was not in any great trouble except with her dad who didn't have the greatest love of the boisterous Yanks whom he met daily in his job as a conductor on a double-decked bus. I silently wondered if he was the one whom I had encountered on the prior trip to London. She said not to worry about her dad; her mum would get him to not oppose Pat seeing me. I was delighted we would see each other again the next time I was in The City. We agreed to write a lot until the next time I was in London.

When I got back to the hut, walking with a joy in my step, I began my candy collection program. I asked each guy to give me what candy they had left over at the end of each mission. I put an open box by my cot where they would dump their boxes of the uneaten High Carbo-hydrate ration. I would take what ever was collected into London on my next trip.

I inadvertently screwed up on my first letters to her and irked her dad all over again. I had put the stamp on the envelope upside down, which back home would mean a kiss. This simple gesture by me had a different meaning to an Englishman. Pat told me when he saw an envelope with the stamp bearing the face of the King was put on upside down, he bellowed, "He's disrespecting the King!"

It seemed I had a lot to learn about how to be suave and debonair in dear old England, or anywhere for that matter.

Chapter 10

Hamburg to Buzz Bombs

WE had had a relatively quiet spell when on November 4th we were awakened to a harsh hut light turned on by the orderly. He then called off the names of those of us who were to fly this date. As I awakened and lit my morning cigarette, I reached over for my canteen cup to take a sip of water and found it to be ice. With my usual grumbling about how damn cold it was in this country, I got dressed. The washroom next to the hut was our source of water but it had no hot water to wash with. During the day we would heat water on the coke stove but in the morning I just got enough cold water to brush my teeth. We slowly moved out and got into the trucks parked by the Squadron Orderly Room that would take us to breakfast.

Our hut mates had informed us that a breakfast with fresh eggs was not a good sign because it usually meant a tough target. A worse sign was when the Mess Officer was personally serving the eggs to us; this meant a really big mission. We came in from the cold black of night into the comforting warm light of the mess hall, and the welcome smell of coffee. I noticed with satisfaction we were having oatmeal and powdered eggs along with toast and coffee. Hot dog! I thought, maybe seven is a lucky number; this being my seventh mission, I hoped so. After a warm filling breakfast, we climbed into the waiting trucks and were driven to our respective locations on the flight line areas to get ready for the day's mission.

Somewhere along in this time frame, Andy, our navigator, had decided that he and I would cooperate on each mission to record any significant information I observed as we were flying to and from the target. When he, along the others who had been to the mission briefing, got to our plane he would open up his maps and give me a mini-briefing. On the maps he showed me our planned routing to the target and areas we would be flying over. He sometimes pointed out special things for me to look for on the routing. I was to call on the interphone and give him pertinent information on what I was seeing on the ground. As an example, when we flew over the Rhine did I see any barges; how many, and headed which way? Did I see any barrage balloons deployed somewhere, if so how many? This was information that was to be reported up the line and over to the 9th Air Force for the fighter pilot's usage. I was pleased to have this assignment because it kept my mind busy and off of what may lie ahead for us. Much of the time, I had an 8MM movie camera installed in my turret by the Photo Lab to take bomb strike pictures if the weather permitted. After the bombs had been dropped, I did use the movie camera also to take pictures of activities of interest such as planes in flames or crews bailing out, etc. But Andy was talking about collecting information that would be turned over to the Intelligence Officers immediately during Interrogation and not necessarily that which would be filmed.

On November 4th, we flew to Hamburg, Germany to bomb an oil refinery with our Group Commander, Colonel Harry Leber, in the lead ship. We flew at 25,000 feet altitude in –40°F air temperature, over complete cloud coverage. This was to be our first mission as the complete Goldin crew. Sam was finally our first pilot with Lt. Windsor having signed-off that Sam was ready to lead his own crew.

We were met with heavy flak, as you would expect protecting a major target area such as Hamburg. However, and fortunately, their barrage was not as accurate as the Cologne anti aircraft gunners had been a couple of weeks ago. I don't think our ship ended up with any significant battle damage.

Prior to reaching the Hamburg area I was constantly scanning the bright blue skies for German fighters, even though none as yet had been reported in our area. What I did see were our P-51 Mustangs as they patrolled looking for any Germans who had designs on shooting us down. We were not to see any Me 109s or FW 190s that day. By this stage of the war, primarily due to the shortage of aviation fuel, Germany was having to restrict when and where their fighters attacked the massive bomber formations that were pounding them regularly.

As we left the Hamburg area, we were flying over broken cloud cover where I could see sections of Germany laid out before me from my turret hanging under our ship. I observed a group of B-17s bombing an airfield with apparently good results. But when I reported this to Andy, he told me it was a dummy airfield that had suckered the bombardier of the other group into bombing it. I suppose there were a couple of extra toasts that evening in the local German beer hall to celebrate their cleverness in getting the Yanks to waste some bombs. Oh well, he who laughs last laughs best, as the old saying goes.

With seven and one-half hours of the constant deafening roar of our ship's four Wright-Cyclone engines; which as usual had left my ears ringing, and with the six or so hours crammed in the ball turret, I was old man tired. But we were home to the beautiful English countryside where Ridgewell is located and a warm meal awaited us. After stiffly pulling myself out of my turret, I stood at a waist window and looked out. I stretched and gazed at the peaceful sight of the Essex farms and villages as they slipped below us. Many of the farms had little pond like depressions made by stray bombs dropped by German aircraft. The farmers were undeterred and apparently just plowed around them and went on with their important work.

I was grateful for our effective and safe mission. I didn't fully appreciate then that Sam, Al Reynolds, with Marty's steady assistance, still had serious work to do to bring us safely down one more time...which they did. In later years I was to regret I never told Sam how much I admired his piloting skills and now wished I had then recognized how tough a job he had.

CREW CHIEF'S QUARTERS

Each crew chief built along side of his ship a little hut constructed mainly of empty bomb boxes and wrecked aircraft pieces. These huts varied greatly depending on the inventiveness of its owner. Each had a stove to heat the hut. Some were coke stoves but many burned used motor oil. Most of the huts were quite comfortable even in the clammy cold English climate. They were certainly better than the tents issued by the Army. Many were big enough so there was room enough for the flight crew to wait out of the weather for their time to fly.

As an aside I remember one morning, while we were waiting in a crew chief's hut, there came the distinctive *gung-gung-gung-gung* sound of a .50 cal. machine gun firing a few rounds. Sam immediately said, "Where's Gilbert?" Everyone laughed but the reason for his question was the ball turret was the only gun position where the ammunition had to be fed into the gun and the cover-lid closed while the ship was still on the ground. Every once in a while a ball turret gunner would close the lid too hard and it would kick off a few rounds; but never me I hasten to add. In any case that deadly sound of wildly flying bullets would give everyone a start and wake up all the dozers waiting take off time. No one wanted to be shot anytime, but while sitting on the ground would be uselessly tragic.

On November 5th, when we arrived at our plane to get our guns ready for a mission to Frankfurt, one of the guys went into the crew chief's hut to ask him a question. The hut was warm and the crew chief was apparently asleep in his cot, which was unusual. Our guy jostled the cot and said in a loud voice, "Hey, Sarge, I have to ask you a question."

From the form under the blanket came a feminine voice timidly explaining, "The sergeant isn't here."

It developed he was off somewhere with a bout of intestinal discomfort. We had to wait for him a few minutes more before he sheepishly appeared out of the dark. He was lucky we had found him rather than Sam or Marty because he had some pre-flight work yet to be done.

Crew chief peccadilloes aside, we had to get about our business which was to bomb a target in another major German city. On this date we had been awakened in the wee hours to once more carry a load of explosives to a German target. In our part of this war, we were like a trucking company hauling explosive cargo into a dangerous neighborhood guarded by armed people intent on stopping our deliveries by shooting us down or blowing us up. For the most part, it wasn't a very glamorous task and was hard work under trying circumstances.

We bombed from 25,500 feet with a temperature of –30°F. Our target was the marshalling yards on the outskirts of Frankfurt, Germany, which easily could be seen from my turret. We were able to visually bomb today and the results were impressive. I tracked our Group's bomb load as it fell unerringly toward Frankfurt's vast rail yards. An interesting visual phenomenon that could only be witnessed by the ball turret gunners happened when tracking a bomb load. As the bombs fell from the planes toward the target they appeared to steadily shrink and then begin to lag behind the bombers. But as they neared the ground they would appear to speed up and would impact the ground immediately under us.

We were a part of a force of some 360 bombers of the Eighth Air Force's First Air Division that were sent to cripple that important railway hub with 1,612 tons of bombs. Our Group's bombs went directly on the target area where I could see massive explosions and fires as locomotives and war materiel were being destroyed. It was a good feeling to see that we were being successful in disrupting Hitler and the Nazis' military campaign.

The 88mm anti-aircraft flak bursts were of moderate intensity and accurate. Scarily we were bounced and thumped about from near-by concussions as flak pieces tore into our ship. In addition, we saw quite a few anti-aircraft rockets being fired at us, which were also rather accurate. The rockets left a larger explosion cloud in the sky, which was white rather than black. Though the explosion clouds were larger they appeared less ominous to me than did the regular flak for some reason. I suppose being white smoke they didn't look as mean as the black smoke of the 88mm shells. We also saw the dreaded German jet fighters in our area but none attacked our group, perhaps because of our very good P-47 and P-51 fighter support. We had minor flak damage to our ship on this shorter six hour 40 minute mission. [See photo of flak at the end of the chapter.]

Europe in the winter was snow covered. Dark wooded areas and fields of white interspersed with towns and cities etched in dark detail along the way. Both coming into the target area and returning home while looking down at the ground, I could see areas under attack by artillery. There were burning buildings marking the snow-covered landscape with black. From our altitude it was impossible for me to know who was attacking whom or what. Due to the interphone discipline of no idle chatter, we of course couldn't share what we were individually seeing. So I just silently looked at the sweeping panorama of World War II below us and kept the images burned in my memory.

I saw for the first time a large RAF formation coming across the Channel as we were leaving the continent. I noted in my log that they had, "Awful formation flying." I didn't realize then that they didn't use the tight formations we did because of their different bombing philosophy. We bombed as a group, at the same moment during the daylight; which also required tighter formations as fighter protection. .The RAF bombed individually on the flare of a marker bomb dropped by the lead ship at night so didn't require our tighter formations.

It was getting late, when we returned to the hard stand. The crew chief's guest was no longer in evidence and nothing more was said about her. We had returned home for another mission finale with Interrogation bolstered by an issued shot of warming Scotch. Then we had a welcomed hot meal in the Combat Mess for the mission's end. In a light cold drizzle, we returned to Hut Five for conversation about the day's events and to read our mail. The evening after a mission was a time to recuperate and relieve the stress of flying hour-after-hour in a sub-zero freezing, un-pressurized, unheated, noisy, vibrating machine while some folks tried to shoot us down. Maybe we would; write a letter or two, listen the radio, play a little poker, have a cigarette...these were all options for the tired gunner. But, "Sleep that knits up the ravell'd sleeve of care," as Shakespeare so aptly wrote in *Macbeth*, was the best option. I got to where I could, and probably did, sleep most anywhere at any time in dark or light or in noise or quiet.

THE BLUE ROOM

Though our primary purpose was to fly combat missions against German strategic and tactical targets, the bulk of our time was spent on the base and around the hut. Each hut established its own character based on the current inhabitants. The Squadron didn't impose many normal military rules or inspections to interfere with our youthful creative instincts. Each guy's individual space was his own collection of stuff arranged how and as he saw fit. Thus each hut's interior was unique.

Hut Five became to be called The Blue Room because we had taken the liners from chaff boxes to cover the inside wooden ends of the hut. These were sheets of Kraft paper lined with aluminum foil, which had a shiny light bluish tint. The ostensible purpose for doing this was to block out the wind that blew through the cracks in the joints of the weathered wooden end-sections of the hut. This application did a wonderful wind-proofing job and also gave a rather festive bluish tint to the ends of the hut as light reflected off the foil surface.

To further add to the club-like atmosphere of our hut, we had acquired a wooden table and two benches for card games. To provide a proper card table surface, we nailed a wool blanket over the tabletop. This became a very nice poker table for us, and for other time-to-time drop-ins. The poker games were at times an irritation to some of our hut-mates if they wanted to catch some sleep. However, Foon was never bothered by noise in the hut if he wanted to go to sleep. And usually I would sleep through most distractions. But, to no avail, others at times did complain.

THE HOME PHOTO LAB

Frank Hrehocik was the hut's expert on photography. He was a very inventive and talented young man who spoke with authority on most subjects and maturity beyond his years. Being from New Jersey, he had that East Coast man-about-town persona that could be impressive to most of us. Even though we were not supposed to have any personal cameras, he had a still and a movie camera. For developing the still camera pictures he obtained the necessary chemicals in town somewhere and set up a small photo lab in our hut. He, with the aid of Dan Adair I believe, made contact prints of his snapshots and gave them to us as we asked. [See group photo at the end of the chapter.] He ingeniously made a photographic enlarger using a bellows type camera, two coffee cans soldered together, and a powerful light. He was able to make decent enlargements with this rig. On the opposite side of the storm door vestibule from the poker table, Frank set up his photo lab. There was a faint chemical smell in the area and he had prints drying on lines at times. Our austere hut was becoming a comfortable home in the UK. The 8mm movie film that he shot went home with him to be developed later. As an aside, I had never seen any of that film until 2005 when Frank's cousin Jerry Gergasko had it transferred to DVD and was generous enough to send me a copy.

THE MONSTER STOVE

One early evening there was a large explosion in the ordnance area by the flight line where a number of buildings had blown up. Most of us hurried down there out of curiosity and to help in any rescue attempts if needed. When we got there we weren't needed, so we wandered around and looked at the smoking devastation. Then one of us spotted a large coke stove that had been thrown out of a building during the blast. Some creative mind saw the potential for increasing the heat in our hut. It was "GI requisitioned" (meaning stolen) by us and loaded on a Jeep found nearby. No one was using that particular Jeep at the moment so it was used to relocate the stove to The Blue Room. This wonderfully robust stove would surely provide enough warmth for our hut's busy social schedule. Ah, we thought, the end of our heating problems at last!

The Army issued coke stove put in each hut was very small to conserve the scarce coke. We were rationed one bucket of coke each day from a stockpile by the Orderly Room. This would provide heat for only a few hours each day. With our new acquisition, we thought we could now have heat for much longer times each day. It turned out we hadn't thought this situation through too well. The monster stove needed more than the rationed measly bucket of coke a day. We now had to turn to stealing coke from a larger coke compound nearby, which was under armed guard. We developed elaborate plans involving distracting the guard so coke could be "acquired." A section of the fence was altered to allow an easy gate-like opening, etc. A complication to handling coke and not being detected during coke acquisition was that it has a very hard surface and quite noisy when a shovel was jammed in it. Therefore, to solve that problem we hand loaded the coke into sacks to keep the transaction quiet and hopefully undetected by the hapless guard. The coke acquisition duty was spread out to all of us so it didn't become too onerous on just a few.

A further detail needed solving, which was what to do with all this additional supply of coke. We couldn't leave it outside the hut where some less than honorable souls would take it, or turn us in to the squadron commander. We couldn't just have a pile of coke sitting on the hut floor, which would be a little messy and obvious should we ever have a visit by an officer. We decided to acquire some empty bomb boxes because they were often used as footlockers for our personal property and wouldn't look out of place. We eventually had twenty or so bomb boxes filled with coke stashed under every cot and on top of the storm door vestibule area. All this effort paid off in our very comfortable quarters...The Blue Room.

Though we had never had a quarters inspection before, one day we did have an unannounced one. A young fresh-faced 2nd Lt. who was unknown to us, followed by his neatly dressed aide with the usual clipboard, entered our hut. They walked importantly from one end of the hut to the other. As he took his walk, the inspecting officer had to go around the monster stove parked in the middle of the hut. He went down the aisle and looked at all our haphazardly arranged stuff by each cot. He silently observed the poker table, the photo lab equipment, the shiny blue end walls and the monster stove. When they got back to the front door, and as they were leaving, he turned and said to his aide with the clipboard, "I never saw so damn many footlockers in all my life!"

And with that they left without further comment. I don't think he really wanted to know what was going on because then he would have had to require us to do something about it. The Blue Room had passed its one and only official inspection.

COMBAT AGAIN

On November 10th we returned to our old nemesis, Cologne, but an airfield rather than the rail yard was the target today. The very cold temperatures continued this date at –41°F as we bombed with radar from 26,800 feet. I could observe the bomb strikes through gaps in the clouds and they appeared effective. We once again experienced Cologne's very accurate flak that had ripped through our plane and caused some random battle damage. In another squadron of the 381st, a bombardier was killed as bombs dropped from another plane crashed into the greenhouse where he was seated. This sad accident caused Sam to give me another duty on the bomb run. Although I usually kept track of planes around us, he specifically wanted me to report during the bomb run any aircraft about to slide under us on our path. Which action I'm sure I would have taken as routine, but the specific order was a good reminder.

EMERGENCY LANDING

Our ship's brakes hydraulic system had been damaged by the flak at Cologne. Consequently our plane wouldn't be able to stop on the runway when we landed. As we returned to the Ridgewell area, Sam reported our brake hydraulic difficulties to the Control Tower. To avoid messing up the runway in case we crashed, he was told to circle around the base until all other aircraft had safely landed. He was instructed to execute an emergency landing without brakes on the long runway. Sam was talked through what he had to do by command personnel in the Tower. Meanwhile, the rest of us in the crew were ordered into our crash landing positions and told to prepare for a wheels-down crash landing. Gathered in the crash landing positions in the Radio Room we couldn't see anything. We could hear and feel as Sam reduced the landing speed as much he could without stalling and set the plane down on the first part of the runway. After touchdown as we thundered down the runway, it seemed to me we were not slowing down very much. Finally the tail dropped down as we lost some speed, I prayed there was enough runway left to keep us from going off the end and crashing.

We could only wait and trust in Sam once again. And then, as we neared the end of the runway, we felt a sudden lurch to the right with an increased engine roar. The plane almost immediately came to a stop without a crash. Sam was able to execute a perfect ground loop off the runway onto the soft dirt and wet grass on the right side of the runway. As directed by Tower personnel, he had applied what little fluid was left in the brake system on the starboard wheel brake. And then at the same time he revved the port engines to pivot us off the runway to the right. When we climbed out of the ship, awaiting us were several vehicles and people with smiles all around. Besides the ambulance and the fire truck was the worried crew chief of the plane we were flying. He scanned the plane for the visible battle damage, and then thanked Sam for saving 'my plane', as he put it. A few days later at a regular combat crews' meeting, Sam was commended for his fine flying and cool attention to instruction from the Tower during our successful emergency landing.

The next few days were spent in routine as the worsening weather was limiting flying operations and no combat missions were scheduled. A few of the permanent party ground personnel first three grader enlisted men established a private club for Staff, Tech and Master Sergeants. Membership fee was £10 British, which was the equivalent of $40 American. The membership fee was for operating capital only. When one wished to no longer be a member, or were returning home, the £10 was refunded, no questions asked.

On the base there had been a small mess hall that was used by the RAF when they had the base, but not by the USAAF. This building was donated for our usage. It was rehabilitated, painted and modified into a very nice club complete with; a cocktail bar and lounge, restrooms both men's and women's, a dance floor along with a stage with parachute curtains for stage presentations. We had a members-only entrance controlled by paid enlisted men. Officers, or lower graded enlisted men, were only allowed in on special events and by invitation only.

The master sergeant in charge of buying liquor for the Officers Club, was given a free membership for acquiring the liquor for our bar. Similarly, the mess sergeant for the Combat Mess was also given a free membership, for which honor he supplied the bar with sandwiches and snacks to be sold for modest prices. I believe we also had an antique slot machine, if my memory is correct, for a little gambling income.

Mostly, it was just a place to hang out that was a little non-military and was never over crowded. I remember one party wherein the officers were invited as a gesture of friendliness. There was a stage show put on by a group from London with lots of pretty girls. After the show there was some dancing with the girls who were mostly quite attractive. It was a fairly civilized affair with only one broken arm as I recall. Most of the club members were ground personnel who worked very hard on vital tasks keeping our aircraft and our base in good and safe working order seven days a week and 24 hours a day. They believed they needed a quiet place free of officers and of lesser grade enlisted men; a haven from responsibility and conformity. We were honored to be able to join the Senior NCO Club. Today these are called Zebra Clubs on airbases all over the world. As an interesting aside, I'm told in the current day Air Force they have done away with the separate Officers', Enlisted, NCO Clubs in the interest of political correctness.

They apparently have just one club for the use of all from the General to the Private. How dreadful!

AIDING THE GROUND WAR

The Eighth Air Force's primary responsibility was strategic bombing of industrial and transportation targets. Rarely had it been used in tactical missions which were the forte' of the Ninth Air Force with their aggressive close-in support by fighters and medium bombers. The U.S. Ninth Army was preparing for an assault on the Aachen, Germany, area, which had massive heavy artillery emplacements defending Germany from the advancing American armies. On November 16th, our crew along with 489 other B-17s, dropped 1,776 tons of 250 pound fragmentation bombs on those artillery gun installations to assist the Army's assault on the German Fatherland. Bombing was visual. I was able to see the direct hit on those artillery emplacements, which were located down in a vast stone quarry. For us this was a milk run, with only light flak and no bandits in sight, but it was satisfying to know we were directly helping our brothers on the ground.

BUZZ BOMBS

The next days were spent in training again with visits to the local pubs. At around this time, I was awakened in the middle of the night by the sound of a buzz bomb droning toward us. I listened and wondered if I should wake everyone up and head for the bomb shelter, or wait it out because it would probably just pass by and explode somewhere else. Deciding to just sweat it out...I listened. It seemed that deep groaning sound kept coming forever. I waited in the dark as it passed almost directly overhead vibrating the hut as it moved on beyond us. With that I reached over, got a cigarette and lit it with my lighter when several matches and lighters also lit up all over the hut. It seemed most of them were awake, excepting Ralph who could sleep through anything, were doing as I was...just listening and hoping and maybe a little praying until it was beyond our base.

The V1 Buzz Bomb was as much a psychological weapon as a tactical one. As they lumbered their way across England before dropping and exploding, they had affected thousands of people hearing that ominous pulsing sound...and wondering. The V2 rocket on the other hand fell silently from out of the sky without warning. It was the world's first ballistic missile. It's liquid rocket engine only fired 4 seconds as it climbed up off its launching pad across the Channel. More than once, on a clear morning while preparing for a mission, I watched the bright contrail of a V2 seem to squirt up into the atmosphere. We knew there was a V2 aimed and heading somewhere with its 2,000 pounds of explosives. If the contrail were perpendicular to the horizon, you were on its path though probably not the distance it was targeted for, which was likely London forty miles away. But unlike the Buzz Bomb, no one's sleep was disturbed as it fell to earth, except for those unlucky souls who would be at or near where it crashed to ground with a mighty explosion.

We were given another 36 hours pass and I was going to return to London. I checked the box where I had been collecting the unused high carbohydrate candy ration donated by my crew and hut mates and found it full. I estimated that it was about five pounds of candy and gum.

I carefully packed my candy cargo for its trip to London and my next visit with Pat.

CANDY MISSION TO LONDON

For day-to-day enjoyment we could go to local towns for an evening if we were not on flight status the next day. Our permanent Class B Passes were all the authority we needed. There were the dances held with the WLA girls in a local hall of some sort. We would visit Cambridge, Braintree, Halstead and even Chelmsford in the evenings on Liberty Runs. These times were a few hours of pub time and socializing with the local girls. I enjoyed these diversions for the friendliness of the people and the great sing-a-longs. We were very fortunate to have the lovely countryside with its towns and villages to visit when we could leave the base. But my heart now was in London.

A trip to London however required a Class A 36 hour pass for which we were normally authorized for every week and a half or so. It was a big deal for me. A London trip was special because I had become really fond of that tough old city and because of being able to visit Pat of course.

I was going to London with my Class A pass to be with Pat and to deliver the box of candy and gum I had collected from my hut mates. Maybe, I thought, I could spend some time in her part of London and we could get to know each other a little better so I called her right away. When I got through on the phone to her house she was happy to hear I was coming to town. She then put the phone down to talk to her mother about something. She picked up the phone and said, "If you would like to stay here, you could sleep in my brother's bedroom. Mum said it would be a good idea because my dad wants to meet you."

Oh, God, what have I gotten myself into, I silently wondered. I tried a little verbal dancing around about I didn't want to put them into any effort, etc, etc. It seemed her brother was in the British Army on duty in North Africa, so there was plenty of room. It was agreed I would come down to London and Lower Edmonton Friday afternoon and would stay the night at her place. This was not what I really wanted to do, but was probably necessary if we were ever to see each other again.

When I arrived at the Liverpool Street station, I called Pat to let her know I was on my way up to Lower Edmonton. I carried a bag for my personal items and had put the box of candy in it. When I got off at the end-of-line bus stop in Lower Edmonton, I saw Pat waiting for me by the fish and chips shop. It turned out her mother had suggested we should pick up some fish and chips for the family evening meal and had given Pat money to pay for it. We picked up a large package of warm fish and chips freshly fried and wrapped in newspaper. I insisted on paying for the food of course. Later when her dad found out I had paid for the meal he was a little miffed. Once again I had made a social mistake with the best of intentions.

When we got to her house, I met her family. Her little sister was about 13 or 14 years old, cute and very girly. Her mother was warmly friendly and welcomed me to their home with a soft handshake. The father was a smallish man and a little standoffish, but polite. We traded the usual firm handshake routine as I smiled and looked him in the eye. He asked a few questions the answers to which didn't seem to matter. More, it seemed he was trying to figure what kind of chap was this whom his daughter seemed so taken.

I found the fish and chips were really good and for me thinking that was unusual. I didn't normally care much for fish but this was not fishy tasting nor smelling, and no bones to worry over. As a kid I had a fish bone lodged in my throat one time, which my dad had to remove with a pair of pliers. So, eating fish for me was usually a concern, but not this fish.

We chatted as we ate. Mostly the conversation was about where I came from and what did I do back there. I don't recall any questions about my flying duties. Frankly, I was a little disappointed. I had thought I could impress them by calmly answering their questions about combat. I needed some points with the family and thought my best chance was the daring-do of bombing missions over Germany. But they were more interested in California and what was it like living there. Maybe they had had enough talk about the war over the past few years.

In all the activity of my arrival and eating dinner, I had forgotten about the candy I had collected for Pat. When I suddenly remembered it, I went to my bag, took out the candy box and opened it to gasps of wonder from everyone. None of them had ever seen so much candy. Sensing a little wariness from her father, I carefully explained that it hadn't cost me anything, and that I just wanted them to have what was very scarce for them during this long war. After a little hesitancy, they helped themselves and of course were delighted. Pat's mother took control of the candy fairly soon to keep anyone, particularly her youngest daughter, from eating too much. I heard that later they gave some of the candy to neighborhood kids who wolfed it down with great glee. Later that evening Sid, Pat's father, asked me to join him for a "mild and bitter" at the local pub.

Sid introduced me to a few of his mates at the pub who seemed friendly. As we ordered our beer, I was smart enough to let him buy. We smoked my American cigarettes, which were quite a hit and talked about general events. Though I was a little ill at ease with Sid I had a good time and joked some with his pals. He even let me buy a round of beer after a bit. I assumed that pub visit was all a test of some kind. Whatever the test was, I apparently passed, or at least I didn't fail, which seemed more likely. As we casually walked back to the house, our conversation was friendly. When we got there, Pat was waiting for me in the living room reading a magazine. The living room provided some privacy, but it had no heat. The family spent their evenings in the kitchen because it was the only room in the house that had any heat. I think this had to do with the scarcity of coke just as we had back at the base. We spent the evening in that chilly living room of her home getting to know each other a little more. That quiet time just being with each other was really nice and comfortable as we chatted away getting to know each other.

The next morning I was awakened, (or knocked up as the English used to say), from a deep sleep by Pat. She gave me a gentle nudge and presented me with the nice English custom of a cup of hot tea. Her brother Jack's bed was the most comfortable one I had slept in for the past year or so. To sit up in that soft clean bed and have a cup of tea delivered by this smiling girl was extraordinary. I warmly relaxed inside. It was as if all were perfect in the world at least for those few minutes. And a permanent lovely image was etched in my memory.

I Commit a Gaffe—Once Again

After a breakfast of fried bread, which tasted surprisingly good, and a cup of tea, we went into Central London rather then her neighborhood. Pat showed me London from the perspective of her eyes. Much of what we saw and where we went is indistinct and jumbled with image fragments in my memory. But, I believe it was on this trip, or perhaps a later one, we went to visit Selfridge's Department Store, which had been hit by a V2 rocket some days before. Though a portion of the store was walled off, due to the destruction, most of it was open for business. The building had steel divider doors that were rolled down at night between sections of the store. These were to localize the effects of any blasts should they occur. We saw a line of these roll down doors that had been bulged by the explosion of the V2. But where we were walking, business was going on quite normally. We were strolling through a lady's wear section when a comfortable looking soft wool coat caught my eye. I had noticed that Pat's coat seemed rather thin and worn so I thought maybe I would get this coat for her. The price was quite modest and something I could easily afford and wanted to do. It was like the caveman bringing home an animal pelt I guess. Anyway, I asked her to put it on and she loved it. I bought the coat for her and she wore it for the rest of the day. Her old one was folded up and carried in a bag. Later Pat told me that once again I had irritated old Sid.

"We don't need anyone to buy our daughter clothes...etc.!" he was reported as fuming to Mary, Pat's mother.

I seemed to have an ability to do the wrong thing time after time. He let her keep the coat though, but never mentioned it to me.

After a day well spent that seemed to go too fast, and with a lingering sentimental goodbye, Pat returned to her home and family. Although our life situations and our backgrounds, as well as some physical distance separated us, we had bonded emotionally. It was awkward and uncomfortable to have to deal with adult situations with only teen-age experiences as a background. But that's the way it was.

Alone on the train and our romantic interlude over, I watched the countryside rattle by and was lost in thought. I reluctantly returned to Ridgewell and my life there with periods of combat over Germany and longer periods of routine on the base.

An example of heavy and accurate exploding flak throwing chunks of steel, spreading potential death and damage. [USAAF]

Blue Room crew, the gang from Hut 5, Site 5, Ridgewell, England. Back Row: Bob Gonnering, Dan Adair, Jack Bressie, Marty Tremble, Bob Gilbert, and Frank Hrehocik. Front Row: Frank Clemens, Ralph Engleman, Bill Hiney, unidentified.

THE VIEW FROM THE BOTTOM UP

Chapter 11

The Dog Fight

TIME OUT FOR CHAPLAIN BROWN

DURING the last weeks in November, we endured almost daily penetrating cold rain or drizzle. Everything was wet and dreary. When the low steel-gray clouds lifted, the weather cleared and got colder. During those nights, we had heavy frost that by morning had coated everything which wasn't moving. Fence wires were so heavy with frost they looked like white rods between the weathered fence posts. The bleak colorless landscape of the airbase seemed like an old black and white photograph and looked as if it had snowed during the night...but it wasn't snow.

On the Sunday after my candy mission to London, I attended, as I did occasionally, the church service conducted by Captain James Good Brown, Chaplain, 381st bomb Group. His services had a lot of attendees from the local English families as well as 381st personnel. We were a mixed bunch of officers, enlisted men and civilians.

I had never been much for going to church in my civilian life. I had read portions of the Bible from time-to-time, and participated in many lively discussions with other guys on the issues of religion. Spirituality and powers greater than human power were of interest to me, but formal religions were not. However, in his sincere and easy manner, Chaplain Brown could make a believer out of most anybody. His sermons I found were very down-to-earth and translated well to both the AAF guys and the English civilians.

On this date his sermon in part was a defense of the pin-up pictures we had all over our quarters. Most religious folks would, publicly at least, tsk, tsk at such displays of scantily clad women as being immoral and leading to the decline of civilization as they knew it. In fact the pin-up pictures of those days were quite benign. There were no violence or pornographic images involved. Chaplain Brown's thought was pin-ups were a normal sign GIs were showing esteem for something other than them. He went on to opine that this was a step toward believing in a spiritual power greater than themselves, which was needed to come to believe in a loving God, as he understood Him to be. That may not be exactly what he said but that is what I heard, and I liked it.

Chaplain Brown was a unique Chaplain in many ways. He understood some of the problems having to do with airmen and flying combat. He was always in the Interrogation waiting area after a mission for anyone who needed his counsel. He would wander about and inquire, how did it go today? His friendly presence was a welcome and reassuring sight to me even when we didn't speak.

In his chapel he had a heavy punching bag installed in the back area. He explained that the bag was there for our usage anytime, excepting during services of course, to help relieve tension. Unreleased tension comes from being attacked with no ability to fight back such as happens during flak barrages. This often would result in emotional and physical problems. He knew what he was talking about because he actually flew on a number of combat missions. Eventually he was ordered to stop this practice because chaplains were non-combat personnel and specifically prohibited from engaging in combat operations.

We had a number of Hollywood celebrities come by the base and perform or maybe just say a few words of appreciation to the troops. James Cagney, Bing Crosby and Edward G. Robinson were a few of those who stopped by the 381st. Robinson, when he met Chaplain Brown, was surprised to find out he was a chaplain. He was reported as saying he looked more like a boxer than a man of God and he noticed the chaplain didn't wear the usual cross symbol on his collar. When asked why, Brown told Robinson he didn't want to appear to be separated from the other service men. So he wore the Air Corps wings collar symbol instead of the Chaplain's Cross.

On the 21st one of our hut mates, Dan Adair and the crew he was flying with on a mission to the oil refineries at Merseburg had major damage to their ship. They were reported as missing in action (MIA). It was also reported that Dan had bailed out over the Continent. This event has a bit of irony in that the pilot Dan was flying with was Dale Windsor the veteran pilot who shepherded the Goldin crew on our first missions.

THANKSGIVING 1944

On Thanksgiving Day, the 23rd of November, the Combat Mess personnel put on a wonderful traditional turkey feast. The mess hall was decorated in a Fall-like theme. We were served our meal sit-down style at the table on white tablecloths and on china dishes instead of the usual Army steel trays. With that atmosphere, and a meal of first class quantity and quality, we were indeed blessed and thankful. Second helpings were encouraged and I for one ate way too much. I slowly walked back to our hut rather than ride to help digest that wonderful meal, which had reminded me of home.

As I strolled along back to the hut, I thought of my family back in California with fondness. On this day they will be gathering and would in some hours be enjoying a festive meal together. As I saw it in my minds eye, probably they would be at my folk's house in Long Beach. Mom and my aunts would have the house smelling wonderfully of roasting turkey. The sounds of laughter and quiet adult conversations would fill the air. The kids would be outside raucously playing games.

Where ever the family gathered it was always a festive time for all of us. This year, like last year, a number of us were away in different parts of the world serving our country. I felt sure we guys in the service would be missed at today's meal. Maybe next year we will all be home...I prayed.

BACK TO COMBAT

As a part of the First Air Division, we bombed the I.G. Farben oil refinery at Mersberg, always a tough target, on November 25th . The First Air Division put up 355 bombers against Mersberg, 50 of which were damaged. The flak was very intense but somewhat inaccurate as far as our ship was concerned. The sky was black with flak bursts all around us, but we seemed to be quite lucky and suffered little damage. However, the Third Air Division that sent 315 bombers to Mersberg had 147 of them damaged. We proceeded home from this successful mission without further incident.

However, things were very different for Bob Gonnering (our original crew member and hut mate) and the Riza crew. On this mission they suffered major damage to their plane and crash landed in Belgium. They were reported missing in action just as had happened to Dan Adair's crew a few day's earlier. Things were getting tougher.

THE DOG FIGHT

The next day November 26th, we attacked a railroad viaduct in the northern Ruhr Valley at Altenbecken. We had to resort to bombing by radar when clouds covered the target just as we approached.

The flak was meager and accurate, but of greater concern was we had a huge group of Me 109s attacking our task force. On this date the Luftwaffe launched a major effort to attack our 8th Air Force bombers. According to Roger Freeman, in his *Mighty Eighth War Diary*, this amounted to some 500 fighters. Later we learned that 34 of our 8th AF bombers had been shot down, mostly by fighter attacks. I watched as a wolf pack of 100 or more Me 109s flew past and down below us looking like a swarm of angry bumble bees, but out-of-range of our machine guns. There were so many of them I thought at first they must be our P-51s. Then when I quickly realized they were Luftwaffe Me 109s, I called them out to the crew.

"Bandits two o'clock low...a bunch of them!" I reported.

The threatening dark outlines of the Messerschmitts continued to fly off to the side and below us but still out-of-range. Once past us, they rapidly climbed up high above us and then, in one mass attack, slashed down through the group flying behind us. Why they chose the other group instead of us I of course don't know. Perhaps we presented a tighter formation and thus not as vulnerable as would be a looser one.

I watched in horror, as several bombers in that Group immediately exploded and fell toward the ground trailing parts of airplanes and crewmen. The unfortunate Group's formation began to scatter as the fighters passed through it. Oh my God! I hope they don't come back for us, I prayed as they flew down and away from us. I must confess at that time I was more concerned about my safety than for those poor souls scattered about the German landscape.

From seemingly out of nowhere, came a smaller group of P-51s screaming right past us to get to the '109s. As scores of fighters engaged in swirling aerial combat, I watched the battle that ensued with heart-pounding fear and excitement at the same time; I couldn't tell who was being shot down. Like a demonic New Year's Eve celebration, the azure blue sky was filled with streamers of color hanging in scattered profusion. Streamers of white condensation trails, and of white and black smoke trailing the red flames of burning aircraft all swirled together. As I rapidly turned my turret looking about the sky, I fearfully wondered who was winning, and would the Germans come after us if they vanquished the Mustangs? At one point, two Messerschmitts roared right passed us being chased by one gutsy P-51 pilot. The whole scene was pure chaos. According to Christer Bergstrom, the Swedish air war historian; subsequent reports indicate three B-17s destroyed, six badly damaged, also nine P-51s and 38 Me 109s were shot down.

After a while things began to settle down; the streamers faded into limp smeared memories of the fierce fighter aircraft battle. It became clear the P-51s had prevailed as they patrolled a sky now empty of Luftwaffe. Heart rates slowing down, we were just starting to relax as our B-17 droned on, when from his waist position Clem called out a Me109 at two o'clock low coming out of the clouds below us and climbing.

"Can you see the bandit, Gilbert?" he excitedly asked.

I quickly spotted him and replied, "Yes, I got him in my sights."

He was well over a mile away with his nose aimed right at us. I tracked him outlined against the white clouds with my Sperry computing sight as he climbed toward us. But he was out of the accurate range of my guns. For my turret the effective range of accurate shooting was 1,000 to 1,200 yards, whereas the waist gun that Clem had the range was only about 600 yards, and the bandit was still around 2,000 yards away.

In the Sperry sight, there was a light reticule that consisted of a horizontal light line with two vertical light lines. We moved the turret to put the horizontal line through the center of the fighter's fuselage. And to operate the computing sight we moved the vertical lines to the wing tips with the foot pedal. When the image of the fighter's wing tips didn't yet reach to the vertical lines, he was well over a 1,200 yards away and out of range for accurate or effective shooting.

At this point I had to discontinue talking on the interphone. One problem with my long legs in the ball turret was I had to shift to one side when using the pedal for the turret gun sight. The turret had two foot-pedals; one operated the sight and the other was the interphone switch. And as I discovered during our combat crew training, I couldn't have both feet on their respective pedals at the same time. So when operating the sight, I couldn't talk on the interphone. I was tracking our intruder and eagerly hoping for him to get in range of my guns. The fear I felt when watching the massive attack on the other Group was replaced by eagerness. This wasn't like a flak attack where you can do nothing but hope or pray. I could finally do something! Being confident in my ability firing guns from the ball turret, I believed this was going to be a chance to get back for the '109's gang-attack on the group behind us. I held my breath waiting for his image to fill my sight; when he would be ripe for my two 50 Cal. machine guns to nail him

But my silence on the interphone apparently caused some doubt and concern about what was going on with me. Clem began to get excited and started yelling.

"Shoot him, shoot him!"

I had the '109 in my sight, but he was still out of range. However, I had to start shooting to calm things down on the interphone. I hammered 15 or 20 rounds from each gun directly at the Messerschmitt. He immediately broke off his climb toward us and dove back into the clouds. He must have detected he was being fired at even though we didn't use tracer bullets. There was neither smoke nor fire from the '109 that I could see. Disappointed, I didn't know if I hit him or not. I continued to search the area under us for any more bandits, but none appeared. Slowly my heart rate returned to normal.

We continued on home without further action or incident. We were all a little wound up when we got to Interrogation, and excitedly talking about our first exposure to a mass fighter attack. The hot steaming coffee tasted great and I think most of us took our shot of the Medic's issued Scotch before we went in for our interrogation. During our crew report in Interrogation, Sam told of our direct encounter with the '109. The Intelligence officer wanted to know if we were claiming a kill or a probable, Sam and I both said no at the same time. I felt disappointed, and frustrated because given another 30 seconds I believed I would have smoked him. I thought it was possible I had hit him. But I didn't see any fire or indication of physical damage and thus no claim could or should be made.

We went off to chow and back to our refuge in the Blue Room for a little rest; then maybe write a letter home and a quiet evening listening to the Andrews Sisters or maybe it was Clem's pet, Dinah Shore. Again I experienced the emotional paradox of being; between the tension and fear of aerial combat at 25.000 feet, and just hours later being back in the relative normalcy of the Blue Room having a cigarette listening to the radio.

We had a couple of days off to enjoy sleeping in. And later in the day, a visit to the Senior NCO Club for one or two of those meat loaf sandwiches with a warm beer. I don't have many specific memories of my times at the club; they were just nice times in a quiet atmosphere. I do remember when someone came into the club and told us the good news that Dan Adair, who had been MIA, had safely bailed out over Belgium and was OK. Also, the Riza crew including Bob Gonnering, our other MIA hut member, had been recovered by the British and returned to London. So our Blue Room cast-of-characters was back together. Our time-off went by swiftly and all too soon we were back to work.

The View From the Bottom Up

On the 29th of November, we were back at it as we hit another oil storage facility this time near the town of Misburg. Due to the unavailability of flyable aircraft in our Squadron, we flew a 535th Squadron plane on this mission. We bombed once again by radar through the cloudy undercast. For me bombing by instruments was not as satisfying as visual bombing. When clouds obscured it, I couldn't watch our bomb load hit the target with satisfying large explosions scattered about. Results of bombing were determined later by camera aircraft that were often either a British Mosquito or an American P-38 Lightning. These special aircraft were stripped down to remove all nonessential weight. They were extremely fast and virtually untouchable as they flew in low, took their pictures of the bombing results and scrammed for home. They usually beat the bombers back to the base.

We had good fighter support and the flak was light but accurate. The German radar had us locked in but only a few guns were protecting Misburg. Our ship had some serious flak damage to one fuel tank but Marty was able to close off the system to where we didn't lose too much gasoline or develop any fire.

The next day, the 30th of November, once again in a 535th plane, we hit another oil storage facility. This time it was in Zeitz, near Mersberg. The flak gunners had a clear sky to target us with heavy and accurate flak. The flak was so heavy it almost looked as if we were flying into a black cloud. The press the following day reported 57 bombers and 30 fighters had been shot down. The headline in Stars and Stripes, the official U.S. Army newspaper, was, "The Sky Was Filled With Flak and Death." We were bounced around some and our ship had minor battle damage. Our toggelier was knocked off his seat when a hunk of flak hit his flak vest. Andy was hit a glancing blow off his flak helmet. There were no injuries to either of them.

We were able to bomb visually. I watched our bombs falling directly under us toward and finally smacking the target. We had good success evidenced by massive explosions as our bombs hit their target. All over the area I saw bright red fires with boiling black clouds of smoke. I noted in my log that, "It looked like all Germany was on fire" as other Groups were also hitting their targets. The power on my turret burned out due to malfunction or battle damage. To maintain my turret's operation, I had to hand-crank it for the rest of the day. It was important to keep the turret moving because I still had to look for bandits, and also to not appear inoperative and thus vulnerable to the

Germans fighters. This was a seven hour 30 minute mission at 26.400 feet and at –44°F.

Zeitz was our fourth mission in six days and we were losing efficiency due to fatigue. The sharpness needed to be an efficient crew in combat formation flying gets dulled when there isn't enough time in between to restore the crew's physical and mental resources. An eight-hour mission actually took around 12 hours or more out of the day. So when you have two such missions back-to-back it is like constantly being involved for 48 hours in preparing for and performing combat. It was good to get a lot of missions completed and thus be a little closer to completing your tour. Unfortunately, though, having so many missions so close together, was like driving your car for eight or ten hours straight without any rest stops for several days in a row. You can do it but when you have not had enough rest it is dangerous to operate equipment and conduct precise technical operations.

LONDON AGAIN

At around this time we were given another 36 hours pass. Several of us had decided to go to London once again. I had collected another box of candy for Pat and her friends. When I called I found out Pat would be working the next day. We could only spend the afternoon and evening together. We met in Leicester Square. She looked pretty and happy wearing the new coat I had bought her on an earlier trip. Pinned to the lapel she had a little sprig of a small flower. Pat seemed quite proud of her new coat and did a fashion turn to show me how nice it looked. I felt a flush of pride having been able to do something that pleased her so.

We went to a movie, sat in the balcony, cuddled and snacked on the candy I had brought. It turned out that the last box of candy was now gone thanks in part to the neighborhood kids. She said her little sister got sick from eating too much at one time, so her mother would see that this box would last longer.

I don't recall the movie, but it was something light and entertaining. We ate a nice meal at the Lyon's Corner House after the movie and spent the rest of the evening talking and still learning more about each other and our respective cultures. Late that evening we quietly rode the bus to Lower Edmonton where I walked her to her home for another sad goodbye until next time. I returned to Russell Square to stay at the Red Cross Club that night.

The next day I went with the guys to visit some of the sights around town. Particularly I remember Madam Tussaud's Museum. It was an exhibition fixated on the bizarre and the criminal. The accent was on infamous murders, the bloodier the better. After spending an hour looking at one lethal contraption or another, and one murderer or another I wondered why this place was so famous. It seemed rather cheap and tawdry.

As we strolled along, the public parks were serenely beautiful amid the hustle of the great city with its bomb shelters and damaged buildings. I liked Hyde Park particularly for the street orators who ranted on any subject that suited them. They reminded me of back home. In Long Beach we had a similar area by the foot of Rainbow Pier called The Spit and Argue Club. When I was a youngster, I liked to listen to the rabble-rousers who regularly spoke there. I don't think I ever really learned anything from them, but I enjoyed their enthusiasm and at times outrageous propositions to solve the world's problems.

We grabbed a lunch at a café called Wimpy's (after the character in the Popeye cartoon strip) that advertised American hamburgers and hot coffee. We sat at the counter and the place did sort-of look like an American diner. As we awaited our order, we heard a GI in a harsh New York accent complain to the waitress, "Hey, sweetheart why don't you marry a GI," he rudely barked, "then maybe you can learn how to make a cup of coffee!"

He left as our orders for hamburgers with everything on them arrived with the coffee. Being American we were embarrassed by him, so one of us apologized to the waitress for the loud-mouthed GI. Then as I tasted the hot so-called coffee I knew what he was unhappy about. It was bitter yet flat and tasted like the grounds had been used a few times before. The "hamburger" was at best a disappointment. The mystery meat patty was a meat loaf like mixture that contained primarily bread with some sort of meat stuff for flavoring. The lettuce role in the hamburger charade was played by what appeared to be clover or something kind-of green. This meal was even worse than the waffle we had at George's American Restaurant on an earlier trip. The message was clear; forget eating any place that pretends to offer American style food.

Later after cruising the penny arcades in the Piccadilly area, we caught the train back to Yeldham and returned to the base. To get Wimpy's out of our taste buds, we stopped at the bar in the Senior NCO Club for a wonderful meat loaf sandwich and a glass of beer.

CIGARETTES

On the 4th of December, the sales of cigarettes at the PX were again happening for non-combat personnel. We in the UK in the recent past had been under a strict rationing on the sale of cigarettes due to severe shortage. Combat personnel were allowed to buy five packs a week and non-combat personnel were not allowed to buy any. At this time, combat personnel were still to be allowed to buy five packs a week but non-combat personnel would now get to buy two packs a week. The Stars And Stripes', London Edition, feature story of November 30th had been about a Japanese internment camp in Tule Lake, California. There was a photocopy of the camp newspaper, Tule Lake Cooperator, dated October 16, 1944. The front page told the story of how they, the Japanese internees, had sent two cases of Lucky Strike cigarettes "as a gift to the Japanese Imperial Soldiers." This story did not sit well with the GIs in the UK, and still doesn't to me to this day. I assume this was carried out by the International Red Cross and was probably legal but the timing was poor.

On the 6th of December we had a six hours training mission over an area called The Wash on the eastern coast of England. These training missions were boring after combat flying but we needed to keep proficient in our various duties. For the gunners it was shooting at a tow target. To minimize the time for tow target shooting, we aimed for the forward attachment of the tow target. If we got lucky, and shot off the target connecting cable anchor we were through for our part of that day's training. Once finished shooting we could curl up and take a nap. Meanwhile the officers tended to more important matters, such as flying, bombing and navigating. Normally we had two of these training flights each month and everyone generally disliked them.

December the 7th, the third anniversary of the Japanese unprovoked attack on Pearl Harbor, happened quietly at Ridgewell. We remembered it was also a quiet peacetime Sunday in 1941, when naval forces of Japan started World War II for the United States with their sneak attack. We remembered those whose lives were taken so treacherously by Japan that fateful day and silently promised them justice.

DISRUPT THE TRANSPORTATION

We hit the Marshalling yards of Stuttgart on the ninth of December with good results. Although we had prepared to bomb with radar due to the cloud cover, as we neared the target the clouds parted and revealed the target. We bombed using visual bombsights. I was able to see accurate bombing results as our bombs fell to the rail yards creating a huge series of explosions.

We encountered moderate and very accurate flak causing substantial damage to our ship. We were being bounced about by insistent flak shells exploding all around us and tearing at our ship. Then suddenly number three engine failed due to flak damage as we were being pounded once again. Flying with only three engines, between the efforts of Sam, Marty and Reynolds, we were able to keep up with the Group all the way home. Andy was hit again, in the shoulder this time by a glancing shot that ripped his flight suit but didn't cut him! Curled up in my turret I carefully watched the underside of our ship to see if I could see any obvious damage. I looked particularly for any damage to the tires and for evidence of leaking gasoline or oil on the underside of the wings. The inspection of the tires and wheels and underside of the ship for evidence of damage was a routine I performed after each time we encountered any flak. The lower 35 percent or so of the tire was visible with the wheels retracted. They would rotate slowly in the air stream so all of the tire could ultimately be seen. A tire exploding upon the pressure of landing could likely cause a serious crash so it was important to check them while still flying as best we could. We had flak damage holes too numerous to count throughout the ship, but we all survived the day once again. At our bombing altitude of 25,000 feet the temperature was a bitter –55°F as we moved into Europe's coldest winter in memory.

Two days later on the 11th of December, we took off at 6:30 A.M. for Germany once again. Though the sky was clear over England we encountered complete undercast of clouds as we approached our target. Using radar we bombed our target a railroad bridge which ran between Ludwigshafen and Mannheim on the Rhine River. Results were unobserved due to the clouds. We had heavy and accurate flak thrown at us resulting in a large hole in our Plexiglas nose. Norman, our toggelier on this mission, covered the hole with his body to hold down the flood of air disrupting Andy's navigation maps. Norman spent so many hours blocking the hole in the nose with the –41°F below zero wind ripping at his back that he was in a lot of pain. When we got back to the base, he couldn't straighten up and looked like an old man when he walked. Duty up front in the greenhouse was starting to be unpleasant for the navigator and toggelier. We had a number of large holes throughout the ship as well as the nose, but no critical damages.

On this date the Eighth Air Force put up 1,600 four engine bombers over Germany, which was a record number at that time. The majority of them attacked targets in the industrial Ruhr Valley.

The next day on the 12th of December, at 27,000 feet and −45°F air temperature our primary target was a railroad yard at Ludwigshafen. On our way to the primary target, two of our squadron's ten ships had a mid-air collision causing both to make emergency landings in Belgium. Due to bad weather, the target at Ludwigshafen could not be bombed by visual sighting, which was required to minimize collateral damage. We then proceeded to the dangerous Merseburg to bomb the oil refineries there. This was a nine-hour mission wherein we met somewhat inaccurate but very heavy flak that caused minor damage to our ship. By the time we returned to Ridgewell there was 100% cloud cover. The ceiling had lowered to 1.000 feet. The Group disassembled above the clouds and carefully proceeded with landing operations down through the cloud cover. Observing great care to avoid each other, the Group was able to land all ships without incident at around 5:00 P.M.

Having flown three missions in four days, we finally got lucky and had a couple days of rest because of Group stand-downs due to weather. It was time to snooze and maybe play a little Snooker at the Aero Club.

On the 15th of December, at dawn we took off into a cloud filled sky. We proceeded to Germany and bombed the railroad yards at Kassel, which was our secondary target. This was my 18th mission, which was called 'going over the hump', meaning I was more than half way through my tour of duty of 35 missions. We were superstitious about saying how many missions we had left to fly. We would never say we had so many missions to fly, for instance we would say "I have 28 in," not "I have seven to go." But it was OK to say, "I went over the hump today." In any case, my luck prevailed as this was the first milk run since our first mission. We had no flak and no fighters in the area.

On the subject of superstitions, earlier Clem had a bad experience that added to our superstition on mission count. We were in the back of a truck taking us out to our plane with another crew. Clem was kidding around with one of the guys on the other crew whom he knew. The guy had said he had nine missions completed when Clem jokingly said, "That isn't such a big deal, it means you still have 26 missions to finish." They were shot down later that day over Germany. Such superstitions may sound silly today, but Clem was really distraught and felt responsible in a way for that awful coincidental event.

THE VIEW FROM THE BOTTOM UP

The Children's Christmas Party

On December 22nd, the 381st held a Christmas party for the local children on a cold and bitter day. The Aero Club was the site for this event that featured candy, gum and homemade ice cream. Santa was there with presents for the 350 or so children and parents from the surrounding villages and farms. Many, if not most, of these kids had never tasted ice cream before. After eagerly eating this delicious concoction from our mess hall, they laughed with happy ice cream smeared faces as they opened their presents. Their joy made this a truly Merry Christmas time for we Americans far from home at this family time of the year.

This was to be my second Christmas away from home. Christmas for me was a family gathering time featuring our family traditions of gift exchanging and a big home cooked turkey feast.

When I wasn't home with my family on Christmas Day, it was a nice holiday but it really wasn't Christmas.

Me removing .50 cal. Machine guns from the ball turret, Ridgewell Airbase, England, circa December 1944. [Frank Hrehocik]

THE VIEW FROM THE BOTTOM UP

Ralph Engleman on a rare sunny day, Ridgewell. [Frank Hrehocik]

Frank Hrebocik with an unidentified nurse, England. [Frank Hrebocik]

Chapter 12

The Battle of the Bulge

BACKGROUND

THE largest land battle ever fought by the United States was the Ardennes Salient, which involved over a million German, American and British men. It started on December 16th, 1944 when German forces mounted a massive counter attack against advancing U.S. and British forces. It took place in the Ardennes Forest on the Belgian and Luxembourg borders. The Germans used the fierce weather, which was historically cold with heavy snows and fog, as a cover from Allied air power.

Though officially designated The Ardennes Salient, it was commonly known as The Battle Of The Bulge. For eight days the world watched helplessly, as the initial thrusts by Germany were successful. They had stopped our advancing forces and in fact encircled and isolated large numbers of Americans. To us Army Air Corps guys waiting in England, it was a frustrating and anxious time. Due to the heavy weather that had most planes grounded for days, only a few small missions were flown at all and none in the Bulge area. Everyone I knew would have given up any pass or furlough time they had earned to come to the aid of our ground troops pinned down in Bastogne and such places. We in England read daily of what was happening in the Bulge and were very concerned, not that Germany might win the war, but concern for our guys slugging it out in the bitter cold and snow without the American and British airpower to assist them.

Then on Christmas Eve day, the 24th of December 1944, the weather dramatically cleared and the United States and Britain were able to unleash their air forces. The fighters and medium bombers of the 9th Air Force were deployed in direct troop support by attacking German tanks, fighters and troops. We in the heavy bombers of the Eighth Air Force were used to box in the Germans' chance to effectively re supply and protect their troops or even to be able to make an orderly retreat and save some of their resources. This date was the turning point for The Ardennes Salient. It officially continued on until January 25th, but most military historians would agree that the start of the end was on this day, Christmas Eve, 1944.

MAXIMUM EFFORT

On December 24th, to assist in the Allied response to Germany's incursion at Ardennes, we in the 533rd Squadron were assigned to bomb the German supply lines and temporary airfields at Kirchgons as other squadrons in the 381st were hitting Ettinghausen. We all were calmly elated because we finally were going to be able to help our guys on the ground. It was exciting to be directly a part of stopping and turning around the German advances. We encountered light flak coming in on the target but suffered no battle damage. Bombing was visual and excellent results were observed with all bombs hitting the target area designated.

We were in our favorite ship today, *Dreambaby*...a beautiful ship on a beautiful day with crystal clear skies. I saw other bomb Groups hitting rail yards, with excellent results, throughout the area. This day was a Maximum Effort by all bomb Groups. The 381st launched 51 bombers. In a maximum effort, it was required of each Group that every ship which could fly to be launched. To give understanding to this number, normally we would put up 30 ships or so on a good day. The 381st Bomb Group also participated in a combined wing, which was made up from one squadron of the 91st and of the 398th Bomb Groups plus the 533rd Squadron, which included us. The Eighth Air Force had 2,046 heavy bombers airborne against the German incursion, which turned out to be the largest heavy bomber deployment of World War II and, therefore, in the history of aerial warfare.

Take that, Herr Hitler!

CHRISTMAS 1944

Also memorable on this Christmas Eve was the bad weather we crews encountered when we returned to England. As they tried to return, many Groups couldn't land at their home bases due to fog and ice. Ridgewell was clear and 50 of 51 of our planes safely returned. However, 74 planes from other groups also landed at Ridgewell!!. The base had airplanes parked all over the place, wing tip to wing tip including the cross runway. The additional personnel and aircraft had to be accommodated for housing, food and flight preparation for when they all eventually left our base.

Our ground personnel were astoundingly diligent and efficient in handling all this extra work. They also had to almost immediately begin to prepare all of these aircraft for the next day's scheduled mission. They worked all Christmas Eve, as they refueled and armed 124 ships, four times their normal workload! On Christmas Day the mission was scrubbed due to the weather and then all these planes had to have their bomb loads removed!

I have an incomplete memory of a Christmas Eve sing-a-long event. We stood out in the dark with headlights from a few trucks to provide some light. We sang Christmas carols being led by a GI dressed in his dirty work fatigues. He sang *a cappella* the song *I'll Be Home For Christmas* better than I've ever heard anyone sing it. I'm not sure of the nature of this get together and whether it was formally arranged or not. But I can still hear that wonderful voice in the cold clear night while moving our feet on the crunchy frost to keep warm. Yes, I thought, next year we'll be home for Christmas...I hoped.

On Christmas morning the sky hung low with gray flannel clouds. From the near-by farm houses, light smoke curled lazily up and over the white fields and dark bare trees. England had had its heaviest frost in 50 years. Ridgewell and the countryside looked as if there had been a light snowfall. There were icicles hanging from some of the trees and building eaves. This was truly a White Christmas.

Another high performance on Christmas Day was when the Combat Mess served an excellent sit-down Christmas turkey dinner, and all the usual side dishes, to an unexpected additional 600 plus crewmen! The only evidence that this was unusual was the long line and wait to get into the mess hall. The mess hall was beautifully decorated with tablecloths and candles on each table. Also on each mess table, there were heaping platters of warm sliced turkey along with steaming bowls of mashed potatoes and pungent sage dressing. Combat crews always got special notice for their efforts, but these folks in the Combat Mess at Ridgewell deserved very special recognition for what they accomplished without much advanced notice on this Christmas Day 1944.

Also an unusual event this date was that we first three grader enlisted men were invited to the Officer's Club for a friendly Christmas drink. For those unfamiliar with military life, be assured this was not at all common. Commissioned officers and non-commissioned officers were not allowed to socially co-mingle. The Air Corps, though a part of the Army, had an independent view of such things and from time to time ignored those requirements.

After Christmas Day I had a chance to spend a day and a half in London. I grabbed my bag, a box of the Hut 5 guys donated "mission candy" and was off to London. I spent time with Pat and her family and stayed overnight in her brother's bedroom. We exchanged small gifts and Christmas cards. Later Pat and I went to a movie, in Edmonton I believe, which had a Disney cartoon running with the movie. It was about the character Goofy playing football (American style) that was hilarious to me and no one else. Apparently it wasn't funny if you didn't understand the game. I stuck out like a sore thumb in this audience of Englishmen, and drawing unwanted attention to myself was an embarrassment.

For the most part, my time with Pat's family was very pleasant, except for her dad. He was polite to a degree but seemed to find any way he could to challenge my American ways. He even asked me why I wore my ribbons on my Army blouse when I came into town, which seemed like bragging to him. Particularly the European Theater of Operations ribbon bothered him. He questioned why someone should get some sort of decoration for just being in England. The fact that we were conducting bombing operations on German and German occupied territory industrial targets from England, and thus a part of the European war theater, didn't penetrate his bluster. He also asked what the Oak Leaf Cluster on the Air Medal ribbon meant. When I explained it meant a subsequent award of the Air Medal, he sniffed,

"Well, for our boys it means that they had been mentioned in citations back to headquarters." It seemed to me that we were a matter of snobbish amusement to him for anything we did that was not as they did.

To be honest, I was a little irked with him too for never once acknowledging that in flying combat bombing missions I was risking my life to help protect his country and his family. I had the good sense to keep my irritation to myself. Perhaps in his job as a conductor on a double-decked bus he had met some obnoxious Yanks, because they did exist and were an embarrassment to the rest of us. I do know there was a cultural difference that made our American positive self-confidence seem like bragging to some of the older Brits. But what we needed was mutual respect, not just snide comparisons based on differences alone. I tried to explain I had no choice but to wear my ribbons as I would not be allowed off base without them being worn on my uniform. I wish I had been more assertive with him, and not so defensive, but at 19 years I was still pretty immature.

His attitude was not the usual I found from the British people who were gracious and even understanding of our differing ways. There is a very sweet poem written in 2005 by an English woman, Kate Kirkum, titled *The Old Airfield*. Kate lives near where the 95th bomb Group was based during World War II at Horham, England. The poem expresses what she feels walking around where the aircraft rumbled so long ago. She says her appreciation of the American airmen who flew off from Horham, and other airfields, to engage the Nazi war industries and resources, is also felt by many other Brits. I have included a copy of her heartfelt poem at the end of the chapter.

I now wish I had had the nerve to have said to him, "You're damn right I wear my ribbons and proud to do so. Because they show my country's respect for what we are doing over here for you folks...even if you don't like it!" But that would have meant the end of my relationship with his daughter Pat, I'm sure. Further, I doubt at that time if I saw things as clearly as I do today as I look back.

The next day Pat went into London with me for a little quiet time alone. We spent the time mostly strolling or sitting in one of the many parks. After a late lunch, and when it was time for me to go, she went along to Liverpool Street station and saw me off on the train with a sad farewell. She stood there looking a little forlorn, huddled against the chill, as the train pulled away from the platform and we waved good-bye

I didn't keep log entries of my many London visits with Pat so they somewhat begin to blend in my memory and I don't have specific memory of each trip. But, I finally was beginning to realize she was getting more serious than I and I didn't know what to do about it. I really enjoyed our times together and our letters back and forth, but I was years away from being ready to settle down. Besides, I had missed some of the normal post high school socializing with my peers in Long Beach. Paradoxically I felt in some ways old for my years but in other ways socially underdeveloped. In any case I felt, if I survived this war, I wanted to be irresponsible and carefree for a time and not married for some years to come.

RETURN TO GERMANY

On December 30th, as 1944 wound down, we targeted the rail yards at Bischoffsheim. Our crew was flying a GH ship today and we led the Squadron and Group to the target. In a GH ship there is no ball turret because that is where the GH signal-receiving dome was located. The GH system was a way of locating a target by receiving focused radio beams from two sources that would intersect at the target as a signal of when to release the bombs. I got to fly as a waist gunner as a consequence of having no ball turret. I had forgotten how nice it was to not be jammed into the ball turret. In my log I noted on this date, "I was the left waist gunner. What a life!"

At 26,400 feet altitude, we had meager and inaccurate flak with a few anti-aircraft rockets thrown at us. This finished 1944 for us, as we were not scheduled to fly on New Year's Eve day. However, there was no chance to celebrate New Year's Eve because we were scheduled to fly on New Year's Day. We would be getting up for our pre-mission breakfast when most celebrants were just crawling into bed and calling it a night.

1945

As the United States entered its fourth year into World War II, on New Year's Day, 1945, we took off in the dark on a cold clear moonlit morning. Our primary target, an aircraft plant at Magdeburg, had to be bombed by visual sighting because of some non-military facilities, which were close to the aircraft plant. Once in the area of our primary target, we encountered light flak. The Group started its bomb run on Magdeburg, and the flak continued. However, the clouds covering the aircraft plant stubbornly remained. Not being able to bomb by visual sighting, we closed our bomb bay doors and the Group moved on to a secondary target at Koblenz. As an aside, this mission proved to me, and should to any doubters, that the Eighth AAF would subject itself to additional peril to avoid civilian facilities when possible. Due to cloudy conditions, while leaving the Magdeburg area in the confusion of the day the high and low squadrons got separated from the lead squadron. The lead squadron proceeded to Koblenz as briefed. The high and low squadrons under the lead of the 533rd Squadron then flew to yet another secondary target, the railway yards at Kassel. We bombed there by radar and were met with intense and accurate flak. Due to all the changing of targets, we were subjected to on-and-off flak for hours. We were growing weary with the almost constant flak bursts throwing pieces of iron into and through our plane.

Me 109 fighters attacked another squadron in our Group and shot down two bombers. Though our Squadron wasn't attacked by the Me 109s, we did see two of the new Me 163 rocket ships for the first time.

They appeared to be stunting, showing off their immense speed rather than attacking anybody. Later during interrogation we were asked to sketch what these new birds looked like to us. This confusing mission took 8 hours and 30 minutes whereas our earlier mission to Kassel only took 7 hours and 10 minutes. Upon landing at Ridgewell we found we had a lot of flak damage, but luckily nothing critical to the operation of the aircraft, nor the safety of our crew.

On January 3rd we once again returned to Cologne to attack their marshalling yards. We bombed by radar and met only meager and inaccurate flak. It seemed something had happened to the once deadly accurate flak of Cologne. Perhaps their guns and efficient gunners had moved deeper into the Fatherland to avoid the hard driving Allied ground forces. My turret burned out and I had to hand-crank it around. Later, when there was no more flak, nor fighters, in the area, Sam allowed me to move to the waist area for the rest of the mission. The turret door was left open so I could return to it rapidly if need be. When we arrived back at Ridgewell, it was raining steadily giving us a cold wet welcome home. In the smoky crowded Interrogation waiting area, Clem accidentally splashed hot chocolate on a visiting Brigadier General's camelhair short-coat. The brass in the immediate area of the General looked as if they were going to have a group heart attack. Clem made a swipe with his free hand to brush off the General's coat. He looked at him and said, "Pardon me General," and casually walked away.

Everyone held his breath waiting for the General's response...except Clem who was just standing in the corner lighting his cigarette. To his credit the general took no outward note of his messy coat as an aide furiously wiped at the chocolate stain.

A couple of days later, on the 5th of January, we were involved in another tactical mission in support of our ground troops. Our target was the Heimbach communications center between Duren and Aachen, Germany. On the bomb run, we encountered meager flak and no fighters. We bombed by GH instruments through complete cloud cover so we couldn't observe the results. Our mission was a comparatively short one for us of six hours and 30 minutes and pretty much a milk run.

On the 6th of January we had a V2 rocket hit and explode on the edge of the base, near the town of Halstead. It was around 11:00 P.M. in the evening and really shook up the base. If we needed a reminder that even here in Essex we were vulnerable to attack, this provided it. It is hard to know what the rocket's target was. It logically was London but if so it was a big miss. If the target were the base, it was only a near miss, but a miss none-the-less.

The next few days were the usual routine, and then on the 10th, the group took off for Ostreim in a snowstorm. Our squadron commander Lt. Col. Shackley had to leave the Group and make an emergency landing at Ghent, Belgium. Also this mission was ill fated for Stu Newman, our former bombardier, flying as navigator for the Roush crew. They had to make an emergency landing in Belgium after massive damage to the tail area and the wounding of their tail gunner. Upon landing the gunner was rushed to a near-by British hospital where his leg was amputated. One of our hut mates, Jackie Nichols was also wounded by flak. The flak hunk was about the size of a package of cigarettes and lodged in his husky thigh. He was given immediate first aid by others on the Steinwinter crew and survived well to his arrival in our base hospital. He was doing well when we visited him in the hospital. He asked for someone to bring him the piece of flak that was removed from his leg. He wanted to show the other wounded guys what a real piece of flak was when they began to compare notes on their wounds. I ran into Jackie in Los Angeles after the war in the lobby of a movie theater. He suffered no permanent disability due to his wound. He was going to college and playing football for that school.

MORE TACTICAL SUPPORT

On the 13th, we again were brought into a tactical type raid and this time on a railway bridge at Germersheim. We took off on an icy runway with a heavy cloud overcast. Each aircraft took off in timed sequence and made its own way flying in zero visibility to get above the heavy clouds to assemble in our bombing formation. Flying blind through heavy clouds, while other aircraft were doing the same, was a very tense time. I was at a waist window with my eyes straining to see through the clouds while looking for any other flying aircraft. At times our wing tips would disappear in the clouds. This was a very dangerous time and success is based on everyone flying exactly as briefed to avoid a mid-air crash. As we flew the clouds began to lighten and we finally broke free of their clutches into a brilliantly blue sky. One-by-one I saw the other bombers breaking away from the billowy white clouds and joining up as we assembled into our formation. We could breath easily again.

When we entered Europe, there were cloud free patches where I could observe in places the snow-covered battlefields. But at the target

THE VIEW FROM THE BOTTOM UP

our Group had to bomb using GH instruments due to cloud cover. At the IP and on the bomb run, we began to see heavy flak bursts up ahead that were right on our altitude. We encountered flak bursts thumping away at us and rocking the ship as the bomb bay doors opened up. While looking forward for the bombs to drop, I began to get speckles of black gunpowder, from the flak bursts, collecting on my turret window glass. I followed the bombs as they inexorably raced for the target. As luck would have it, the clouds separated and I got to see our bombs hit smack on that railway bridge. All other considerations aside that was why we were here. It felt good!

We had minor battle damage due to that heavy and accurate flak defending the bridge. A plus for this mission was its length of only five hours and 30 minutes and as such was our shortest mission. As a minus though, the temperatures were really low at 53°F below zero. We returned home without further incident. The Group had to disassemble above the clouds and make our way individually down to the base. This is just as scary as climbing up through the clouds as we had done in the morning. We had a near miss when we were landing. Another plane, dangerously close, suddenly appeared in front of us during our final approach to the runway. Some good piloting by Sam avoided a deadly mid-air crash. The Medic's Scotch issue at Interrogation came in handy as we rehashed what we all were thinking during this scary event. Sam just smiled that self-confident look of his.

The next day on Sunday the 14th of January, with absolutely clear skies, we were sent to Cologne once again. This time we were to destroy a highway bridge over the Rhine River. [See photo at the end of the chapter.] Cologne's accurate and heavy flak unfortunately had returned and we were buffeted by constant flak blasts. We had one bomber in our formation shot down over the target. Our ship however had only minor flak damage. Our bombing was visual and very accurate. I reported to the Intelligence Officer in Interrogation I had seen two 1,000 pound bombs hit the bridge directly. We were delivering these thousand pounders on the bridge because of their greater destructive power than the 500 pound bombs we usually dropped. This was my 25th mission and I was starting to truly feel like a veteran.

On January 17th Andy, Reynolds and I were assigned to fly spare with Lt. Riza's crew due to three of his crewmembers not being available. The target was the marshalling yards at Paderborn, which is near Kassel. Bombing was from 23,700 feet using radar through complete cloud coverage. We flew in –35°F air on a six hour and 50 minute mission, which was fairly routine. Flying spare along with my usual Navigator and co-pilot seemed comfortable. The flying spare assignment meant that someone on another crew couldn't fly due to illness or injury and you had been selected to fill in for him temporarily. I had flown spare one other time and thus I finished two missions before Sam and the bulk of the crew.

More important than getting another mission in, we were to leave the next day for a week's rest and recuperation in a rest home, better known to us as the Flak Shack.

We were ready!

THE OLD AIRFIELD

Strolling through these fields so green
Where once a throng of life has been
A feeling so invoked of me
Of sadness amidst tranquility

For beneath where now grows golden corn
Bonds as strong as steel were born
Laughter, tears and stories shared
Amongst the comrades of the air

And as on concrete strips I tread
The backbone from whence missions led
I can almost hear the roar
As engines to the heavens soar

"We count them out, we count them in"

Through the ever ascending din
This, by those who watched and cared
For men whose lives might not be spared

Day after day, night after night
Into another enduring flight
The hardcore now so cracked and worn
Each tell a story for those who mourn

Yet now looking up to the clear night sky

Over the airfield on stars on high
I feel sure that in this patchwork of land
Our faithful friends stretch out their hands

This land which now yields sheaves of gold
Will forever breathe a life of old
Never forget—they came, they went
And for you and me their lives were spent

—Kate Kirkum, U.K., 2004

Originally published in the 95th Bomb Group (H) web site
http://www.95thbg-horham.com

Included by permission of the author who lives next to the Horham
air base in England from whence the 95th Bomb Group (H) flew combat missions during World War II.

THE VIEW FROM THE BOTTOM UP

Chapter 13

At the Palace Hotel

THE RESPITE

UNDER the control of the U.S. Eighth Air Force were a number of private manor houses and a few small hotels that had been acquired for usage as rest homes for AAF personnel. These were assigned for the use of combat crews for rest and recuperation either late in their combat tours, or after a significantly traumatic mission or series of missions. For our rest home week, the enlisted men on the Goldin crew were sent to The Palace Hotel in the town of Southport in Northern England. The officers of our crew were assigned to go somewhere else I don't recall where.

The Palace Hotel was on a 3 acres beachfront site on the Irish Sea in a town of some 80,000 people. We arrived on January 20th, 1945, and checked into the Reception Desk manned by an elderly Englishman in a tired dark blue suit. He looked as if he probably came with the place when the Air Corps acquired it. On the wall behind him was a sign that proclaimed, "THE AIR CORPS TAKES CARE OF ITS OWN." This was an overt statement of the Army Air Forces' independence in personnel matters such as the rest home practice. We were checked-in by the reception clerk to whom we paid three Pounds and 10 Shillings for the seven days stay. That amount was the equivalent of about $2.00 (American) per day and paid for our room and meals in the hotel.

During World War II a service man or woman was not allowed to wear civilian clothes at any time. Contrary to this regulation, as we checked into the Palace, we were issued civilian clothes; tweed jackets, slacks, sneakers and sport shirts for our use while there. If we went into town, we were required to wear our uniforms, but inside the hotel property we were as non-military as we wanted.

We loaded into the European style lift (elevator), which was an open wrought-iron cage with cast iron ornate flourishes. The desk clerk closed the well oiled accordion gate and moved the control handle to bring us up to our floor. On the way up to the third floor, he showed us how to operate the noisy lift cage, which we were required to do because there were no lift operators on duty. He led us to our rooms, wished us a pleasant stay at the Palace and returned to the main floor

The hotel beds had been removed and several Army cots placed in each room. The sleeping arrangements were similar to the Red Cross Hotels in London in that regard. We dropped our baggage and immediately changed into our civilian clothes issued by the Reception clerk. Already feeling more released from the military way of things, we sat down to read the instructional handout we had been given when we signed in. It gave us our rules-of-conduct and listed all that was offered for us at The Palace. There apparently was most anything you might reasonably want within the hotel. The Red Cross ran the recreational and entertainment activities. In the daytime, there was horseback riding, golf, tennis and swimming; weather permitting. But during the Winter time, these were not attractive options due to the cold weather. In the evening there were to be presented movies and dances with local girl volunteers, or your own date if you wished. All of this time was charged as TDY (temporary duty) and not charged as leave or furlough time. The Air Corps did indeed take care of its own!

In our civilian clothes, we could walk out on the hotel grounds for a stroll just to feel more unmilitary. Opposite the ocean side, the grounds abutted a city street where traffic sometimes included convoys of American Army trucks. There were reports of some of our guys wearing their civilian clothes waving at the GI convoys passing by and yelling, "Give 'em hell Yank!," with fake English accents.

It was thought this might cause some confusion for the GIs seeing so many young "English" guys not in the Army.

More than anything else, just the wearing of civilian clothes was the most therapeutic for me. I felt like a regular person slouching around in comfortable clothes and wearing sneakers. Sitting in a soft chair in the lounge of the Palace while sipping a hot cup of coffee or tea, made being five miles up in the freezing sky over Germany, looking for bad guys, a story of someone else's life.

The large comfortable lounge off the reception area was a favorite place to sit and talk or even to just doze. It had comfortable overstuffed sofas and chairs with small tables with magazine racks. To add to the civilian nature of the room, there was a grand piano in the lounge, which was played by anyone who knew how. The selections you would hear were anything from "The Moonlight Sonata" to "The Boogie Woogie Bugle Boy." In the evening there was usually a professional pianist playing requests. To keep contacts with civilians under control, all the floors above the ground floor were off-limits to guests.

However, we could invite guests to any of the ground floor facilities or functions.

THE NAKED GUNNER

Although we didn't have many rules on how we dressed, there were apparently some strictures about nudity on the ground floor as we found out. One time a few of us were going down to the main floor for a snack and a Coke. But there was one guy from another crew who said he wanted to stay in his cot and take a nap instead. A buddy of his insisted he join us. We helped him pull his fellow crewman out of his cot so he could come down to the snack shop with us. He turned out to be a guy who slept in the nude, but, no matter, he was made to join us in the lift down to the lobby. Because the lift cage was made of open ironwork, he could easily be seen as nude when we arrived in the lobby. The elderly desk clerk seemed rather alarmed as he looked up and saw the cowering naked man in the lift cage. He yelled, "Boys, boys, you can't bring a naked man down here!"

As the lift arrived in the lobby and stopped, I slid open the cage door and stepped out. The naked gunner tried to hide in the corner. Someone inside the cage pulled the door closed as the red-faced desk clerk apprehensively approached. To avoid the clerk, they ran the cage back up away from the lobby.

As this was going on, I found a comfortable chair facing the action, sat down and serenely lit a cigarette. The old gentleman hurriedly huffed and puffed up the stairway that was along side of the lift. As he neared the first floor, the guys reversed direction and returned in the lift to the lobby.

"Boys, boys, BOYS," he loudly pleaded as he came charging back down the stairs, "you mustn't do this!"

As a crowd gathered, drawn by his loud outcries, everyone began to point and laugh...most of the girls giggled nervously. As my friends tried the patience of the desk clerk, I acted as if I didn't know them; I was just another person enjoying the show.

After a couple more trips up and down, and finally bored, they returned the reluctant nude to the third floor and his cot and went upon their day's important activities. They came back down to the lobby, blithely walked past the out-of-breath desk clerk, collected me and we went into the snack room as if nothing had happened. I suspect the old Palace never had such a playful bunch staying there before or since.

SOUTHPORT

In Southport there was a pier that had a dance hall and other beach town diversions. This place reminded me somewhat of my hometown back in California. The ocean, at low tide particularly, was quite a long way out with sand dunes in between it and the promenade. Walking along the beach area, with its constant chilly sea breeze coming in off of the Irish Sea, one could hear the many sea birds squawking to each other. With that familiar smell of a fresh sea breeze, which never stops, I was again transported home to Southern California. And once again I was alone with my thoughts of home.

It was rather pleasant walking around Southport. Though it was January, and a little chilly, oddly enough it was still warmer than down south at Ridgewell. One of the girls I had met at a dance at the Palace and I walked along a street with many shops in quaint Victorian buildings. Southport, particularly in peacetime, was apparently a popular tourist destination. So many of these shops sold the types of items designed to relieve the tourist of any excess Pounds or Shillings he might have. Of equal, if not greater interest, were the many pubs some of which actually had cold beer.

In the evenings there were many diversions both at the hotel and in town. I don't recall many specifics of what we did in the evenings but I do remember we were very busy as one might guess for young guys. While there we had many interactions with the young ladies of the town and spent money freely, which will make you popular anywhere. I had arrived in England just four months earlier and had changed from a slightly shy teenager to a rather self-confident American flyer. I met several girls while there who were engaging and a lot of fun. There was one particular girl named Carla who was nice to be with and also movie star gorgeous. Her father was Scottish and her mother Spanish. The combination of her mother's skin and hair along with her father's blue eyes was very attractive. She and I enjoyed being with each other during the daytime and nights in Southport and at the Palace. At the hotel there was a pretty good cafeteria and snack bar, which we visited often as well as enjoying the evening entertainment being offered.

It wasn't all chasing girls and drinking beer, although that was quite nice. I fondly remember sitting in the Lounge slumped in a soft chair sipping Champaign someone had bought. Earlier there had been a contest trying to hit a chandelier by popping Champaign corks, which no one won as I recall. We just relaxed there in civilian comfort, had a cigarette and talked of back home. What we were going to do when the war was over also came up a couple of times, but it was a subject not indulged in very often...it could be bad luck we thought. It was a good time to take a nap and get ready for the night ahead.

But then as quickly as we came to this oasis on the Irish Sea, for a brief respite from flying combat, our week was over. Our time of being irresponsible young guys resting and just being silly was quickly slipping into memory. When we checked-out at the reception desk, and reluctantly had to turn in our civilian clothes, it now became real. The knowledge of what lay ahead pressed in our minds, whether we wanted it to or not. We were a quiet bunch going back to Ridgewell...each lost in his own thoughts.

The rest home time was a wonderful experience but it made going back to combat very difficult for me; and I assume everyone else as well. Prior to our time at Southport, I had developed a fatalistic attitude about surviving the war. Having such an attitude gave me the ability to take just one day at a time and to not worry too much about tomorrow. But after spending a week with no responsibilities and living a civilian-like carefree pleasurable existence, life was now more precious. And thus my final nine missions now were to be more anxious for me.

A few weeks later, after we had returned to Ridgewell, Carla came to Yeldham and stayed at the Waggon & Horses Inn for a night. She had stopped by on her way to London to visit a girl friend with whom she had gone to school. This was only a brief wartime relationship; we wrote for a while after her trip to Yeldham but never saw each other again. Also, now back at home in Ridgewell, it felt uncomfortable for me being with Carla. I was feeling disloyal to Pat even though she and I had no committed relationship to respect.

And then we once again returned to the war in the skies over Germany.

Chapter 14

Big B and Valentine's Day

AFTER our time at the Flak Shack, the first morning getting up at around 4:00 A.M. in a cold icy hut was tough. It was somewhat as if you had been having a fantasy dream in full color; with pretty girls on white sandy beaches, under a warm bright blue sky, and you are rudely awakened to a cold black and gray reality. For a microsecond or so after waking, you likely would be confused and then would say, "Oh, crap! It was just a dream."

And so it seemed to me that morning when we returned to combat.

It was a cold blustery January 29th morning as I swung my feet over the side of my cot to the cold concrete floor, lit a cigarette and grumbled once again about "the miserable weather in this country." We laboriously dressed and made our way out of the hut into the dark and a scattered snowfall with near freezing temperatures. As we were riding to the mess hall, we learned while we were enjoying the rest home time a terrible tragedy had happened for the 535th Squadron as they returned to Ridgewell from a mission on the 21st of January. Two planes crashed into each other as they were making their peel-off maneuver to land. Their wreckage was strewn about the farms and towns near the base but no one on the ground was injured. Unfortunately all eighteen crewmen were killed. This was a grim reminder that death could lurk even in the most peaceful place such as the beautiful Essex countryside.

After we had breakfast, and over hot coffee in the comfortable warmth of the Combat Mess, the conversation centered on the probability of flying on this date. Were we to go through all the preparations for flight only to have the mission scrubbed due to weather? The consensus was we would not fly today. Clem and a few others thought otherwise.

"Y'all be flying for sure," said Clem our gloomy prophet...he was right.

After our week of R&R at the rest home, this whole morning was feeling a lot like that morning last October Ninth ...our first mission. Getting my guns ready and installed in the turret with the falling snow and bitter cold was uncomfortable to say the least. Later, it was still swirling snow outside our plane as we huddled in the radio room waiting to begin our takeoff. The engines had been warming up and sounded strong and ready to go. It was 7:30 A.M. and we slowly moved along the perimeter track making our way to the head of the runway and our turn to takeoff. Arriving there Sam pivoted the plane, put on the brakes and began to rev up the four powerful engines to take-off power. She vibrated as if in anticipation and eager to get aloft. Someone said what we all were thinking, "If we survive through this take off and the assembly above the clouds, the mission itself will be a gentle afterthought." Some of us were holding to their faith in luck, and some in God, to get us through the day. Some of us also had an unshakable faith in Sam Goldin with the able aid of Reynolds and Marty to get this heavy lumbering bird safely on our way. The brakes squealed as they were released and our war bird, filled with her human and deadly cargo, slowly started through the slush and down the runway. Picking up speed, as she hammered away at the runway with engines roaring, her tail lifted as her sign flight speed was near.

We finally lifted up free of the earth and on our way to Germany once again. Once we were aloft, the wheels were retracted and we each moved from the radio room to our flight positions. After getting my turret ready, I stood at a waist window to help watch for other aircraft also climbing away from the base through these clouds. The immediate challenge flying through dense clouds heavy with moisture was avoiding any mid-air crashes. We needed to get to the clear air above the clouds where we would meet up with the rest of our group and assemble into a combat formation. When we finally broke out into the almost unreal looking clear sky of brilliant blue, with a floor of bumpy cotton underneath us stretching to the horizon, I let out a big breath of air and relaxed. Breaking out of the clouds and into the clear blue sky was always eerily beautiful to me, and a sight to which I never became accustomed.

FIGHTER SWEEP

Our target was Neiderlahnstein and our ostensible mission was to bomb the marshalling yards there, but our real mission was to perform a "fighter sweep" where we would act as a magnet for any German fighter aircraft in the area. It was not formally called that but the crews knew the routing we were to take today was not normal. In a "fighter sweep," a Group is sent on a circuitous route in areas known to have heavy fighter presence to attract them while the other Groups went about the business of bombing targets. In other words we were to be sacrificed in the greater good. We were provided fighter escort aircraft to confront any bandits, which might come for us. Upon such event our fighter escort hopefully would engage them in dogfights prior to their getting to us.

In my intense desire to pick up any bandits before we were in their range I almost made an embarrassing error. I was using a tactic many ball turret gunners used so the turret would continue to move slightly without the controls being touched. We would adjust the turret's drive system to add a little creeping movement as the default setting. With this creeping movement, the turret would appear to be manned to the Luftwaffe even though the gunner were to be incapacitated. On this day I was probably a little more intense in my search for fighters because we knew it was a fighter sweep. As I was looking down along the tops of the clouds, I saw a dark shape moving along with us. I tried to identify whether this bandit was an Me 109 or a FW 190 fighter who was stealthily tracking us. It was so far away it was hard to be sure. As I touched the turret's control handles, the "bandit" then moved faster as I moved my control handles! I realized what I was seeing was a spot of dirt that had become stuck to my turret window and not a fighter a long way off. Fortunately I had not called out this "bandit" to the rest of the crew.

As it turned out, the Luftwaffe didn't take the bait and we never saw any enemy fighters. When we had finished our "fighter sweep" portion of our flight plan, we bombed our target at Neiderlahnstein through light flak. I couldn't observe the results due to clouds over the target. We returned home without incident. However, there remained the dangerous approach through 100% cloud cover to Ridgewell as we tensely awaited our landing as the final challenge for our pilots.

DOWN TIME

The bitter and snowy weather that had been keeping our ships on the ground was also making it difficult to move around very much on the base. In fact on January 30th, riding bicycles on the base was specifically prohibited until further notice. Other than chow times, we pretty much stayed in the hut, read, wrote letters and played a little poker. I had a wild streak of luck in an all-night 6 Pence (10 cents) limit poker game at this time. I won enough to send home a $200 money order to my parents to save for me. I knew if I kept the money with me it would be gone by the time I got out of the service. I needed to start saving up for a car for when I got home.

Letter writing was difficult. Because of the censorship rules we couldn't write anything about combat missions or even that we were flying combat at all. When you take away the most important things going on in a man's life from being mentioned in his mail, it leaves very little.

Having too much time to think, and still fresh from the liberating Flak Shack experience, I began to really get incensed about all of the terrible costs of the war. People on all sides were paying the price for the actions of Hitler and his evil pantheon of fellow Nazi leaders. This was not the usual thought process for me. We bomber crewmen, to function best, had to be deliberate and unemotionally dedicated to perform our tasks irrespective of any actions by the enemy. We just slugged it out one mile and one mission at a time. But having recently experienced a taste of "normal" life, while we gamboled at The Palace Hotel, and knowing the reality of aerial combat, I became angry at those bastards who had caused all of this mess. I began to spout off about how we had to somehow convince Hitler he should give up, because to continue to fight was useless and would only further destroy his own country.

Tex, who was usually quiet and would just let me ramble on, finally spoke up, "Back home my Daddy used to say, about a stubborn mule we had, 'Get a two-by-four and hit him square between the eyes. That won't hurt him none, but it *will* get his attention!'. Maybe, we just need to get ole Hitler's attention," he concluded.

It was an old joke I guess but there was wisdom in it.

The Bomber Stream to Big B

Major General James H. Doolittle [see photo at the end of the chapter] and the brass at Eighth Air Force headquarters in High Wycombe must have been listening to Tex. On February 3rd, we were launched on a massive mission to Berlin. Because of its strategic importance and the defenses around it, the bomber crews called Berlin, Big B... and we were going there at last.

Each Group was to bomb strategic targets in and around the city primarily to assist Russia in its attempts to take Berlin. Our effort was to be part of a 1,000 bomber force to deliver 2,250 tons of bombs on that one target. Berlin was the very heart and mind of the Nazi Third Reich so we were going to "hit them where they lived." We learned that the Eighth AF would fly in a bomber stream today rather than the usual technique where Groups would be routed in many different directions to get to the same target. In a bomber stream, all the groups flew in a straight-line corridor aimed directly at the target...Berlin. Apparently the Army Air Force was confident enough with our allied air superiority that there was no need for deception as to what the target was. The fighter escorts flew back and forth along side of and giving protection to the stream, as the lumbering bomb laden formations headed for their specific targets in the Berlin area.

As we entered into European air space, everywhere I looked, from my seat under our ship, were B-17 and B-24 groups flying in the same direction. The bomber stream was illuminated by bright white contrails following each bomber Group as they boldly and inexorably moved toward Big B. For the first time, I believed this was clearly the beginning of the end of the war in Europe. Looking right and left and behind I saw huge collections of bomber formations inexorably heading to Hitler's last stand...Berlin. The exhilarating feeling of being a part of something so righteously powerful was worth all the hours, days, weeks, months and years of dedicated effort it took all of us to get here. The petty sniping of people like Pat's dad were forgotten. We were doing good work that will help shorten this disastrous war.

In the 381st we were one of the earlier groups to reach Berlin and yet it was almost surrounded by smoke when we arrived. We received light but very accurate flak. A number of our ships suffered extensive battle damage and our Group lost two bombers to the flak. Our target was at the Tempelhof Aerodrome and the nearby marshalling yards. I watched, and filmed with the movie camera installed in my turret, as our bombs fell exactly on target erupting in large explosions as they hit. Smoke from earlier hits from prior groups almost covered the target, but there was good visibility for our bomb drop.

After I had taken the bomb strike footage, I decided to film the periphery of the smoking areas to give a view of the extent of the total area involved. I moved my turret along looking at the edge of the smoke. There appeared in my sight a B-17 from our group, which looked to be in trouble. She had dropped down below us. I kept my camera on her. If the crew needed to bail out, I thought I would have an accurate count of how many crewmen made it out. I used the rest of the footage loaded in my camera on that ship, and watched her fade in the distance as we moved on toward England and...left her behind. I don't know if that was one of the two ships of our group shot down by flak or if she was just straggling.

When we were returning home, and approaching the western shores of Europe, I could see there were still bomb Groups heading for Berlin. These 1,000 bombers in two corridors, one going in to Berlin and one coming back, was an unprecedented display of aerial might. It was unlike anything the world had ever seen before and should have penetrated the soul of even the most ardent Nazi. Maybe as in Tex's dad's homily, we got their attention.

There was great excitement in Interrogation about the successful bombing results of today's efforts by the Eighth AF generally and the 381st specifically. During our crew report, I mentioned to the Intelligence officer the film I had taken of the straggler below us for whatever use to them that might be.

The next day there were large headlines in the British papers about the February 3rd raid. In one London tabloid paper, there was a half page picture of a B-17 with the Triangle L (meaning 381st BG) identifier on the wing and Berlin burning below it. [See photo at the end of this chapter.] Figuring that it must have come from our photo lab, several of us from the hut went to ask if we could get a print of that picture. The photo lab guy at the counter gave each of us a print of the photo. As we were looking at the picture, it dawned on me it was the same view as I had with my ball turret mounted camera. I asked him what was the source of the picture and he said he believed it was from a ball turret's movie camera footage. At a subsequent combat crew meeting, there was a chewing-out of the ball turret gunners generally for not using all the film in the camera when they were installed in their turrets. The Berlin mission was used as an example, we were told that out of five cameras installed, "...only Sergeant Gilbert shot all of the film in his camera." This picture has since become famous and I believe it may have come from my camera, but so far I haven't been able to find any proof one way or the other.

ROUTINE

In early February the weather was very wet, cold and windy. Several missions were scrubbed due to bad weather. On the 7th of February, a mission to Osterfeld was ill fated. The crews slated for this mission couldn't take off until 9:30 A.M. due to bad weather and then had to be recalled when the Group neared Germany as the weather got worse. Unfortunately they had to go through all that effort and still didn't get credit for a mission flown. One ship in the 532nd Squadron got separated from the group and didn't hear the recall order. They went on their own and successfully bombed Essen as a target of opportunity and thus got credit for their one bomber mission.

Finally, on the 9th of February the weather eased up enough to where missions could be flown. Our target was a motor road viaduct at Arnsberg south east of Düsseldorf. The cloud cover on the way in from the North Sea was broken but became total in the target area. We encountered some light flak on the Dutch coast as we flew in over the Zuider Zee. I could see vast areas of the Netherlands that had been flooded due to the dikes being opened by the Dutch to make the land unusable for the Germans.

When we were on our bomb run we were met with clouds at a higher altitude than had been anticipated. As a consequence, we were actually in the clouds when we dropped our bombs. This had no effect on our bombing accuracy because we were using radar once again, but flying in clouds is not conducive to safe formation flying. I didn't get to observe the results of our bombing efforts.

THE NEW BIRD

On February 14th, Valentine's Day, we were given a rare gift. Being an "old crew"; the Goldin crew had finished 27 missions, I had finished 29 and Andy had finished 31, on this date we were assigned to fly a "new" B-17G still fresh from the States. We were not sure whether it had flown any combat missions or not, but it sure didn't look as if it had. We were all nearing the end of our combat tours and it looked as if we would finish in-style in this shiny new bird. We had flown several different ships from time-to-time and *Dreambaby* had been our favorite, however, a "new" ship was rare. She was beautiful; no oil stains on the wings, no missing relief tubes, no flak holes or patches anywhere...she was bright and shiny and even smelled new. This was only the second "new" ship we had ever flown, the first being the one we flew overseas from Hunter Field, Georgia, which was later shot down over Berlin. We talked about naming this bird if we got that chance. No consensus was arrived as to which name would be best. This was Valentine's Day so maybe something about a heart would work? But we decided it was best to get our mission done before talking about naming her.

The February 14th, 1945, raid on Dresden historically has been the subject of much discussion by historians, it is often described as the "night and day firebombing" of Dresden by the combined forces of the RAF and the 8th AAF. I don't have the desire or ability to enter into that controversy. What I do know is we in the 381st Bomb Group, as a part of the First Air Division, were briefed to bomb the Dresden rail yards and not the city.

In a maximum effort, the 381st put up 37 bombers. We took off at 8:30 A.M. for what turned out to be a mixed-up mission. Over Munster the First Air Division became disrupted by heavy flak and had to reroute to maintain a proper position for the planned synchronized attack on Dresden. The 381st encountered cirrus clouds and massive contrails of other groups ahead of us and we got separated from the rest of the Division. The bombing at Dresden was to be a very synchronized attack of many Groups coming in on a well-coordinated plan of headings and timing. When we became separated, the 381st elected to go to a target of opportunity rather than foul up the coordinated effort at the Dresden rail yards involving many Groups. Riding in the ball it was clear to me there was something unusual going on. Upon becoming clear of all the clouds and contrails, as a Group we seemed to be alone in the wide blue sky. Also we had lost one of our squadrons! We were down to 25 ships now...alone and on our way to somewhere. Sam explained the 381st was going on its own to a target of opportunity minus one squadron, which was now separated from the Group just as the Group had become separated from the Division. It was not looking good. Once one thing goes wrong usually the problems multiply.

BRUX

As a bit of luck, however, our lead bombardier spotted a large industrial facility near Brux, Czechoslovakia It turned out to be a long time Eighth Air Force high priority target the large S.I.T.O synthetic oil refinery. He was able to set up for a visual bomb run. Sitting in the ball turret, I was eager for us to finally make a bomb run. We had been under attack twice by accurate flak as we roamed about Germany but hadn't dropped any bombs. Now as we approached Brux, and heavy flak again, we were finally on a bomb run. I was somewhat concerned though because our bomb load contained RDX Compound B explosives. Not to get too technical, but the reason for my concern was an RDX bomb could explode by a sharp impact alone. Conventional explosive bombs would not explode by impact alone, they had to be fused and armed. As we approached the target, we were encountering heavy flak.

The refinery was heavily defended by many 88mm anti-aircraft guns accurate flak, which exploded all around and under us. Everything was happening at once. As we started our bomb run, we were being bounced around with loud WHUMPS of ack ack as pieces of flak ripped through our beautiful new bird. I was looking ahead and, just as the bomb bay doors opened, one shell exploded directly under us and in front of my turret. Our ship lurched sharply upward. Number 1 and number 3 engines were damaged by flak and the superchargers ceased to function properly. I had black powder from the near miss shell caked all around my turret's Plexiglas windows. I worried about the RDX bombs detonating because of being subjected to the bouncing from the near misses of flak, and flak pieces tearing through the bomb bay and the rest of the ship.

In spite of the thrashing about, our bombs were released on time along with the Group's. I tracked our bomb load down as it joined with the others from our Group falling unerringly toward the refinery. After the "bombs away" call, Tex, as was his assignment, opened his radio room door and looked into the bomb bay to verify that there were no bombs still hanging on their shackles. As he looked in the still open bomb bay, he saw damage in the bomb bay was extensive and looked like a sieve with flak holes. He also saw a couple of the bombs were hung up and had not dropped and immediately informed Sam of this dangerous situation. We could not land back at Ridgewell with hanging bombs. These bombs would likely fall out upon the normal landing impact, and destroy the plane and the runway...not to mention our crew.

As I watched from underneath the ship at our bombs falling toward the target, there continued to be serious difficulties with our ship and its lethal cargo.

Marty quickly responded he would take care of the hung up bombs. He had to remove his parachute so he could squeeze in between the inboard bomb racks. He set about to dislodge the bombs from the frozen bomb shackles using his big screwdriver. He climbed into the open bomb bay as we continued to be hit by flak. Tex also stepped into the open bomb bay from the radio room to help steady Marty as he worked getting the bombs loose. Holding onto the bomb bay aft bulkhead with his left hand he held onto Marty with his right while Marty gingerly worked on the stubborn bomb shackles. They were both standing on the narrow catwalk over the open bomb bay looking at the ground some five miles below. After the last of the bombs were finally released by Marty, his walk-around oxygen bottle was hit by flak and the regulator severed. With the regulator hanging uselessly from his oxygen mask hose, he was still able to get back to his turret's oxygen supply in time.

Chaos continued as we finally lost all power on the two flak damaged engines. The oxygen system on half of the ship was shot out. It was bedlam. But we had not been stopped from delivering our bomb load. I watched the bomb load visually shrinking as it neared the large industrial complex. The target exploded violently in yellow and red fire with black smoke as our Group's bombs, in spite of the heavy ack ack defense, hit directly on the oil refinery. Finally something had gone right! I then rotated my turret up and watched, from my position right behind them, to check as our damaged bomb bay doors laboriously closed.

However our troubles were not over. With the loss in power of two engines, and our shot up oxygen supply, we had to immediately get free of the Group formation and to a lower altitude. To avoid a mid-air collision, Sam told Reynolds to take over and fly us out of the Group towards the right hand side because that was the area with the fewest aircraft. A third engine was under-performing due to a problem that ultimately Marty was able to correct. We successfully slid through and were free of the formation. Dropping below and immediately lagging behind the Group, we were alone deep into Europe without too many options. We were a lone straggling and wounded bird over 700 miles from home...and one that the Luftwaffe would love to pick off.

Sam got on the interphone to let us know what our options were. We were deeper into Europe than we normally flew and it was a long way home without fighter protection. He calmly explained with just two engines producing power we could only fly at lower altitudes and we would be straggling for several hours alone across Europe. During briefing the pilots had been told if they developed problems that wouldn't allow them to get back to England there was another option. Arrangements had been made with Russia if any of our bombers developed problems over these deep targets. We were to take a certain heading, fly for 20 minutes and then bail out! Our ally whom we had been helping would now not allow us to land our aircraft. He went on to carefully explain the risks of bailing out over our Russian friends and maybe being returned to U.S. forces in a timely manner or maybe not. Sam also wanted us to know the risks of flying alone across Germany at altitudes low enough for us to be picked off by small arms ground fire as well as any bandits that may spot us. There was a little discussion and then when Sam asked for a vote on our preferences; not one guy wanted to trust the Russians. Position by position, just like in an oxygen check, the answers came in; "Tail to Pilot, lets try for home,

Waist to Pilot, lets go home, etc" until everyone had reported. We all elected to stay with our New Bird as long as she was able to fly.

The next hours were extremely tense. We limped along in a gradual descent down to around 2,000 or 3,000 feet altitude over Germany due to our lost power. Not knowing if anything else on our aircraft might cease to function we worried and waited. Surely a third engine might begin to fail I wondered, or the oil or fuel supply might be damaged or otherwise compromised, etc. We couldn't know for sure. I was constantly on the move in my turret looking for enemy fighters. If you can hold your breath for three hours or so, we did. After we left Germany, Sam had us check for any obvious damage to operating and landing systems and got an all OK. He then decided our plane was going to be able to get back to England and there was no need for an emergency landing in Belgium. In spite of her extensively damaged condition, after an eventful eight and a half hours flight, the New Bird got us safely back to Ridgewell.

Our New Bird had performed her most important task on this Valentine's Day, 1945; though almost fatally damaged she got us back alive. We were told at the time the New Bird was never to fly again, and that she was to be cannibalized to keep other ships flying. However, I don't know if that is a fact or not. But from the looks of her we were lucky she held together as long as she did. Of the 37 381st aircraft launched on this date, 18 did not return directly to Ridgewell. Thirteen ships landed on the Continent and five on other bases in England due to damage or low fuel. As a group we were pretty well shot up, but had performed our jobs well.

Truth be known, on this date I thought I would never see England again. This was a very long and trying day. We would return to the older planes for the rest of our missions. But the New Bird would always have a special place in my heart for her valiant performance in spite of massive and crippling damage done to her by the German anti-aircraft shells.

DRESDEN

No rest for the weary, on the next day, February 15th, we were awakened early for another try at Dresden. I felt drained and numb inside from our ordeal on the Brux mission of the previous day. I went through breakfast and the preflight operations without much energy. When we were issued our boxes of High Carbohydrate Ration, I immediately started eating the candy for an energy boost. It seemed to help.

Our targets were the oil refineries in the Dresden area, which we couldn't see due to cloud cover. We had light flak over Europe but no fighters. Then 45 minutes before bombs away, we lost one half of our oxygen system. Half of the crew had to use walk-around oxygen bottles to continue at altitude. After bombing we had to leave the Group and head for England on our own. Now two days in a row we were straggling alone across Europe. Because there were no bandits reported in the area, when we got down to 20,000 feet altitude Sam had me leave the ball and go to the radio room to fill oxygen bottles for the half of the crew that had no oxygen. While there I found I could go quite a few minutes without oxygen with no negative effect even at 20,000 feet or so.

When we got back to the Channel there was another ship of our Group circling low over the Channel. They asked for help looking for their tail gunner who was in the Channel. They had been returning on their own due to mechanical problems when an engine blew up as they started across the Channel. Their ship was thrown up by the explosion and then fell into a backwards motion, after which they went into a dive. The tail gunner thinking they were going to crash, jumped out of his hatch holding onto an emergency inflatable raft and parachuted into the Channel. Just before it was about to crash into the Channel, the ship was pulled out of its dive. That their ship held together in this violent maneuver, which was essentially a loop, was more evidence of the B-17's toughness and structural integrity.

After their ship had been righted, they had been looking without success in the Channel for their tail gunner and his raft. I went back into the ball turret and scanned the choppy waters of the Channel for their guy, but with no luck. We couldn't stay too long and had to get on our way to Ridgewell. Air Sea Rescue had joined the search as we flew on our way home. He was never found. I found out later that it was Frank the bicycle repair guy we all knew and liked so well who had died in the Channel on our way home from Dresden. For some reason, it is harder to accept the death of someone who is as vital and active as Frank was. In the following months, I had a few occasions when I thought I saw Frank somewhere in a crowd or coming into the mess hall, etc. But it was just my mind not accepting his death I guess.

I was starting to get edgy. It seemed like the closer I got to my 35th mission the more unsure things had become. I had just four missions to go and was beginning to think ahead too much. Finishing my tour was so close I would find myself thinking what it would be like to know I was going home in one piece. Then I would have to make myself not think ahead. It was bad luck, we thought, to allow yourself to think about being done with your tour of duty.

It was time for a pass to London and a peaceful visit with Pat.

Cologne Cathedral. Bridges on the Rhine River and other buildings show extensive damage while the cathedral remains basically intact due to care exercised by Allied bombers. [USAAF]

THE VIEW FROM THE BOTTOM UP

ACME

Major General James H. Doolittle

To Bob:
With kindest personal regards.
J. H. Doolittle

This picture was signed for me by General Doolittle in 1965.

Berlin, February 3, 1945. Picture I believe may have come from the film I shot from my gun turret. [USAAF]

THE VIEW FROM THE BOTTOM UP

Chapter 15

The Combat Tour Closes

I went off to London for a little time away from the base and all things military. When I got to the end-of-the-line bus stop in Lower Edmonton, I popped into the fish and chips shop. I had a quick snack of hot deep-fried fish and chips with a little vinegar sprinkled on them, as the English like to do. I felt a little guilty for not having checked with Pat first to see if she wanted to join me, but it was enjoyable just sitting by myself on the bench and watching the locals going about their normal routines. They were chatting away and going to the green grocer's or the butcher shop. It was a remarkably normal scene.

After finishing my snack, I was walking toward her house when I was suddenly assaulted with snowballs thrown by young boys. Mindful that being in uniform whatever I did in response to this boyish action would reflect on my country, I just kept walking up the street and did nothing. Then as I was really getting pelted, a door opened and a housewife came out and yelled at the boys to stop.

"Don't you dare throw snowballs at one of our Allies. You should be ashamed!" she scolded. The boys scurried off and left me alone. I smiled and thanked her as she waved and returned to her home. She had saved me from an awkward situation. It dawned on me then I had been treated very well in England other than this minor incident. Considering the tens of thousands of us crammed into this small island, it was further evidence of the strong bond between our peoples.

My visit was a very quiet one. We stayed in the local areas and just walked, window-shopped and talked. At no time did I see another American. It felt like we were a normal young couple just enjoying our time together. For the most part, the evening was spent in her home mainly with Pat and her sister in that chilly living room. Her folks spent their time in the warm kitchen reading the paper and talking. We listened to the radio playing popular music, mostly American.

I stayed over night in her brother's bedroom again. Pat came by when she was ready for bed dressed in pajamas and a cotton robe and we talked a while. The same act by a less naïve girl could be misunderstood as provocative, but she was just a young girl infatuated with a romantic wartime situation. After a while her dad loudly said, "Pat, go to bed." We kissed quickly, said a soft good-night and she returned to her bedroom. It seemed everyone knew she was there talking with me. I was so happy I hadn't misunderstood the situation and done something I would have regretted to this day.

The next day, which started with the lovely cup of tea and a couple of pieces of toast, was spent doing nothing in particular. As the day wore on, Pat rode into Central London with me where we had lunch. While walking, talking and looking we came upon a tobacconist's shop. This guy not only sold packaged cigarettes, but he specialized in custom-made cigarettes and pipe tobacco. Entering the shop, out of curiosity, we were greeted with the pleasant aroma of various types of tobacco. We watched as he combined strands of apparently different types of tobacco and chopped them up. Then he rolled the tobacco and cigarette paper together and cut them into proper lengths. I only mention this little incident because it shows for those who could afford them there were hand-made things available in London during the war. I was fascinated people would pay what it must cost for these custom made cigarettes, which were probably inferior tasting to my Lucky Strikes.

On one of my earlier trips, we visited a boot maker's shop, filled with the comforting smell of leather, where you could have shoes custom-made. They started with a tracing of your foot outline along with a series of foot measurements. From these they would make a shoe, or boot, which I was told would fit like a kid-leather glove. Later I wished I had ordered a pair of shoes made. Some of the guys had Chukka Boots made at this shop. The Chukka Boot was an ankle high boot favored by pilots for its comfort. They were beautiful but I didn't want to pay the price of £10 ($40 American at that time). My pay was £44 a month, including flight and overseas bonuses, so £10 would have been over a week's pay.

We ultimately went to the cavernous Liverpool Street Station. It was a huge place with a several stories high open area as its hub. The vast open area muted the sounds of hundreds of people arriving or leaving London. The appearance contrasted in my mind to the Union Station in Los Angeles. The mood here was somber and functional. Whereas the station in California, though equally busy, was filled with warm colors and seemed more restful.

We moved out to the. loading platform and waited for my train. The whole area was drab and monochromatic. Smoky air pollution caused by the trains covered everything. Anything that wasn't dark to begin with, became so in time. Here and there would be a bright splash of red or yellow, usually adorning a young girl, but mostly it was a grim picture. Even the advertising posters were faded. It was a fitting place for goodbyes.

I was becoming more concerned about Pat's attachment to me, and her apparent desire for something more permanent, which I didn't share. Yet, I wasn't mature enough to face the situation openly with her. I didn't want to end our relationship, because I enjoyed our time together. But, our goodbyes were getting more and more difficult. I knew the day was fast approaching when I would be going to the States, Good Lord willing, and how would I handle that? Later, as my train pulled out of the dark station, we waved a sad farewell to each other one more time. This was beginning to look more and more like a corny old wartime black and white movie.

CROSS YOUR FINGERS

I was coming up on my 32nd mission and feeling a little superstitious. Most of the Steinwinter crew was about to go home except Dan Adair who had gotten behind his crew on mission count due to that bailout over Belgium. The old Blue Room was not as festive as it had been when we all were "young" and in the middle of our combat tours. A time that seemed truly "long ago and far away," as in the then current song, and yet was just a few months ago.

Saying goodbye to fellow airmen, at least in our time, was usually quite casual. All debts were cancelled and emotional attachments ignored. We traded home addresses and promised to "keep in touch," but rarely did. It may sound a little cool but it was a habit that offered protection from emotional turmoil. These guys, the Goldin and Steinwinter crews, were closer to me than anyone, other than my immediate family, had ever been. Yet as they each left to go there was little more than a, "Can I help you with those bags?" and later a handshake and maybe a slap on the shoulder. A final, "See you later," were the usual hopeful last words. The guy who had left soon dimmed in my consciousness like a smoky apparition.

As more and more guys were leaving, I kept thinking about finishing my tour and what it would be like to know for sure I was going to survive to go home. The odds at this point were pretty good I would finish in good shape, but I was becoming somewhat morose and focusing on the negative. It was hard to understand; I should have been happy. I had completed 31 missions without a scratch and now I had only four missions left to complete my combat tour. Even with all that, I was not the usual carefree Bob. I wasn't sleeping well, which was not normal for me.

Then on February 21ˢᵗ it was a cold frosty morning when I awoke, the lights were on and the hut was empty of my crew. I tried to remember what had happened. Then it came to me that we were scheduled to fly today. I could remember Marty shaking me and saying, "Hey, Gilbert, we are leaving for chow; you better get your ass in gear or you could be in big trouble!"

Now fully awake, I quickly dressed and was going to find a ride to the Combat Mess when I looked at my watch and realized it was too late for breakfast. I had to get directly to the flight line and join my crew or it was courts marshal time for me. I supposed the least charge would be absent without leave (AWOL) and could be as serious as dereliction of duty. When I got outside of the hut, I found my bicycle had a flat tire as usual so I decided to walk to the flight line. Fortunately for me I have a good sense of direction and knew where the 533ʳᵈ Bomb Squadron's flight line facilities were from our hut's location. Unfortunately, however, this meant crossing a farmer's plowed field. I stumbled across the field of frozen tilled earth, which was like walking over an expanse of large broken rocks. Why I didn't turn or break an ankle I don't know. I picked up my equipment bag and hitched a ride out to our ship for the day. Ralph and Clem had just arrived ahead of me and were starting to get their guns ready. I picked up my guns and began to disassemble them and removing the excess oil used for storage. I acted as if nothing unusual had happened as we completed our pre-flight routines. This screw-up by me didn't help any of my feelings of impending doom.

It was Andy's next to last mission, and he seemed his usual happy self. We left Ridgewell at 7:30 A.M. for our target, the marshalling yards at Nürnberg. It was bright and clear over England, but we began to encounter clouds over the Continent. Although we had to bomb by radar, I could see the ground from time-to-time. We were met with light but accurate flak at the target. From what I could see through a break in the clouds after the bombs were dropped, we did hit the rail yards. We had good fighter support and there were no bandits reported in the area.

My gloomy mood persisted as my personal black cloud was apparently still working when my interphone burnt out. I couldn't hear anyone and could not be heard by the rest of the crew. When the interphone burnt out, I opened up my turret door and told Clem what had happened. We established that if an emergency developed, Clem would bang on the turret with a wrench and I would come up for information or get out of the turret if needed. He let Sam and the rest of the crew know of my interphone problems. No emergency developed and I had a mission bereft of conversation. Under normal conditions it was easy to feel isolated in the ball turret with no visual connection to anyone. However, without any interphone conversation it was as if I were alone on a solo airborne voyage droning across a sea of clouds. With the steady roar of the ship and the view of an unchanging sky, it was almost hypnotic as I was lost in personal thoughts. I had to fight dropping off to sleep. Finally at the Channel, I was allowed to get out of my turret. I stretched out in the radio room and got connected up to the interphone like everyone else.

We returned by 3:30 P.M. without any damage. I had eaten all of my high carbohydrate rations and some of Tex's too as I sat in the radio room. It had been over twenty hours since my last meal and I was starving for real food thanks to missing breakfast. After Interrogation I couldn't get to the mess hall fast enough. We were having an inventive stew-like concoction made with corned beef. For a change I didn't bitch about having corned beef again. Our mess staff even with their limited resources went out of their way to keep meals interesting. With enough ketchup, that night even the corned beef tasted good.

OPERATION CLARION

I met with Andy for our last pre mission mini briefing, but there was of course no mention of this being his final mission. It was the 22nd of February, and after a wet and drizzly take-off through a low cloudbank, we headed toward the Gardelegen marshalling yards north of Magdeberg. Today we were a part of the *Operation Clarion*, a major assault on German rail and road communications by the Allied air forces. However, in the crowded sky we got diverted off course by traffic pattern interference from other outfits. The Group then proceeded to a secondary target, the rail yards at Klotze. Flying without oxygen masks at what was for us a very low altitude of around 12,000 feet, we could see a lot of fighter action and dog fights in the clear blue sky ahead of us. I was watching a B-17 being attacked by Me 109s when it exploded in mid-air. Nine more families were to receive those telegrams dreaded by every family who had loved ones in combat that began, "The President of The United States regrets to inform you..." I had to force my thoughts to my job at hand and not dwell on the negative possibilities.

We were approaching the I P of our bomb run when Marty spotted a bandit zeroing in on us at 12 o'clock and a little high. He had him in his sights but Jerry was still out of range and closing quickly. Marty said he could see the sparkling lights of machinegun fire from the bandit's wings indicating he was shooting in our direction.

I whirled my turret forward to the 12 o'clock direction and turned on my gun selector switches. I waited for the attacker; if he should make his pass under us I would pick him up. Then Marty yelled, "He got the bandit! A '51 came out of nowhere and nailed the bastard!" I could see the flaming wreckage falling from the sky ahead of us and a blossoming parachute as the pilot bailed out. The pilot in his parachute drifted under us, I had him in my sight with my thumbs on the trigger buttons. I was still ramped-up emotionally ready to attack this plane that had been firing at us. My heart was racing, and as a reaction, I was about to shoot the pilot suspended from his parachute. It reminds me now of being on the skeet range when a clay bird would be partially hit and as a reaction I would go after and shoot the rest of the bird as it spun off. But fortunately I didn't respond to a reaction and shoot him hanging helplessly from his 'chute and no longer a threat to us. I'm very glad I didn't, but it was a close call. In the heat of battle things do happen that are immediate reactions and not evil acts. I think this incident speaks well of the training we received that we were taught to make sure before we shot. I doubt that Luftwaffe pilot ever knew how close a call he had that day.

We finally bombed at 11,500 feet and put our bombs right on the rail yard. My viewing position today was exceptional. Everything was very clear as I witnessed the bombs smacking into the rail yard with large explosions. It was satisfying to be able to see and know we were doing something positive against the enemy's ability to move his war materiel and personnel. Bomb strike photos are fine but watching the real thing in real time is exhilarating.

While we were flying back home, I was able to watch P-47s and P-51s as they rampaged over the German countryside primarily shooting up locomotives and other transportation targets of opportunity. I particularly remember watching two P-47s making a low level run firing with tracers into a wooded hill. Then their bullets hit something hidden there in those woods that erupted in a massive explosion. They both peeled off to avoid the explosion debris. It was exciting to watch, and made me jealous of those fighter pilots as they slammed their way flying on-the-deck across Germany firing at trains and other targets of opportunity. We returned home without further incidents of note.

Andy had finished his tour of duty with this mission. When we got back to the hardstand he strode around as he was being congratulated. He had a smile so big I didn't think he could ever stop smiling. [See photo at the end of the chapter.] Andy was a very gregarious, likable guy and someone I would miss. Asking me to report my ground observations to him, he had made me feel I had something important to do besides manning my guns in the ball turret. I was to miss our little mini briefings before each mission when we went over the planned flight for that day. As it developed we would really miss him on our very next mission the next day.

OOPS

February had been a busy month for the Goldin crew and would continue to be so right up to the end. On the 23rd we again were scheduled to fly as *Operation Clarion* continued. This was another low altitude raid at just 11,000 feet. We in the 533rd Squadron got separated from the 381st Group due to cloudy conditions. I don't recall how it happened but before the Squadron's bomb-run our ship also got separated from the squadron. The Squadron successfully bombed the rail yards at Adelsburg as a target of opportunity. At this time we were by ourselves somewhere over Germany. The primary duty of the navigator was at all times to know exactly where his plane was. When the formation was together, the lead navigator guided the lead pilot and all planes followed that lead ship. But in each ship the navigator had to be ready in the event of an emergency to guide his pilot should they become separated from the formation. We had a rookie navigator flying his first combat mission and he didn't know where we were, nor where should we be.

Bandits had been reported in the area and we were alone. After searching the skies for our squadron, we finally visually spotted them some miles away in amongst the clouds. Alone we bombed a target of opportunity, a rail yard somewhere, and were able to catch up with the squadron. But by now we were running low on fuel after flying all over the place trying to locate the squadron. We stayed with them for a while and then left them over France near the Channel to go on our own straight to Ridgewell to save fuel.

Somewhere in clouds or contrails we were lost again and our navigator had become disoriented. Sam had me get back into the ball to help look for landmarks on the ground. We had been over water that was apparently the Channel when I first got back into the ball. Then I spotted land, which had to be England. As I was about to get out of the ball, I looked and we were over water again! We had apparently cut across the southeastern corner of England and were now over the North Sea and heading for the arctic. Sam began to dead-reckon and got us back to England. As we crossed the English coast, we almost flew into two large radio antenna towers that suddenly appeared out of the mist. Sam quickly banked away from the towers and I watched close up from the ball as we just cleared them by what seemed just a few yards. He ordered me out of the ball and all of us into our wheels-up crash landing positions. Our fuel was almost gone now, he was going to find a farm field somewhere and do a wheels-up crash-landing. As I locked the ball turret in place, I was reminded that in a wheels-up landing the ball turret would impact the ground first. We hadn't had time to disconnect and drop it, so we had to hope the ground was soft. If we hit hard rocky soil, the ship could break open at the ball turret location just aft of the radio room where we would be in our crash landing positions. We could then be ejected out onto the fast rushing-by ground.

We crew members, who were waiting in the radio room, could see nothing. We were scrunched down into our proper crash landing positions and were hoping and praying we would survive the upcoming crash. Doubts crowded my thoughts. I was thinking that maybe this was it. Was this some more of that recent bad luck? But no, damn it! I suddenly thought. I'm going to get out of this mess no matter what it takes. As we came closer to contacting the ground, my self-confidence and determination paradoxically returned. We were going to survive this crash somehow...I knew.

Then all of a sudden the ship rose slightly and banked to the right. With the engines almost at an idle, I could hear the landing gear grinding down into place. Sam expertly landed our ship with hardly a bounce on a runway that seemed to have appeared out of nowhere. We all were excited and wondering what had happened. I quickly stumbled back into the waist area for a look-see. Gawking out of a waist window, I saw an unfamiliar air base with RAF bombers parked all around, including one that had belly-landed before us. It turned out we had landed at RAF Station Rivenhall, which Sam had spotted just as we were about to crash-land into a farmer's field. It had taken us 9 hours and 45 minutes, but we were safely back in England at last.

THE VIEW FROM THE BOTTOM UP

RAF Hospitality

The RAF guys treated us royally (no pun intended). Our officers went off with the RAF officers and we were taken to the Flying Sergeant's mess for a great meal. After we had eaten, they got us situated with places to sleep. We were then taken to the enlisted men's club where they wouldn't let us spend any money. We were treated to a great evening of drinking and singing. I always carried a few packages of Lucky Strikes in my flight suit to be used as currency if needed to avoid capture in Germany. I found out that American cigarettes were also liked by some of the RAF guys, so I handed them out to those who wanted them.

Before the evening's festivities got started, several of the RAF airmen came up to bid us good luck on our return to our base tomorrow. With typical British understatement, they said they had, "... a bit of a do over Germany tonight...," and wouldn't be back, "... 'till you lot are fast asleep."

This whole scene gave me a flashback to movies I had watched as a youngster back home. The RAF was greatly admired by us then because of their valiant stand against the Luftwaffe and their unstoppable bombing of Germany. And here I was talking and laughing with them as peers. What a wonderfully unique experience.

Bragging Rights

The next morning after a hearty breakfast we returned to our plane that had been loaded with enough fuel for us to return home. The coordinates needed to return to Ridgewell had been clearly marked on his map for our novice navigator if they were needed. Sam had obtained the necessary clearances to return to Ridgewell and we were ready to go. Sam apparently had to defend some competitive type claims he had made to our RAF brethren. He had one thing going for him, the B-17 to begin with was a sportier aircraft than the larger RAF birds. Then when you have no bomb load and the weight of only minimal fuel the plane is at its lightest weight and quite agile. Sam had told the RAF guys to watch our takeoff if they wanted to see what a "real" airplane could do, or some such friendly bravado.

He warned us to hold on if we were standing when we took off because he was going to jump off this runway. I was at a waist window with my arm around the ammo box as I recall. He held on the brakes and revved up the engines until they were screaming in a high-pitched demand to be turned loose. When he let the brakes go, we shot down the runway and were 100 feet off the ground by the time we got to the control tower located mid-field. Holding on for dear life I looked out the window as we rapidly climbed away from the runway. He then made a 180 degrees turn and flew back across and away from Rivenhall. After gaining speed he made another 180 degree turn with wheels up and dropped down on-the-deck. He headed toward and back down to the same runway and buzzed by the control tower at max speed. Normally traveling at say around 200 miles per hour at thousands of feet of altitude one would not be particularly aware of any speed. But being on-the-deck, the ground moves by in a heart-pumping blur. We waved at the RAF guys on the ground and the control tower balcony as they waved back to us. What a rush! Boys will be boys. [See drawing at the end of the chapter.]

Our little RAF base detour of the 23rd had an advantage beyond avoiding a crash landing, we couldn't be scheduled to fly on the 24th. We all could use a breather. We had been very busy of late and it seemed that either they were short of crews or someone in Operations may have been interested in having us finish our tour as soon as practical.

WITH A BANG AND WITHOUT A WHIMPER

On the 25th we were scheduled to fly once again and for me this was to be my last time. There was going to be a little celebration today for the ship "Stage Door Canteen," which had been adopted by the British and American movie people. It had reached 100 combat missions in February! On the 25th there were to be several movie star types at the base for a celebration with a birthday-like cake. We probably wouldn't have bothered going to watch anyway, but the decision to not be available for the event was made for us by Operations.

Now, I had finally come to the real target of all crewmen, my thirty-fifth mission. Everyone was careful to not mention to me this was my final mission. No one wanted to jinx me. This was a superstition akin to when a baseball pitcher is working on a no-hitter; no one talks to him about it until after it is a fact. We went about our usual pre-flight routines while we waited for Sam and the others from the mission briefing. I was eager to know about our target for today. How about a short milk-run? That would be nice, I thought.

It turned out our mission on this date was not going to be a short one. We were going to Munich deep into Germany near the Bavarian

Alps. This was another bit of personal irony. My last mission was going to be Munich...Munich where Hitler had his first action to occupy and terrorize Europe seven years earlier. Our target was the marshalling yards there. In the recent past, our missions had been focused on destroying the Nazi transportation system more than the industrial factories. Munich was no exception.

We had a beautifully clear day. In sharp outline I could see the magnificent Alps covered with snow as we headed for Munich. Where the sun was hitting the snow they were bright white with sharp canyons of pink and blue. When we neared Munich I saw the other groups ahead of us catching hell from very heavy and accurate flak. The Germans had a large installation of 88mm anti-aircraft guns protecting Munich. They were creating a huge black cloud of exploded and exploding anti-aircraft shells that we were going to fly through. The Eighth Air Force's bombing technique of precision strategic bombing did not allow for any evasive action. The Eighth's operating philosophy was that it had never been deterred from, nor avoided, a target due to enemy action. So we knew that we were going to fly into that black maelstrom up ahead. As we approached the target area, a Fortress ahead of us suffered a direct hit and blew up before it could drop its bomb load. Well, now it was for sure...this was not to be a milk-run.

The same clear sky that was allowing such accurate flak also revealed our target in absolutely clear detail. With bombs away I tracked the great mass of bombs from our Group falling in a tight cluster directly under us. I followed them as they visually shrunk nearing the ground. Then they contacted the huge rail-yard complex with massive explosions. The Intelligence guys later rated our bombing results as an exceptionally satisfactory job...one of the best they said. [See photo at end of the chapter.]

As we made our way home on this beautifully clear day, I for the last time looked down at Europe at war. From five miles up, I gazed silently at the map-like arrangements of towns, villages and farms connected by roads and rivers. It was hard to realize what was happening down there in that beautiful tapestry of greens and browns, scattered with white, that was Germany in the later months of World War II. I realized in that peaceful looking world thousands were still being sacrificed to finally stop the Nazi war machine, which had so negatively and fatally affected the lives of millions of people.

Coming back from my reverie, I thought we were probably in the best shape physically we had been in for the past month...and I was going home. As we neared England, I got out of my turret and into the waist area of the ship for the last time. I looked out at the other ships in our formation proudly flying back to Ridgewell our English home and felt a buzz of elation inside my chest. Later several of the guys came up and silently shook my hand, but avoiding actually saying I had flown my last mission because we weren't home yet.

I'm Through—But Not the Crew

When we arrived at the hardstand, I slowly climbed out of the waist door and just said, Thank You, as I patted the horizontal stabilizer. I was taking my guns out of the ball, when Sam came back and squatted down along aside of me. He yelled for one of the ground crew to handle my guns for me. He put his arm around my shoulder and congratulated me.

"Gilbert," he said. "you always did a good job down here," pointing at the turret, "...I felt confident knowing you were in the ball."

I thanked him for his kind thoughts. He then asked me if I would fly two more missions with him so the whole crew could finish together. I respectfully declined the opportunity, though it would have been a noble gesture on my part. I didn't want to tempt fate any more.

Though I had finished my tour of duty, I wouldn't allow any personal celebration until the other guys had also finished theirs. I sweated out their next two missions, more than they ever knew.

On the 26th of February the crew went to Berlin. This was actually a bigger raid than the one on February 3rd that got all the headlines. It went well and they returned without a hitch. I had fixed the flat tire on my bicycle during the day while they went to Berlin. Later I rode my bicycle down to the flight line, watched and waited for them with some trepidation. After they had safely landed, I went back to the hut. In a way I felt a little guilty not flying with them, but the guys had told me I would be nuts to volunteer. I met them later at the mess hall where we all acted casually and no one mentioned they now only had one more mission to fly.

The next day, the 27th of February they went to Leipzig for their final mission. In the early days, Leipzig had been a very dangerous target and was highly defended by the Luftwaffe. On this day there were no German fighters and the flak was meager. Once again I sweated out the crew until all ships had returned safely. The Goldin crew had flown six of the last seven days as they finished their tour of duty. We Hut Five guys had agreed that we would celebrate our tour completions together and boy, oh boy did we! I believe our original crew-member, Gonnering, also celebrated with us though he still had several missions to go.

HAPPY WARRIORS

In our outfit when one finished his tour of duty, he was given a Happy Warrior pass of 72 hours. Apparently this was a normally unauthorized amount of time, because the Squadron clerk would not give it to you if there were anyone else in the orderly room at the same time. I had intended to go to London the next morning after our celebration and so I wanted to pick up my Happy Warrior pass in the evening. The first time I went over to get my pass there were a couple of guys in the orderly room so, with a conspiratorial wink, I was told to come back later.

We had been saving up liquor for our little end-of-combat-tour party. We had a couple bottles of Scotch plus some Champaign Marty had picked up in Paris a month or so earlier. From time-to-time the Group had visitors, usually military or governmental, who were considered as VIPs and accommodated as such at the request of higher authorities. We had an Air Force command level officer visiting from the China, Burma, India (CBI) Theater who wished to also visit Paris. Sam was selected to fly him to Paris. All he needed with him was the minimum flight crew of co-pilot, navigator and Marty our flight engineer. While he was in Paris, Marty had bought all kinds of souvenir stuff for us to send home. Also he bought several bottles of Champaign for our later Happy Warrior party in the Blue Room, UK.

Using our canteen cups we mixed Scotch and Champaign half and half for The Happy Warrior Cocktail as we called it (a very foul tasting drink as it turned out). There were a few awkward and controlled emotional toasts to each other. Then we settled down for some serious drinking. I had been back to the orderly room a couple of times and told each time to come back later due to people in the room. Finally the clerk looked at me and said, "Sarg, I think I better give this pass to you now while you can still find your way back to your hut."

We all drank way too much, but we were young and our livers were still in good shape. We made a mess of our hut, but it was memorable and no one begrudged us our release of emotions. The next morning, some officer came into the hut and looked around. He said, "I hear some of you finished up yesterday. Congratulations. Now, clean up this damn mess."

I got my area in order, changed my clothes and went off to London for several days. This was my three days authorized Happy Warrior pass and my planned self-authorized leave extension.

It would be a memorable time and more like a vacation then a wartime leave.

"Buzz Job." *A graphite pencil drawing by Alexandre Jay based on the buzzing of RAF Rivenhall by the Goldin crew.* *[Copyright* © *Alexandre Jay]*

February 25, 1944, Munich, my last mission. An example of very accurate bombing by the 381st Bomb Group. Note concentration of explosions on the rail yard target. [USAAF]

A grinning Andy completes his combat tour. Marty in the background talking to plane's crew chief on her performance today. Co-pilot McLochlyn listens in. [Frenk Hrehocik]

The View From the Bottom Up

Chapter 16

Goodbye

AFTER catching the Toonerville Trolley at Yeldham on my way to London, I had time to muse about what was next for each of my crewmates:

The Goldin crew was no more. One by one we will be sent to a replacement depot in the UK and then shipped back to the States. We each will get a 30-day returnee furlough to unwind a little while back home with our families. After our furloughs we will individually report to a returnee center and be processed for further duty assignments. The war in Europe was getting close to the end, but there was a lot of work to be done with Japan in the Pacific Theater. I was in no hurry to get home because I had been recommended for further combat after a period of rest in the States. [See Combat Experience document at the end of the chapter.] This would probably mean being sent to the war in the Pacific for God knows how long.

I had the three-day Happy Warrior pass to London where I planned to spend at least a week or so. I had never been asked by anyone for my pass on any previous trips to London, so I figured I could safely unilaterally extend it. Back at the base they never took bed checks or had roll calls, so they wouldn't miss me for a while. It was an open door for some creative time manipulation, which I happily planned to do.

FAREWELL TO LONDON

I was able to use Pat's home as my base of operations during my self-authorized "furlough," and ended up spending ten days in London. For some reason I can enjoy sightseeing while alone, which helped because Pat had to work some of the time I was there. On my days alone, I spent time along the Thames River in Central London mostly looking at the historic old buildings such as the Houses of Parliament. The bridges such as The Tower Bridge and The London Bridge were fascinating too. I sat along the slate gray Thames slowly moving by and watched the river traffic on that ancient thoroughfare. I wondered what had happened there in the centuries gone by. My visual memories of London today seem to be in shades of gray like a black and white photograph, yet a color will standout vividly like the red phone booths on the city sidewalks. So it is that Dickensian London I remember...with a spot of color here and there.

FINAL CURTAIN

The time with Pat was almost domestic. We could spend hours together doing very little and yet finding it enjoyable. Ours was a warm an easy relationship. The only negative aspect was the pending final separation when I left England, which was the brooding bear in the room that no one talked about. Mostly we stayed in her neighborhood, but we did go to Leicester Square a couple of times to see first-run movies from the States.

I found out during my absence most of the crew had shipped out for the replacement depot. Gonnering, Engleman and Adair were still around but we Blue Room veterans were a dwindling presence in Ridgewell. So I decided to boldly drop in on the orderly room and have them get going on my orders home.

SAVING THE ROCKER

I casually walked into the orderly room only to hear, "Sergeant Gilbert, I believe. I'm pleased to see you." It was the Adjutant and he wasn't really smiling.

"Good afternoon Captain, I've been looking for you," I bluffed with my best innocent face.

"Oh really? And why was that?" he asked expectantly.

"Well, sir, I haven't received my orders for home yet."

"I'm told Sergeant, we have looked for you for some days now, with no success. Where have you been?"

"Oh, I was around, Sir," I responded vaguely, "over at the Aero Club or the Senior NCO Club. Just around."

"Really? Well that brings up an interesting development. Your mention of senior NCOs reminds me the new Table of Organization has reduced the maximum rank of MOS 611, Career Gunner, to buck Sergeant. You are a 611, as you know, and also a Staff Sergeant. Now, we here in the 533rd wouldn't reduce your rank, but...," he paused, so I could imagine the dire possibilities, "in order to protect your Staff Sergeant rocker and to keep your senior NCO status, we are going to train you to become an MOS 612, Armorer Gunner, which still rates a maximum rank of Staff Sergeant."

"How long will this training take, Sir?"

"Just 30 days for someone as smart as you are."

"OK," I said, walking into his trap, "...when do I start?"

"You start at 2:00 AM tomorrow morning. You will load bombs for the next 30 days. At the end of which time, having been trained into the fine art of an armorer you will be reclassified to a 612, Armorer Gunner. This preemptive action by us will preclude anyone in the States from removing your rocker and making you a buck sergeant." This said with a satisfied smile as if he believed it himself.

A very smart Adjutant it seemed had solved two of his problems at once. There was no record of my being listed on the Morning Report as AWOL. I thought he was pretty sure I had been AWOL but he couldn't prove it. The ground armorers needed help because recently the Army had been reducing the squadron's ground crew manpower. They were taking some enlisted men and sending them to serve with the ground forces in France and Germany.

The only injury I received during my time in England was while loading 50 Kg (110 pound) fragmentation bombs. And it was on my last night loading when I got hurt. We were hand lifting up the frag bombs to attach them to their shackles. I had the tail fin and the ground armorer had the nose. We were each astraddle the bomb bay with one foot on the catwalk and the other on the bomb bay frame. As we lifted the bomb up, my wet shoe sole slipped off the catwalk and I fell sideways throwing out my right arm to catch the catwalk. Unfortunately I held on to the bomb and the guy on the nose let go of his end. I crashed into the catwalk edge with the full weight the bomb pulling me down and cutting into my right armpit. It was near the end of the loading session so I finished up with shaking legs and arms. The cut was minor but the muscle pulls through out my body would be painful. Back at the hut, I went right to bed and slept until mid-afternoon. For the next few days I stayed in the hut and lived on aspirin, instant coffee and hot Lipton's dehydrated chicken soup, which Ralph's mom had sent him. I could hardly move I had so many strained muscles.

Later I was given a regular day and a half pass to London. It was April 13th, 1945, and we had just received the information that President Roosevelt had died in Warm Springs, Georgia, on the 12th. This sudden event of course was headline news in England as well as the United States. When I was in London, I had complete strangers come up to me and tearfully express their sorrow. They wanted me to know how they felt about him as if my father had died. It was very touching. I stopped by the Rainbow Corner to hear what was going on there. There were reporters everywhere from the States as well as the UK. A reporter from the International News Service interviewed me to get an American soldier's reactions. The reporter wanted me to tell how I felt about the death of the President. I expressed how sad I thought it was that after he had given so much, for so many years, he didn't get to live to see the end of this noble effort in Europe...World War II. I don't know if that interview was ever printed anywhere or not.

After a tension filled visit with Pat, I returned to the base on time not wanting to give our Adjutant any chances to get me on any other assignments that would further delay my return home,

THE SWAN SONG

On April 19th I received my orders sending me to the replacement depot from where I would be returned to the States. Ralph had left for the replacement depot several days before. I successfully went through clearance check of all the required areas on the base with no problems of forgotten equipment or obligations yet to be fulfilled. Along with my orders, I was given an unexpected three-day delay-in-route. The Adjutant, perhaps feeling sorry for the delay in processing me for home caused by the bomb loading chore, cut my orders so I would report after the three days delay-in-route. I left a message where Pat worked and told her that I was coming into London that afternoon. When I got to her house, I found out her brother was home on leave so I would have to stay in a Red Cross hotel. I then returned to Central London, and as I was walking by the Imperial Hotel in Russell Square, impulsively I decided to stay there instead of the Red Cross hotel. What the hell, I concluded, I could afford it. And how many times will I have a chance to stay in a nice hotel in London in the future? I asked myself. As it turned out, none was the answer. I was beginning to develop a sense of being aware of where I was and to not leave chances undone that may never re-appear in my life.

The Imperial Hotel as I recall was rather Spartan by today's standards. But it was comfortable and very civilian and only cost 14 Shillings and 6 Pence ($2.90), which included a breakfast and a "boot cleaning." I felt like a real person and not just one of the herd. The Imperial did offer many amenities such as a dining room, snack bar, brasserie, lounge, Turkish bath and a barber. If one wanted a meal served in your room, it cost One Shilling (20 cents) extra. All in all it was quite civilized. I wondered why we hadn't stayed here rather than the Red Cross hotel on any of our many trips to the big town.

Pat and I had a nostalgic but awkward few days and revisited some of the places we had been during my times in London. I finally got to see the world's most famous clock, Big Ben, and hear the Westminster Chimes in person. Our final depressing days are smeared together in my memory. I know we were together during the days and the evenings. That I rode out with her to her to her home at night and she came into Central London in the morning are the most specific things I can remember.

It was a very melancholy time for me because I doubted we would ever see each other again. She was such a sweet but naïve girl and I had strong feelings for her. I knew she believed we would some how meet again. But our paths were parting and our teenage romance would be the stuff of fond memories for both of us as we moved separately into our young adult lives. In a way it was cruelly unfair that our youthful romance was thrust into the charged atmosphere of wartime and was happening 9,000 miles from home. We were both far too young to make sensible decisions, or to make life-long commitments. Somehow I knew the best thing to do was to do nothing and that turned out to be correct, but it didn't make me feel any better. Deep inside I felt guilty but didn't know why.

We waited in the gloomy sepia toned train station. It was time for me to say goodbye and get on with the processes for my return home. We were quietly standing with an arm around each other when Pat said, "Remember when we met on the Tube and I thought of the Trolley Song and how it was like me?"

"Yeah, that was kind of corny but sweet." I smiled.

"Well, you know what went through my mind just now... Casablanca. That film with Bogart and Ingrid Bergman... remember?"

"Sure, I do. We saw it twice. What made you think of it?"

Pat looked up at me, her clear blue eyes shiny with almost tears, and said, "Kinda like us now...in that last scene where they are saying goodbye by that airplane in the fog. Their song, *Time Goes By* seems to fit for us also."

I didn't trust myself to try and talk, I just pulled her close and gave her a hug.

I thought it was odd how we can feel so sad and yet excited at the same time. But that was what I felt as I said a last goodbye to Pat, my sweet girl friend for those several eventful months in wartime London. I was sad to be leaving her forever and yet was anxious to get started on my way home.

As it was time to go, with mixed feelings, I got onto the train for Preston. It slowly pulled out. I leaned out the window of my compartment and waved a misty eyed goodbye to her alone on the platform growing smaller to my eyes. The train crept out of the station with a *chug–hiss, chug—hiss,* from the old black locomotive steam engine, as Pat faded in the distance.

Goodbye.

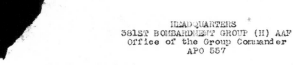

HEADQUARTERS
381ST BOMBARDMENT GROUP (H) AAF
Office of the Group Commander
APO 557

201-Gilbert, Robert B.   25 February 1945

SUBJECT: Combat Experience.

TO   : Whom It May Concern.

1. This is to certify that Robert B. Gilbert, 19207435,
S/Sgt., Air Corps, arrived in the European Theater of Operations
on 23 September 1944 and has completed his operational tour of
duty as a member of a combat crew on a B-17 aircraft.

2. The record of his combat experience is as follows:

    a. Combat Crew Position: Ball Turret Gunner
    b. Number of Operational Missions: Thirty-five
    c. Date of last mission: 25 February 1945
    d. Number of enemy aircraft destroyed: None
    e. Decorations awarded: Air Medal with five Oak
       Leaf Clusters
    f. Manner of performance of duty: Excellent

3. It is recommended that he be reassigned to further combat
in another theater after a period of rest in the Zone of Interior.

RECEIVED
27 FEB 1945
HQ. 1st COMBAT
BOMB WING

Conway S. Hall
CONWAY S. HALL,
Lt. Colonel, Air Corps,
Commanding.

1st Ind.

HQ. 1st Combat Bombardment Wing (H), APO 557, 27 February 1945.

TO: Whom It May Concern.

Approved.

WILLIAM M. GROSS,
Brigadier General, USA,
Commanding.

-1-

Certificate of Combat Experience.

Chapter 17

VE Day in the Dark

REPLACEMENT depots are facilities to gather and disperse service men and women to their next assignment. I was sent to the Bamber Bridge Depot where Army personnel, including Air Corps, were reassigned to the States, the Continent and to other destinations.

I arrived in the Preston area in the late afternoon of April 21st and caught a ride to Bamber Bridge. We traveled through a peaceful scenic countryside along the way with lots of trees and villages. When we arrived, I was pleased to see this particular replacement depot had a very un-military look about it. It turned out in peacetime it had been a girls' school rather than a military base. This was quite a departure from the stark and massive business-like airbase at Ridgewell.

I checked in and was assigned to a room with three other guys also awaiting shipment home. I was told that I would be there a couple of weeks or so during which time there were a few processing requirements to be accomplished, but in the evenings we were free to go on pass to local areas or even to Blackpool on the coast.

AWAITING ORDERS FOR HOME

Each morning we had a roll call at which daily assignments were given. If we didn't have any processing steps to accomplish, there would be a few work details and sometimes entertainment in the base theater to fill up the day. The entertainment was mostly vaudeville type by English music hall entertainers with some talented GIs thrown in from time to time.

For an evening out, one of my roommates invited me to go with them to a place in Preston called The Red Dog Inn. We went the second or third evening I was at Bamber Bridge and I loved it. It was perhaps the friendliest gathering of people I had ever been around. There was a very used upright piano in the corner that was constantly being played. The singing was mostly drinking songs and traditional pub pieces such as Roll Me Over In the Clover, the Hokey Pokey, etc. We had group singing and request solos by anybody. I went there often while at Bamber Bridge and met many friendly people. Apparently my name was, Hey Yank as we happily socialized together.

I recall a waiter there with red hair (what else in the Red Dog?) who carried his lit cigarette behind his right ear sticking straight up! This created the amusing sight of the hair on that side of his head having a singed groove where his cigarettes burned down while he was busy carrying beers.

Some of the guys who wanted a little more sophisticated kind of entertainment went to Blackpool, which apparently had more urbane offerings. But The Red Dog Inn satisfied me and I never took in Blackpool.

THE CHIPS KID

There's a touching incident that comes back to me when I think of Bamber Bridge, which involved a youngster we began to call the Chips Kid. He lived nearby the replacement depot. The first time I saw him he was sitting on the ground with his feet in a ditch just outside a fence of the depot. He was maybe 8 or 9 years old, had scruffy clothes and didn't look too clean. He wore a gray wool cap pushed back on his tousled light brown hair and was sniffling. On his sad face, I could see where rivulets of tears had coursed down his cheeks removing grime on their way. Seeing him through the fence pathetically sitting there alone, I asked him if he needed any help. With his head bowed, he told me about a nameless and thoughtless GI who had apparently forgotten about him. He clutched a newspaper wrapped bundle in his arms and told me about this GI who had asked him to go buy some chips (French fries to Americans) for him. But more importantly the GI promised for the chips he would give the kid a large Boy Scout knife he had shown him. The kid paid a Shilling (20 cents American) out of his own pocket for the chips and had been waiting about an hour for his knife and yet no GI.

The airman, I found out from asking around, had forgotten about the kid and had gone off to a pub in Preston. I tried to give the kid money, but no, he wanted that knife which was grander than any he had ever seen. His misty gray-blue eyes sparkled when he described it. As he sat there huddled against the cold damp twilight, clasping the chips bundle, I went all around our area to find any such knife. I finally found a guy who had a smaller multi-function knife. We negotiated with the kid. For the, by now cold, chips we offered to give him the knife plus two Shillings Six-Pence (about 50 cents American). He

THE VIEW FROM THE BOTTOM UP

agreed reluctantly, and even though he was making money on the deal besides getting a nice knife...his heart was broken. I could have "killed" that thoughtless GI, but it was the best we could do. In the ensuing days, the Chips Kid got a lot of chips business as the guys heard about the knife story. I wonder if he still has that knife as a keepsake to show his grandkids.

REAR ECHELON THIEVES

On my last day at Bamber Bridge, when our orders shipping us to the ZI (Zone of the Interior) were being cut, we were given a list of tasks to be completed before we could leave. Mostly these were the normal checkouts when leaving any post. One was unique to our situation of returning to the United States. We were to take all of our belongings over to a Security building where they would be inspected to assure there were no banned items in our baggage. All of our souvenirs; silk escape maps (I was given three to keep by the 381st Group), photos both personal, and official (given to me by the Group), pieces of flak, any keepsake items military or civilian, etc. were all to be segregated and put into one container. Then after the inspection, which we were not allowed to observe, these items were sealed in a pouch and stamped as "Inspected-Do Not Open." This, we were told, was to get us past the U.S. Customs Officers without further inspection at our port-of-entry in the States.

As is noted later, when we arrived in the States we were not sub-jected to any Customs inspection. After disembarking in the States, we opened up our sealed pouches and found we were the victims of thiev-ery. They, the rear echelon soldiers with the cushy jobs safely at beau-tiful Bamber Bridge, had stolen what they wanted of our personal items. In my case, they took my most important silk escape maps of Western and Central Europe and left me one of Spain. They had taken some of the pieces of flak I had kept. They took several of the photos the photo lab at Ridgewell had given me. Those things were really spe-cial to me and I was able to survive without them. But, I've never for-gotten those low-life thieving soldiers who stole from the combat vet-erans of their own country. I hope they had some trouble sleeping at least for a little while...but I doubt it.

VE DAY

The group I was assigned to, a relatively small one of Eighth Air Force flight crew combat veterans, was given orders to proceed to the port of Southampton and board a designated U.S. Navy transport ship. Coincidentally, it was May 8th, 1945, Victory in Europe Day (VE Day). The German government unconditionally surrendered to the Allies to be effective this date. On our way to Southampton, from our train windows, everywhere we could see British Union Jacks, and here and there American Stars and Stripes. They were happily displayed on every kind of building and vehicle. People waved and yelled at us as we moved through cities and villages on this happy momentous day. I couldn't sit still for very long. I was up and down looking through and hanging out the windows of our train.

It was almost like a storybook plot for me. On D Day, 1944, I was on a train going to Combat Crew training in Florida. Now 11 months later on VE Day, 1945, at the end of this terrible event in Europe, I was on a train to board a troop ship and sail to New York.

SOUTHAMPTON HARBOUR

We arrived dockside of a gray camouflaged Navy transport and boarded her as the only Army personnel on board. Our little group of Air Corps returnees consisted of around a hundred aircrew personnel. About 35% or so of our group was commissioned officers and they ranged from First Lieutenant to Lt. Colonel. The rest were noncommissioned officers. I never knew why we had been selected to travel on a Navy rather than on an Army transport. Perhaps the Colonel got us this special treatment of being on the Navy transport for his own reasons. Or perhaps the Army didn't want to deal with the sometimes independent Air Corps types on their transport ships. Other than us our ship's passengers were all U.S. Navy personnel who apparently had been on duty in England or mainland Europe. We were amused to watch the Navy groups as they came aboard. Their officers didn't carry their own luggage. They each appeared to have an enlisted man who took care of such things. Our Air Corps officers looked on jealously because they got no such deferential treatment and had to handle all their own stuff.

After all of the passengers were on-board, and settled into their assigned sleeping areas, we began to speculate on what kind of celebration the Brits would have on this night. This was VE Day and after six years of war and privation it ought to be the biggest event ever in this ancient land. Some of us asked our Colonel if we could get passes to go into London inasmuch as we were not going to sail until the next morning. He had already checked and found everyone was restricted to the ship. Then he reluctantly gave us the ridiculous news our ship, as well as the others in our convoy, would be under wartime blackout rules! It seemed there was concern the German U-boat commanders may not yet know of their country's surrender because they were often out of contact with their home bases for long periods. If true this was a sensible precaution for when we were at sea. But we were sitting docked in a major English port, which was ablaze with lights. As our ship lay at anchor tied up to a wharf, we would not be allowed to as much as smoke a cigarette on deck, let alone light one. Ah, the conformist military mind!

LONDON CELEBRATES—WE WATCH

As night fell the harbor was alive with signal flares and fireworks lighting up the sky. Small boats cruised the harbor with flashing lights and sounds of female laughter and music blaring at us standing in the dark. At this time the famed radio newsman Edward R. Morrow was broadcasting back to the States about the contrast between what he saw of London at the height of the blitz and this night with joyous people shooting off fireworks. We were told Piccadilly was jammed with tens of tens of thousands of joyous celebrants. But here we combat veterans stood in the dark; alone and separate and barred from the great celebration. I thought of Pat somewhat nearby in London and wished I could have a final goodbye. I couldn't see her in person but did try to get to a telephone to give her a call. Once again military security would not allow me even that small courtesy. I suppose she, along with everyone else in London, was enjoying a glorious celebration and maybe in Piccadilly Circus

WE SAIL AT DAWN

This sea voyage was going to be a new experience for me and I suspect also for most of the other air crewmen. We had ferried a new B-17 to the UK when we came over and so had not been on a troop ship before. I was now looking forward to our voyage home as another experience to savor. It didn't take long for me to decide, however, I was not good sailing material.

At first light we were awakened to all sorts of strange noises and commands over the loudspeaker system. Our ship it turned out was the convoy lead ship and was being deployed first to await the rest of the convoy to assemble. I hurried up on deck to watch the tough little tugboats pushing and steering us through a crowded harbor and out to sea. As I inhaled the familiar harbor aroma of slightly oily salt water, and could hear the sounds of squawking sea gulls, I was back in Long Beach harbor. As youngsters we had watched the freighters and Navy ships being moved out to sea many times and wondered where they were going and what adventurers awaited them. Maybe here in Southampton there were young English boys curled up on a rock, watching and wondering too as they saw us being prodded out to sea.

The convoy formation operation was a sort of slow motion version of a bomber formation assembly, but instead of just 30 minutes this was taking hours. I don't recall what other kinds of ships were in our convoy. I believe it was mostly, if not all, freighter type ships. At first we didn't seem to be making much headway and the ship was doing a lot of wallowing with the motions of the sea. I was told the shallow green waters closer to shore had more rolling movements than we would feel later in the deeper seas. As a consequence, this was a time when some people were experiencing seasickness. An oddity I observed was we Army Air Corps crewmembers were not affected by any motion sickness. The reason I suppose was we spent so much time flying in lumbering bombers, which are constantly moving up and down and sideways. However, there were a number of the sailors, who had not been at sea for sometime, who did develop seasickness.

Our great voyage lay ahead...the going to America as our ancestors had done.

Chapter 18

The Final Challenge

ROUTINE NOTHINGNESS

BEING on a troop ship is the closest thing to nothing to do that I can imagine. We Air Corps guys were all non-commissioned and commissioned officers and thus had no work obligations to occupy our bodies or minds. On the other hand, many of the Navy enlisted men were busy on work details such as chipping and painting the decks and bulkheads or deck swabbing...

For the first couple of days, I just stood on deck and looked over the ship's rail at the swirling blue waters moving past us as we slowly pushed toward home. I also liked to look for and spot the other ships in our convoy, the transports and the prowling Destroyer Escorts. We had the whole vast expanse of the North Atlantic, horizon-to-horizon, to ourselves, but the ships in our convoy were not alone...we had each other. The vast ageless sea heaved ahead of us as it had for centuries for the generations of passengers headed for The New World...and the promise of a better tomorrow.

I had no particular buddies along on this return to home and family. Most of them had left England before me. For endless hours on the start of this voyage I thought of the Blue Room Crew and our times together back at Ridgewell. Their faces and voices echoed in my head as I stood alone at the ship's rail. And there were nagging nostalgic thoughts of sweet Pat back in dreary old London. She will get on with her life and so will I, but...

BATTLE STATIONS

Then about a day or two out from England the PA system ordered the passengers to clear the decks and go to our berth areas and the crew to their battle stations, "...this is not a drill!!" As we were going below decks there appeared a U.S. Navy PBM patrol bomber skimming over the water and dropping depth charges just off of our starboard side. I immediately thought to my self, Oh, no! I had been counting my chickens too fast, as the old saying goes. I had thought all we had ahead of us were days of boredom sailing to New York. We had been told an eager out-of-touch German U-boat could still sink us with a torpedo, but I hadn't really thought seriously about that possibility. Being in the lead ship, as in a bomber formation, I assumed we would be the U-boat's prime target and that was not a happy thought. Even though this was after VE Day, the war may not be over for some U Boat commander out-of-touch with his headquarters silently stalking shipping in the middle of the Atlantic Ocean.

We could hear the thump of depth charge explosions resounding against the hull. It reminded me of the thumping flak made when it got close to our plane, except now the explosions were trying to protect us. We were all a little tense and wondering what we could do if we were hit with a torpedo and the ship began to sink.

Finally the PA clarified what had happened. One of our Destroyer Escorts had detected the possible presence of a submarine. Apparently to conserve their own munitions, they had called in the patrol bomber because we were still within their range from England. It was announced on the PA the alert had been called off and we could return to the open deck areas if we wished. Now we were back to the tedium of shipboard routine, thank God.

THE TEMPEST

A few days later the skies ahead began to darken and the seas were getting heavier. We were sailing into a storm that really looked scary to me. Huge black and dark gray clouds being lighted inside with flashes of lightening roiled on the horizon. We had intermittent showers of cold stinging rain driven by strong gusting winds. It looked almost biblical. I imagined old Noah looking anxiously at the threatening skies and hurrying his animals to shelter. The other ships in our convoy began to move away from each other. I stood on an open deck and watched with fearful fascination as one or another of those ships would disappear behind heaving huge dark green swells and waves. The scene for me was frightening and wonderfully beautiful at the same time.

The wind driven white caps crested every wave and decorated the ominous scene. As lightening and thunder were shattering the sky, we passengers were ordered below decks. The storm was fully upon us. Our ship was diving into and being lifted up on the huge waves as we made our inexorable progress into the storm. The crew reported that the open decks were awash and we were getting "green water at the bridge." Green water meant that it wasn't foam but solid water was crashing high up on our ship as we dove into the waves. The fantail of the ship lifted clear of the water; the screws vibrated in the air and the ship shuttered in response. Our ship creaked and groaned, as it was stressed by the massive power of the sea pushing it about. I thought, if I ever got back onto solid ground again I would never get on-board another boat or ocean ship.

I had trouble sleeping that night. I tried to calm my imagination, while we were constantly being thrust up and down and rolling side-to-side. I tried to stop myself wondering how I would get out of the below deck metal compartment if our ship should break-up. The storm tossed movements of the ship and my fear wouldn't let me relax. There was a persistent odor of vomit that was a troubling reminder all was not well on our ship. We were being maliciously twisted and tossed about like some giant's toy on this vast angry sea.

After what seemed like forever, but was probably only a day or so, the storm abated and passed. When allowed I came out on deck and inhaled the clean, chilly, fresh salt air. A firm wind tried to lift my cap and the skies were beautifully blue with a few white cottony clouds floating lazily on the horizon. The sea had become an almost serenely deep blue with random white caps. The Atlantic weather reminded me of the little girl in the nursery rhyme. "When she was good she was very, very good, but she was bad she was horrid." Though things were now peaceful, after the last days' events I had no interest in shipboard life...ever again!

ROUTINE

A significant part of each day was spent waiting in line for our next meal. If I remember correctly, we were served only two meals each day because it took so long to feed everyone. We did have a small PX-like store where snacks and candy could be purchased. Fortunately boredom returned as we spent time gazing at the vast endless sea and our band of ships slowly moving toward home. The speedy Destroyer Escort ships that wove in and out of our convoy looked as if they were having fun while protecting us from any stray German U-boats. Again I was reminded of the parallel between a ship convoy and a bomber formation. The DEs were our "little friends" here just as the P-51 and P-47 fighters had been for our bombers over Europe.

LAND HO!

One morning, after about 10 days at sea, the continent of North America was spotted dead ahead. Upon this happy event, all of the ships were released from convoy control. Each ship was free to make a straight run on their own for New York or other assigned East Coast harbors. Our ship, we were told by the ship's PA, was the fastest of the group and rapidly moved out ahead of the others. I went below decks to our quarters to gather my belongings. I rapidly and happily got ready to disembark, even though we were hours away from even being in the harbor. Then suddenly there were a series of loud thumps on the hull of our ship, which I recognized as depth charges going off. I along with many others ran for the topside to see what was happening. Just as I made it to the rail a DE came slicing through the water along side of our ship launching depth charges in the air off its fantail. My immediate thought was, submarines! Not now! For God's sake, am I going to be sunk and drown within sight of my homeland? Then on the PA, it was announced that there was no alert. It was just our Navy escort celebrating a successful crossing. The DE crewmen were waving at us as they sped by and so we returned their salute in gratitude. They apparently had set the "ash cans" to explode at a shallow depth causing massive geysers of white water to erupt in their wake. We out on the Atlantic were having our own belated VE Day celebration.

We were all standing wherever we could find room to watch as the landmass of North America and of New York City began to grow larger on the horizon. I just stood by the rail in joy and satisfaction at the fact of our safe arrival back home. I don't recall anyone yelling or cheering at this stage. It was a highly introspective time for each of us. I can still feel that quiet exhilaration of watching New York slowly come into sharper focus as the day wore on.

As we entered the outer portions of the great harbor, the first thing I can remember seeing clearly was a giant neon Pepsi-Cola sign on an island with the massive city in the background. For some reason, seeing that blatant advertisement for a soft drink told me I was home...that exuberant optimistic place called the United States of America! At that time I remember saying out loud to myself, "If I ever take this country for granted again someone should kick my ass."

We continued into the harbor led by our guiding tugboats. The PA came alive and reminded us we were the first convoy to leave England after VE Day. I wasn't sure the people in the harbor knew it, but we did. The Captain greeted the afternoon in New York with two long steam horn blasts. A fireboat tooted and came along side shooting streams of water from several fire hoses. Following the fireboat was a boat with a brass band of WAC soldiers on an open deck loudly playing Happy Days Are Here Again, and other festive and patriotic pieces. After the endless pushing and shoving by our tugs, we were docked at a wharf. Then we were given the sad news we were to stay on board over-night and could not disembark until the next morning. I never knew why. Maybe it had to do with overtime or some other requirement of the port personnel. It sure as heck wasn't for our convenience.

As dusk faded into night, the area around where we were docked was alit with neon signs offering all sorts of the joys of life in the USA. Once again we the combat veterans were barred from being a part of life on shore as we had on VE Day. Even though we had been fed our supper, a sign offering hamburgers for 20 cents was the focus of several of us. On the pier next to our ship, two workmen stood casually talking. We yelled down to them and offered to pay them a dollar each for ten Hamburgers with "all the fixens." They didn't know it but we didn't have any American money, so I guess we were going to cross that bridge when we came to it. But the monetary problems turned out to be academic. They both looked up to where we were gathered and one of them said,

"F--- you, soldier. I am not your f---ing servant. We don't have time for such crap."

I was stunned and for once didn't have a smart comeback as they strolled off, sat down on a box and lit up cigarettes. To this day I can't understand that vulgar and rude welcome home. Later fortunately we were to experience much different people who expressed a sincere appreciation of what ever we had done for our country. Those two New York dockside despicable clods only standout in my memory because they were such an exception to the heartfelt receptions we experienced everywhere else. I had a fitful night trying to sleep that final night onboard. We were home, no longer in peril but not being allowed to touch our home soil. I thought, "They are going to give me an ulcer if one more delay to my return to my family takes place."

BACK TO THE FUTURE

The next morning we happily disembarked carrying our on-board baggage. We then went to go the baggage pick-up area on the dock to get our barracks bags of gear that had been stored in the ship's hold area. The Red Cross was there and handing out fresh milk and Hershey candy bars to us as we moved along. After eight months of powdered milk, fresh cold whole milk right then was the most wonderfully tasting drink in the world. Finally we found there was no U.S. Customs check of our baggage as the GI inspectors at Bamber Bridge had lied to us there would be. We opened up the sealed packets stamped Do Not Open and found we had been robbed back at Bamber Bridge. Numbers of us talked about letting some one in authority know about the thieves at Bamber Bridge, but were too happy to be home to follow-up.

We Army Air Corps guys were separated from the Navy personnel and loaded onto a ferryboat that was going to take us south to Fort Dix, New Jersey. At Fort Dix we were to be assembled by geographic areas and assigned to various troop trains to be transported across the country to our home areas. I was wondering if I should call my folks when I got to Fort Dix or if I should wait and surprise them. My mom's birthday was the 27th of May, which was just a few days away, so I decided to call them on her birthday to tell them I was back and would be home in a few days for our happy reunion.

Once on-board the ferry, I quickly went by myself to the very front in an open deck area. I wanted to see as much of Manhattan as I could even though I was getting a fine salt spray on my face and salt spotting on my uniform. I was bursting with emotions. I allowed myself to not be the sober adult combat veteran. I was the excited 19 year old kid from Long Beach taking it all in. We moved out into the harbor and, giving me goose bumps, there stood the magnificent Statue of Liberty holding high her torch of freedom for the world to see. She was huge and green! I suppose because when I was growing up our history books had only black and white photographs, I didn't know she was green. A more attentive student would have picked up the information she was made of copper and thus had a green copper patina. There was an older gentleman also standing in the bow area whom I hadn't noticed until he said, "A lot of folks are surprised to see Our Lady of the Harbor is green."

I guess I had been talking out loud to myself about this discovery of mine and he had heard me.

He moved over a little and began to speak to me.

"Well, Sergeant I see from your silver wings you are an aerial gunner. That Eighth Air Force patch tells me you have been flying in bombers over Germany."

As he talked I was distracted and filled with the awe of seeing the magnificent Manhattan skyline and not listening too closely. I could see The Empire State Building and the top of the Chrysler Building. They were all standing there in the brilliant sunshine and blue sky of a May morning... gulls followed our ferry and squawked at us. The crisp air smelled clean as I filled my lungs.

His words were in the background of my consciousness, I finally responded, "Yeah, you're right on all counts".

"What do you think of our fair city, Sergeant?," he asked.

"It is such a beautiful and familiar skyline," I answered, "I almost feel I've been here before. I had a similar feeling in London... as if I belonged there."

As we spoke I was struck with the visual difference between London and New York City, which was striking. Whereas; London was largely of darker earth tones, bulkier and almost brooding but solid looking; New York had lighter building colors, with buildings reaching for the sky and spoke to me of American optimism, energy and drive to succeed.

"Well, this is it; the end to the adventure of my life...this past year and half," I thoughtfully added.

The old man smiled, "Do you mind telling me what your time was like flying in those bombers? This adventure of your life as you called it. We've got time. I'd like to know if you don't mind."

I felt at ease with the old guy. I began to tell him of our home, Ridgewell Air Base, cut out of the quiet Essex countryside, surrounded by doughty English farmers and villages centuries old. As I described it for him, I briefly returned to the Blue Room and its smoky companionship with the guys of the Goldin and Steinwinter crews. Faint strains of "I'll Be Seeing You" flitted through my mind. I recalled the raucous good-natured ribbing, the concerns for each other and the Six Pence limit poker games. I remembered how we once were a family and now were split apart as we each had gone his own way.

I tried to convey what it felt like flying into the unknowns of a bombing mission; the weather, the machines and the enemy trying their best to shoot us down. Staying alive while in sub-zero temperatures and the thin atmosphere's lack of life sustaining oxygen. The odd droning muffled world of being incased in a ball turret looking down at Europe at war. I described for him what it felt like to be alone five miles over the enemy's country while trying to fly hundreds of miles to get back home to England. These were some of the things I tried to explain.

I described walking in a battered but unbeaten London, and talking with those brave people whom I admired. I even told him of Pat and my mixed feelings about having to say goodbye when it hurt so much and yet wanting to be able to go home. About that I thought she wanted more, but I doubted we would ever see each other again

I told him, as I had no other living soul, about my fears at times of being killed or maimed. After a bit I realized I wasn't really telling him much about bombing Berlin or Cologne or those other components of a good war story. I was talking about Bob Gilbert the 19 years old young man who often thought he would never really see this day. I said to the old guy,

"You know... it is kind of fitting the adventure of my life would end here looking at New York, this great city, and opening up to you a stranger. This is the peak. I will eventually return to my normal civilian life in California and look back someday, as an old man, at who I once was when I was young".

"You don't know me, son, but I know you," he gently interrupted, "trust me. Let me assure you, to take a line from Browning, 'The best is yet to be'. You will find your way to be a part of our exciting tomorrow and the great adventure of being a part of the future. To be a loving husband and father is a far greater adventure than you can imagine standing here. The curtain is just coming up on your greatest adventures."

As we arrived at the Fort Dix landing, I left him standing alone and collected my bags. He silently patted me on the back and gave me the warm knowledge that..."the best is yet to be" I couldn't wait to get off that ferry boat and on with my life.

I was completing a giant circle that I had taken over two continents and now was now returning to Long Beach for...

THE BEGINNING.

Youthful Airman Has Air Medal and Five Clusters

Bringing back with him the Air Medal and five Oak Leaf Clusters, S-Sgt. Robert B. Gilbert, 19, arrived home June 1 from an Eighth Air Force bomber station in England after eight months service as a Flying Fortress ball turret gunner.

The veteran will spend a 30-day furlough here with his parents, Mr. and Mrs. Hamner B. Gilbert of 1957 Oregon Ave., and will then report to Santa Monica for reassignment. He has taken part in 35 bombing attacks on German targets as a member of the 381st Bombardment Group and has flown 261 combat hours.

Graduating from Polytechnic High School when 17 years old he won his wings in May, 1944, at the aerial gunnery school at Las Vegas, Nev. He also wears two battle stars and a Presidential Unit Citation awarded his bomber group for daring in action during a great air battle over Oschersleben, Germany.

Long Beach Press-Telegram
news item, circa June 1945.

Epilogue

From the Fortress Over Europe to the Moon

A FTER his air combat tour on Flying Fortresses over Europe, S/Sgt. Gilbert returned to civilian life in October 1945.

As they returned from the various battle fields of World War II, Bob and his friends often got together over a few beers and pretzels and compared their experiences. These bull sessions were unintentional therapy; as they shared their "war stories," lied to each other and returned to being just youngsters. They happily became reintroduced to the girls of their past and met others. The Big Band era was starting to fade but in Southern California it still remained at the local ballrooms where everyone went to meet and dance with girls. For Bob it was a time of being young and enjoying life and not being very responsible. He and his buddies could receive $20.00 a week unemployment compensation for as many as 52 weeks. In addition each discharged service man or woman was paid $100.00 a month severance pay for the first three months after their discharge. Inasmuch as Bob was living back at his family's home in Long Beach, and his expenses were low, he spent the first few months in civilian life doing little besides enjoying being home and alive.

Eventually most of the returnees, including Bob, either found employment or went to college under the GI Bill provisions which paid for one's books and tuition. In addition there was a monthly living expenses allotment of $50.00 for single veterans. Starting college in 1946, Bob had earned about three years credit in a business administration major by 1949. But college was boring to him and, besides, he wanted to get married to his girl friend, Althea.

As a result, in 1949 he dropped out of college and went to work for Douglas Aircraft in Long Beach. He became a template maker in the tooling department and started his career in what is now called the aerospace industry. Bob and Althea were married in 1949 and lovingly took the first steps to establish their own family. Their daughters Kathleen and Lynn were born in 1951 and 1954 respectively, both of whom now have their own families and their children are beginning their own futures.

In the '50's it was a time, particularly in the aviation industries, that allowed advancement by one's demonstrated ability to learn, perform and accept responsibility. Starting in 1951 during the Cold War period, Bob, though lacking an engineering degree, moved through tool manufacturing into engineering at the Aerojet-General facility in Downey, California. He performed as engineering liaison within the company and at customers and sub-contractors facilities solving engineering design problems. As the Space Race began, he was moved into the then fairly new discipline of quality control engineering and was involved in many aircraft/aerospace programs. Starting in 1959 his assignments were basically in supervision and management of quality engineering and quality control organizations.

Throughout those working years, until his retirement in 1991, Bob was immersed in the many interesting and challenging aerospace programs of the day. The later years were even more interesting with involvement on the Apollo Lunar Excursion Module, the Space Shuttle, the Concorde SST, other aerospace vehicle/missile programs including finally the Apache Attack Helicopter. When he retired he was the Senior Manager for quality systems integration at the MacDonnell Douglas (now Boeing) Space Systems Company Headquarters in Huntington Beach, California.

His World War II bomber crew experiences acquired in the Army Air Corps, while still a teenager, served him well in becoming a responsible adult enjoying his involvement in the exciting Space Age.

As Bob would say, "What a ride!"

Afterword

AS an introduction to this memoir, in Author's Notes, I stated, "Where there are quoted conversations... they accurately record events and situations as they occurred."

That statement is factual except for the last parts of the conversation with the old man standing alongside of me on the front of the ferry in New York harbor. That conversation is a literary device wherein actually I am the old man of 2006 talking to me the young man of 1945. Though I did have a loosely similar conversation with someone on the ferry, the words of advice recorded are those I would have said to me with what I know today if that were possible.

—Bob Gilbert
Murrieta, California

The View From the Bottom Up

Combat Missions

S/Sgt. Robert B. Gilbert
Ball Turret Gunner
381ˢᵗ BG, 533ʳᵈ BS, Ridgewell, England

MISSION No.	DATE	TARGET	CREW (Pilot)
1.	10-09-44	Schweinfurt	Windsor (Goldin co-pilot)
2.	10-14-44	Cologne	Windsor (Goldin co-pilot)
3.	10-15-44	Cologne	Windsor (Goldin co-pilot)
4.	10-17-44	Cologne	Steinwinter (Fill-in ball turret)
5.	10-19-44	Mannheim	Windsor (Goldin co-pilot)
6.	10-26-44	Munster	Windsor (Goldin co-pilot)
7.	11-04-44	Hamburg	Goldin
8.	11-05-44	Frankfurt	Goldin
9.	11-10-44	Cologne	Goldin
10.	11-16-44	Eschweiler	Goldin
11.	11-25-44	Merseburg	Goldin
12.	11-26-44	Altenbecken	Goldin
13.	11-29-44	Misburg	Goldin
14.	11-30-44	Zeitz	Goldin
15.	12-09-44	Stuttgart	Goldin
16.	12-11-44	Mannheim	Goldin
17.	12-12-44	Merseburg	Goldin
18.	12-15-44	Kassel	Goldin
19.	12-24-44	Kirch Gons	Goldin
20.	12-30-44	Mainz	Goldin
21.	1-01-45	Kassel	Goldin
22.	1-03-45	Cologne	Goldin
23.	1-05-45	Heimbach	Goldin
24.	1-13-45	Germersheim	Goldin
25.	1-14-45	Cologne	Goldin
26.	1-17-45	Paderborn	Riza (Fill-in ball turret)
27.	1-29-45	Neiderlahnstein	Goldin
28.	2-03-45	Berlin	Goldin
29.	2-09-45	Arnsburg	Goldin
30.	2-14-45	Brux, CZ	Goldin
31.	2-15-45	Dresden	Goldin
32.	2-21-45	Nurnberg	Goldin
33.	2-22-45	Klotze	Goldin
34.	2-23-45	Adelsburg	Goldin
35.	2-25-45	Munich	Goldin

From Schweinfurt to Munich: 261 combat hours

Medals Awarded to S/Sgt. Robert Gilbert

Air Medal
plus 5 Oak Leaf Clusters for subsequent awards of the Air Medal

European Theater Medal plus four Battle Stars:
North France
Rhineland
Central Europe
Ardennes Salient (Battle of the Bulge)

American Theater Medal

Good Conduct Medal

World War II Victory Medal

THE VIEW FROM THE BOTTOM UP

Fortieth Year Reunion
Seattle

381st Bomb Group's ninth reunion, Seattle, Washington, 1985. Bob Gilbert, Stu Newman, Ralph and Mary Engleman. [Bob Gilbert]

References

These references were used to corroborate historical facts.

Brown, James Good. *The Mighty Men of the 381st: Heroes All*. Publishers Press.

Freeman, Roger. *Mighty Eighth War Diary*. Jane's Publishing Inc.

Osborne, David. *They Came From Over The Pond*. 381st Memorial Association, Madison, Wisconsin.

www.381st.org, The Official Web Site of the 381st Bomb Group, War Diaries.

www.historylearningsite.co.uk/battle_of_the_bulge.htm.

www.historylearningsite.co.uk/d-day_index.htm.

www.bergstrombooks.elknet.pl/26nov44.htm.

PHOTO ACKNOWLEDGMENTS

USAAF photos source: 381st Bomb Group Memorial Association, CD-ROM produced by Frank Slomzmenski

Frank Hrehocik photos courtesy Jerry Gergasko

Engleman photos courtesy of Ralph Engleman

Goldin photos courtesy of Robin (Goldin) Lee

Made in the USA
Lexington, KY
28 March 2016